ECONOMIC SUMMITS AND WESTERN DECISION-MAKING

Economic Summits and Western Decision-Making

Edited by
CESARE MERLINI

PUBLISHED IN ASSOCIATION WITH THE
EUROPEAN INSTITUTE OF PUBLIC ADMINISTRATION

CROOM HELM
London & Sydney

ST. MARTIN'S PRESS
New York

©1984 European Institute for Public Administration
Croom Helm Ltd, Provident House, Burrell Row,
Beckenham, Kent BR3 1AT
Croom Helm Australia Pty Ltd, First Floor, 139 King Street,
Sydney, NSW 2001, Australia

British Library Cataloguing in Publication Data
Economic summits and western decision-making.
1. Economic summit meetings
I. Merlini, Cesare
330.9182'1   HF1412
ISBN 0-7099-3512-9

Library of Congress Card Catalog Number: 84-40048
ISBN 0-312-23534-8

The publication of this book has been sponsored by the European Institute of
Public Administration in Maastricht and the Istituto Affari Internazionale, Rome.

The opinions expressed are those of the authors of the chapters.

Printed and bound in Great Britain

CONTENTS

v

PREFACE

Every year since 1975 in late spring or early summer the summit conference of the leaders of the seven major industrial democracies has occupied the frontpages of newspapers and has been the opening item of TV news broadcasts worldwide. The Istituto Affari Internazionali (IAI) of Rome and the European Institute of Public Administration (EIPA) of Maastricht, the Netherlands, decided almost two years ago to combine their efforts, resources and expertise to study this new phenomenon which has become so important in international relations. In view of the interest the two institutes share not only in global developments in general but in Community affairs in particular, special attention was directed to analysing the European participants' role in summitry.

The IAI was responsible for carrying out and coordinating the various studies which made up the research project, six of which were prepared by scholars from European and American research institutes and one of which was written by a former participant in summitry. The EIPA provided most of the financial support and organised the two seminars – one in Maastricht in November 1982 and the other in Valkenburg in May 1983 – at which the authors of the papers met with a number of experts and practitioners of summitry to discuss the formulation and progress of their studies.

The idea for the project sprang from the observation that although seven summits had already been convened, making it a regular event, in-depth analysis of the workings, results and significance of the summitry process was still lacking. In concluding one of the seminars, Horst Schulmann, former Chancellor Helmut Schmidt's personal representative for various summits, commented: 'In a speech I made in 1978, after the Bonn economic summit, I noted that while the media had already developed strong views about the usefulness or uselessness of summits, no scholarly research on the subject had yet been undertaken. As this colloquium shows, this gap is now being filled rapidly. Indeed, reading the papers prepared for this meeting and listening to the discussions you have had yesterday and today, I was surprised, if not overwhelmed, by the multitude of aspects, of facets, of angles you have discovered.'

The scope of the project was to come up with answers to three main questions. First: For what purpose have the summits been convened and what have been the results obtained? At the Valkenburg seminar, V. Backes, secretary general of the EIPA, summed up an answer to this question in the following words: 'Summits have arisen from the urgent need to cope with world or regional problems or crises, to find solutions to common problems, which could not be worked out by a single country, however great its influence.' In the opening chapter, Guido Garavoglia of the IAI provides an overview of the short history of summitry, analysing the premises, deliberations and concrete results of each of the nine meetings held so far. In the following chapter, Robert Putnam of the Center for European Studies of Harvard University suggests a model for interpreting summitry in terms of political relations at both the inter- and intra-state level.

The second issue was: How effective is the summitry approach in dealing with Western interdependence? As Beniamino Andreatta, a former minister of the Italian Treasury, pointed out at the seminar: 'The degree of interdependence among Western economies has kept edging up even in the troubled seventies and up to this day. In spite of stagnation, inflation and exchange rate turbulence, the ratio of trade to GDP, as well as the degree of simultaneity in short-term developments, are today higher than fifteen years ago. This growing interpenetration of our economies has not been accompanied by effective economic management at the international level. Collective management of the global economic system is today inadequate, both at the conceptual and at the institutional level.' In the light of these developments, Jacques Pelkmans, professor of economics at the EIPA, discusses the issue of management of Western economic interdependence and the effectiveness of the existing instances of international cooperation. But Western economic interdependence, which was so central and, indeed, so threatening when summitry began, can no longer be isolated from political interdependence. In his chapter, William Wallace, deputy director and director of studies at Chatham House, deals with the issue of the appropriateness of extending economic summitry to political and security issues. In addition to the mainly economic but also increasingly political aspects of summitry there is another special feature of the process: public opinion as an important protagonist of the summits, consequent upon the widespread diffusion of mass media in Western societies and the strong influence public opinion and media exert on each other. A former spokesman who participated in several summits, Kurt Becker, discusses the role of the media on the basis of his direct experience.

The third question had to do with European participation in the summits, where four out of seven seats are held by European leaders and an additional one is occupied by the president of the Commission of the European Community. The interplay between summitry and the Brussels institutions is analysed in the sixth chapter, co-authored by Gianni Bonvicini, deputy director of the IAI, and Wolfgang Wessels, director of the Institut für Europäische Politik. The final chapter attempts to draw some conclusions about the summitry process in general, laying special emphasis on the relationships between summitry and the national and common or coordinated foreign policies of the Europeans, particularly towards the United States.

The great benefit the authors derived from the discussions that took place during the two seminars makes acknowledgement of the participants, and the expression of our gratitude for their contributions, imperative. The conferees were: M. vanden Abeele, B. Andreatta, V. Backes, F. Basagni, N. Bayne, C.B. Brahmsen, A. Comba, D. Elles, J.M. Hoscheit, M. O'Leary, G. de Menil, P. Morel, H. Nau, H. Owada, T. Padoa Schioppa, J. Pelletier, R. Ruggiero, M.H.J.Ch. Rutten, H. Schulmann, F. de la Serre, J. Swift, E. Thiel, J. Vandamme, F. Verros, E. Wellenstein. M.B. Biesheuvel, former prime minister of the Netherlands, chaired the Valkenburg colloquium.

My gratitude also goes to Diane Cherney for her patient work in editing and harmonising the language of so many different origins, and to the entire EIPA staff who did such an outstanding job not only in preparing and conducting the seminars but also in supporting the entire project.

All of this work has been coordinated by a person whose name should have come first in these acknowledgements: Stephan Schepers, director general of the EIPA. Without his commitment, from the very early stages of identification of the scope throughout all phases of the implementation of the project, this book would never have seen the light.

Rome   Cesare Merlini
                        President, Istituto Affari Internazionali

NOTE ON CONTRIBUTORS

Kurt Becker is currently a journalist for 'Die Zeit' (Hamburg) and was ex-Chancellor Helmut Schmidt's spokesman.

Gianni Bonvicini is deputy director of the Istituto Affari Internazionale (Rome).

Guido Garavoglia currently an official of the Italian Chamber of Deputies, was a research associate at the Istituto Affari Internazionale.

Cesare Merlini is president of the Istituto Affari Internazionale.

Jacques Pelkmans is professor of economics at the European Institute of Public Administration (Maastricht).

Robert Putnam is professor of the US Government Center for European Studies of Harvard University.

William Wallace is deputy director and director of studies at the Royal Institute of International Affairs (London).

Wolfgang Wessels is director of the Institut für Europäische Politik (Bonn).

LIST OF ACRONYMS USED IN THIS BOOK

ASEAN	Association of South East Asian Nations
CDU	(German) Christian Democratic Union
CIEC	Conference on International Economic Cooperation
COCOM	Consultative Group Cooperation Committee
Comecon (or CMEA)	Council for Mutual Economic Assistance
COREPER	Committee of Permanent Representatives
CSCE	Conference on Security and Cooperation in Europe
DISC	Domestic International Sales Cooperation
EC	European Community
EFTA	European Free Trade Association
EMS	European Monetary System
EPC	European Political Cooperation
GATT	General Agreement on Tariffs and Trade
IDA	International Development Association
IEA	International Energy Agency
IFRI	Institut Français des Relations Internationales (Paris)
IMF	International Monetary Fund
INF	Intermediate-range Nuclear Forces
INFCE	International Fuel Cycle Evaluation
LDC	Less Developed Country
MITI	(Japanese) Ministry of International Trade and Industry
NATO	North Atlantic Treaty Organisation
OECD	Organisation for Economic Cooperation and Development
OPEC	Organisation of Petroleum Exporting Countries
SDR	Special Drawing Rights
SITC	Standard International Trade Classification
SPD	(German) Social Democratic Party

UN   United Nations
UNCTAD   United Nations Conference on Trade and
            Development

1 FROM RAMBOUILLET TO WILLIAMSBURG: A HISTORICAL ASSESSMENT

Guido Garavoglia

The Origins

Throughout the nineteenth century and the first half of the twentieth, the basic model for multilateral cooperation among sovereigns and heads of state was the Concert of Europe, born of the Congress of Vienna in 1815. *Ad hoc* conferences were convened when necessary to resolve conflicts, share out territories, and sign treaties, but always for the purpose of what we would today call 'crisis management', totally contingent and essentially political in nature.

The development of institutionalised cooperation, after the failure of the League of Nations, led in the second post-war period to the creation of the modern system of international organisations. However, at the periodic meetings of intergovernmental institutions, whether political or technical, member states are represented in virtually all instances by diplomats, ministry officials, or – for the most important meetings – ministers. The rare exceptions to this rule are certain regional organisations (such as the Warsaw Pact, the Organisation for African Unity, the Arab League) or groupings that lack any permanent structure (such as the Non-Aligned Movement), whose general conferences are held at the level of heads of state and government.[1]

The only analogous instance of multilateral negotiation in the West is the European Council which, though it has no legal status under the Treaty of Rome, has been bringing together the heads of state or government of the European Community's member countries three times a year on a regular basis since 1975 to discuss the main political and economic problems of the moment.

The series of annual summits inaugurated at Rambouillet in November 1975 made it possible for the first time to involve the highest representatives of the main economic regions of the West (North America, Japan, Western Europe)[2] in a process of regular consultations – primarily though not exclusively economic – under a trilateral pattern never before applied.

1

This new experience did not spring suddenly out of nothing. Rather it was the product of the serious crises that shook the world economy in the early 1970s. However, it was also affected by accidental factors, such as the personalities of certain individuals, who as always in history help determine the features of a phenomenon if not its success or failure.

The End of an Era

In the oft-reiterated remark of French President Valéry Giscard d'Estaing, the crisis of the early 1970s was not a crisis of capitalism, but simply a monetary crisis. Though this may not correspond completely to the reality of the situation, it is nevertheless certain that the series of events between August 1971 and February 1973 revolutionised the world economic system. They marked the end of an era of relative stability (established by the Bretton Woods agreements of 1944 and based on the supremacy of the United States and its currency) and the start of a much more complex and unpredictable phase that is still with us today.

In the summer of 1971, for the first time since World War II, the United States recorded not only a balance-of-payments deficit but also a balance-of-trade deficit. This led President Nixon to announce a series of drastic measures on 15 August, including suspension of the dollar's convertibility into gold. By the subsequent Smithsonian Institution accords (December 1971), the United States agreed to devalue the dollar by 7.89 percent with respect to the Special Drawing Rights, and the European countries agreed to help right the US payments deficit by differential currency revaluation.

But neither the Smithsonian agreement nor the creation of the European monetary snake in April 1972 (which went into crisis just two months later with the exit of the pound sterling) could reverse a trend made inevitable by the decline of American hegemony and the growing strength of Japan and Europe. Although the dollar held relatively steady on foreign exchange markets throughout 1972, the US trade deficit deteriorated sharply. So on 12 February 1973 Nixon announced a second devaluation, 10 percent this time, definitively putting an end to the system worked out at Bretton Woods.

On top of the crisis of the international monetary system came the first oil shock, following the outbreak of the Yom Kippur War (October 1973). Within three months the price of oil nearly quadrupled[3] and supplies were cut by some 20 percent, with a total embargo against the United States and the Netherlands.

In the face of this challenge, the West proved unprepared and incapable of a united response. The United States, which had been only marginally hurt by the crisis, proposed to Europe, Japan and Canada a united front among oil consumers. However, the summit meeting of European heads of state and government in Copenhagen (14–15 December 1973) failed to overcome the major divergences of interests among the Community partners, and the US initiative came to nothing. The subsequent Washington Conference (11–13 February 1974) to which Nixon had invited the eight leading industrial oil-consuming or -producing countries, did decide however on the creation of a group to coordinate energy policies, which in the end led to the establishment of the International Energy Agency (IEA) within the OECD in November 1974. France, which feared the formation of a US-controlled Western cartel against OPEC, partially disassociated itself from the decisions made at Washington, refused to join the IEA, and initially opposed the European Community's participation in the new body.

In the spring of 1974, then, the international economic picture was extremely uncertain; and – perhaps even more worrisome – there did not seem to be any imminent solution to the differences among the Western powers over the way out of the crisis.

The Revival of Cooperation

A contribution to overcoming this impasse came from the unforeseeable political upheaval that literally overturned the leadership of the five leading industrial countries within just a few months in 1974. (This script would be repeated, in part, in 1980–81 as well.)

Elections in February ousted Edward Heath's Tory government, and Labour's Harold Wilson came back to power in Britain. After the death of Pompidou, Giscard d'Estaing became the new president of France in May. In West Germany, Helmut Schmidt inherited power from Willy Brandt, forced to resign when his position had deteriorated to the point where his own party had been induced to abandon him. The Watergate scandal, which had been keeping American politics in turmoil for more than a year, came to its conclusion on 8 August with Nixon's resignation and the assumption of the presidency by Gerald Ford. And finally, the Fukuda government fell in a cabinet crisis in November and Takeo Miki became the new Japanese premier.

The start of what Kissinger would call 'one of the best periods of

Atlantic cooperation in decades'[4] coincided with the assumption of the presidency of the EC's Council of Ministers by France, in the second half of 1974. With Schmidt's support, Giscard was the undisputed prime mover in this phase of revival.

Within the Community, Giscard promoted the institutionalisation of the European Council. This decision, which had been discussed over dinner at the Elysee Palace by the heads of state and government in September, was officially adopted at the Paris summit of 9–10 December 1974.

As to inter-Atlantic relations, the French president succeeded in reaching a compromise with President Ford on energy matters at the 16–17 December meeting in Martinique. That encounter, preceded by a visit to Washington by Schmidt at the beginning of the month, concluded with American acceptance of the proposal made by Giscard on 24 October for a tripartite conference among a limited number of industrial oil-importers, OPEC countries and other LDCs. This initiative linked up with the repeatedly stated demand of many developing countries, led by Algeria – most notably at the Special Session of the UN General Assembly in New York, 9 April to 2 May 1974 – to deal with the energy problem in a global perspective covering the broader issue of raw materials in general. Despite French desires, this more far-ranging approach was only partly accepted by Ford, and it later constituted the fundamental obstacle to a prompt start to the Conference on International Economic Cooperation (CIEC), which would not open until December 1975, after two laborious preparatory meetings in April and October.

Still, the Martinique encounter did serve to reopen the dialogue between the West and the developing countries, both oil-producers and not, thus avoiding the confrontation with OPEC originally proposed by the United States. In return, Giscard withdrew his veto on Community participation in the IEA, thus agreeing to collaborate indirectly in the activities of the new organisation, though France itself remained outside.

The new negotiating climate among the Western allies also bore fruit in the monetary field. The agreement to abolish an official price for gold was formalised by the Interim Committee of the International Monetary Fund on 31 August 1975,[5] and a compromise on the exchange rate regime was worked out in time to be announced at Rambouillet in November. Thus the two thorniest issues in the monetary dispute were settled, at least formally.

Genesis of the Western Summits

Giscard's activism did not end with the tackling of the issues involved in France's disputes with the United States but was also concerned with the form of consultations among the three poles of the industrial West. In the French president's view, the monetary crisis could not be properly dealt with if international cooperation continued to be carried on exclusively through the traditional multilateral bodies. The collapse of the Bretton Woods system had demonstrated the inadequacy of the instruments it had created or postulated, such as the IMF, the GATT and the OECD. Their functions needed to be supplemented by a political initiative making it possible for the major powers to discuss their economic orientations in a climate as informal and discreet as possible but at the same time at the highest level of representation.

This sort of consultation was certainly no novelty for Giscard or for Schmidt, who as finance ministers under Pompidou and Brandt had earlier been the promotors of a series of confidential meetings with their American and British counterparts on the problems raised by the monetary crisis. At the meetings of the so-called 'Library Group'[6] (which were later broadened to include Japan) each minister was accompanied only by one collaborator and at times by his central bank governor, while the very convening of the encounters was kept secret.

Once they had become, respectively, president and chancellor, Giscard and Schmidt sought to transfer the spirit and the practice of those encounters to the level of heads of state and government. The purpose was to create the most flexible possible instrument for consultations. It was to be unstructured, without fixed meeting dates, and limited to a very few participants, enabling the leaders of the major Western nations to engage in a totally free and frank exchange of views on the economic measures (especially in monetary policy) necessary to solve the crisis.

The idea of a top-level summit had already been circulating for some time in the United States as well. In 1973 opposition Democratic circles had promoted the creation of the Trilateral Commission, privately grouping together a number of important American, European and Japanese figures. Among the architects of this initiative were many men who would later be part of President Carter's staff, including Brzezinski and Owen, who would be the president's personal representative at the summits for three years. Although the kind of meeting they imagined differed markedly from the model offered by Giscard and Schmidt,[7] the concerns underlying it largely coincided.

Still, the prospect of a summit meeting was not viewed with much enthusiasm at first by the US administration. Even though he himself had encouraged such a meeting a few years before, Kissinger now feared that the United States would find itself under accusation, taxed with primary responsibility for the aggravation of the economic situation that had occurred in the meantime. Intense diplomatic activity by Schmidt was necessary to overcome this reluctance and to convince Ford of the usefulness of the tripartite initiative, on the occasion of the new president's first visit to Europe at the end of July 1975.

The proposal for holding an economic summit in the fall among the heads of state and government of the five leading industrial nations (United States, West Germany, France, United Kingdom, and Japan) was put forward concretely by the French president on 31 July at Helsinki, on the occasion of the final session of the Conference on Security and Cooperation in Europe. During a luncheon at the British Embassy attended by Ford, Schmidt, Wilson, Giscard and their respective foreign ministers, it was decided to form a group composed of personal representatives of the participating leaders. These aides, subsequently dubbed 'sherpas', were assigned to study the ways and means of preparing for the summit meeting.[8]

Once Japanese Premier Takeo Miki's approval had been obtained, the personal representatives met for the first time in New York in early October. In the meantime, Italy's request to take part in the summit had been granted (this was then employed in an effort to justify exclusion of the European Community: Italy held the presidency of the Council of Ministers at the time, and the summit was presented as a one-time occasion).[9] US pressure to include Canada instead went unheeded until the following year, due to strong French resistance.

On 10 October it was announced in the six capitals that the summit would be held from 15 to 17 November at the Château de Rambouillet in France. This first gathering would be followed by eight more: in San Juan, Puerto Rico (1976), London (1977), Bonn (1978), Tokyo (1979), Venice (1980), Ottawa (1981), Versailles (1982), and Williamsburg (1983).

The Development of the Summits

Rambouillet (15–17 November 1975)

At the first summit, it became clear that Giscard's and Schmidt's idea of holding as informal and restricted a meeting as possible was an illusion. Despite the secluded location, the autumnal climate and the functioning fireplace, those present were fairly numerous and the delegations included not only the heads of state and government, their personal representatives and foreign and finance ministers, but also various other officials. Reporters numbered about two hundred, and though they were forced to stay in Paris, the publicity coverage was still incomparably greater than that accorded to any ordinary gathering of economic ministers. In later years the situation gradually worsened, but it should be noted that not even Rambouillet, widespread subsequent opinion to the contrary notwithstanding, was truly a private meeting of the industrial nations' top leaders.

Preparations for the summit, brief as they may have been, were not left to chance either. In their last meeting, just a few days before Rambouillet, the six personal representatives finalised details on the issues that would be the focus of the talks and which the various leaders would take turns in introducing (Schmidt gave a report on the international economic situation, Miki on trade problems, Wilson on energy, Moro on East–West trade, Ford on relations with developing countries, and Giscard on monetary problems). These issues would be on the agenda of all subsequent summits, though from time to time one or another of them would take on greater and in some cases exclusive relevance.

The most important event at Rambouillet was the announcement of the monetary agreement between France (which abandoned its demand for a return to fixed exchange rates) and the United States (which pledged greater efforts to prevent erratic fluctuations of the dollar). This understanding was not a direct product of the summit but the fruit of negotiations that had already been going on for several months between delegations of the two countries, headed respectively by Edwin Yeo and Jacques de Larosière. The issue had also been discussed at the IMF Interim Committee and Assembly meetings (Washington, 31 August–1 September 1975) by the US and French finance ministers, Simon and Fourcade, and the Rambouillet summit provided a political endorsement of the operation. This agreement made possible the monetary reform of the exchange rate regime that was passed at the subsequent meeting of the IMF

Interim Committee (Jamaica, January 1976), centring on amendment of art. IV of the Fund's statute.[10]

For the rest, the summit acknowledged that top priority had to be
given to economic recovery, which was deemed to be already under
way. On trade, fears of a massive return to protectionism produced
a promise that every possible endeavour would be made to maintain
an open trading system, and the gathering recommended respect of
the anti-protectionism pledge adopted in May 1974 by the OECD
Council of Ministers (and periodically reiterated thereafter). Special
responsibility for the expansion of world trade was attributed to the
economic policies of countries with balance-of-payments deficits,
such as Italy and the United Kingdom. As to the multilateral negotiations under way in Geneva in the framework of GATT, the summit voiced the desire to speed them up and bring them to a successful
conclusion by the end of 1977.

These intentions turned out to be largely theoretical. The declarations in favour of free trade may have had some weight in preventing
adoption of over-drastic restrictive measures by the Italian and British governments. On the other hand, the Tokyo Round, which had
begun in September 1973, gained no impetus from the pledges made
at Rambouillet, and it would drag on until April 1979.

The final communiqué – a document that would thenceforward
accompany every summit – contained a series of generic statements
on the other topics broached by the leaders taking part. The statement called for growth of East–West trade together with a rapid
conclusion of the negotiations among Western nations on export
credits. It underscored the need for more cooperation with the LDCs
and the urgency for the IMF and other multilateral forums to adopt
appropriate measures to help stabilise LDC export earnings and to
finance their balance-of-payments imbalances, with particular regard to the poorest countries. Satisfaction was voiced over the calling of the Conference on International Economic Cooperation,
which would begin proceedings in December 1975.[11]

Even though the energy emergency had been one of the original
causes for the convening of the summit, the final communiqué at
Rambouillet dismissed this issue with a few quite generic phrases,
calling for a reduction in the West's dependency on energy imports
by means of energy savings and the development of alternative sources. Devotion of such scanty attention to so important a topic reflected the relative calm of the energy situation in 1975, after the major events of 1973 and 1974. In the absence of specific commitments,

progress in this area was slight, and it was not until the Bonn summit in 1978 that there was a move from generic pronouncements to the adoption of more concrete measures.

The Rambouillet summit ended with a press conference given by its protagonists, and like the final communiqué this has become a constant feature of all the subsequent gatherings. The leaders present were optimistic and in some cases even euphoric over the way the summit had gone, and confident that their respective countries were on the way to a prompt economic recovery. The press also gave a positive evaluation of the meeting, on the whole, and in later years there would be frequent − and possibly overstressed − references to the 'Rambouillet spirit'. At that time, however, there was no agreement on repetition of this kind of meeting. On the contrary, the final communiqué referred to existing international organisations as the primary forums for further development of the issues dealt with at the summit.

Puerto Rico (27−28 June 1976)

In May 1976, when President Ford invited his Western partners to spend two days in an isolated hotel a few kilometers outside San Juan, Puerto Rico, it could not be said that there was any especially strong feeling that a new summit was really necessary, just seven months after the first one. Had elections not been so near at hand in the United States and West Germany, the gathering would in all likelihood have been held all the same, but some months later, leaving more time for better preparations.

The practice of Western summitry was being consolidated. Though it remained non-institutional, it took its place alongside such other meetings as those of the European Political Cooperation. This made it clear − especially for the European Community − that a new decision-making forum, at the top level of political representation, was taking its place on the world diplomatic scene, with as yet undetermined effects on the activities of existing institutions.

The problem of EC participation at the economic summits had already been raised at the European Council meeting in Rome (1−2 December 1975), at which the Community's smaller members had harshly criticised the decision of the French, German, British and Italian governments to participate individually at Rambouillet. With the convening of the second summit, polemics broke out anew. What was proposed by the Commission − and by Gaston Thorn of

Luxembourg, who at that time was president of the Council of Ministers – was that the Community be represented by the presidents of the Commission and the Council. But this was not agreed to, owing to rigid French opposition. So there was no Community representative at San Juan, and in the final communiqué the four European participants did not go beyond a vague promise to intensify cooperation efforts within the Community framework.

However, the French opposition to increasing the number of participants – due to Giscard's desire to stay as faithful as possible to an unlikely 'fireside climate' – did not succeed in preventing an invitation for Canada, strongly urged by Ford. On the whole, though Canada's role in the summits could have been more incisive than it has appeared, Ottawa's mediating function has nevertheless been exercised with some effectiveness on a number of particular issues, on North–South relations (let us recall the preparations for the Cancun summit in October 1981), on trade policy and on the inclusion of political topics in the summit agenda.

As to individual participants, aside from the presence for the first time of Pierre Elliot Trudeau, the only new face was James Callaghan, who had replaced Wilson at the head of the Labour government.

The Puerto Rico summit made no major innovations in terms of content, which in large part followed the pattern of Rambouillet. The first few months of 1976 had seen a gradual recovery from the 1974–75 recession in the leading industrial countries, although the most significant basic problems had only been contained and papered over, certainly not solved. With few exceptions, inflation continued at historically high rates, the prospects on unemployment remained a cause for concern, and there was serious doubt about the possibility of raising investment spending to a level high enough to ensure satisfactory long-term growth rates.[12] Schmidt declared that the industrial countries had emerged from the recession together and, like Ford, underscored the importance of the joint decisions made at Rambouillet.

The optimistic climate of the moment was amply reflected in the final communiqué, which recognised the progress made in some countries – though not in others – in the fight against inflation and unemployment and declared that a return to balanced growth was within reach, thanks in part to the policy adopted in the previous months (and confirmed by the ministerial session of the OECD held just a few days before the summit). The aim of this policy was to avoid uncontrolled expansion of the economy and creation of any new barriers to trade and capital movements.

On monetary matters, the agreement reached in Jamaica in January was welcomed. However, the relative stability of the dollar with respect to some currencies contrasted with the grave losses of the lira and the pound sterling in exchange markets and with the difficulties of the French franc, which had left the European snake again in March just eight months after its re-entry.[13] Italian and English hopes for financing to help with their massive payments deficits were not acted on by the other countries, who did no more than remand possible concession of aid to the initiative of such multilateral organisations as the IMF.

With regard to Italy, this decision was strongly influenced by the outcome of a reserved meeting among the leaders of the United States, West Germany, France, and the United Kingdom, held on the margins of the summit. At this meeting it was decided to make concession of a large loan to Italy conditional upon exclusion of the Communist Party from government responsibility, after the sensational advance made by the PCI in the elections of 20 June 1976. This incident was revealed to some American reporters by Schmidt during a visit to Washington a few weeks after the summit. The revelation was highly embarrassing to the other capitals involved and even more so to Italy's Christian Democratic Party, which was engaged in difficult negotiations with the PCI on the formation of the new government. The prime minister's office hastened to specify that neither Moro nor Foreign Minister Rumor nor Treasury Minister Colombo (all Christian Democrats) had known of the meeting. But this did not stop vehement protests on the part of opposition forces in Italy and in other countries, such as France.

In any event, this incident revealed for the first time the habit of holding behind-the-curtains meetings on issues not included in the summit agenda. The importance of this practice would emerge more and more clearly in subsequent years.

On trade matters, the summit recalled the anti-protectionist commitment assumed with the renewal of the OECD Trade Pledge and reaffirmed its desire to see the Tokyo Round concluded by the end of 1977.

The discussion on East–West commercial relations revealed two opposite positions. Schmidt, followed by Giscard and Moro, favoured development of economic relations in the broader framework of détente, while Ford was considerably more prudent. However, the level of confrontation was not comparable to what would be witnessed later at Ottawa and Versailles, as is shown by the cautious tone of the communiqué.

The final declaration also expressed satisfaction with the reaching of an agreement among the participating countries on export credits. The European Commission deemed this agreement illegitimate, in that it was made independently by individual member states on a matter under Community competence,[14] but in the end accepted the substance of the accord in March 1977.

Another theme discussed in Puerto Rico was North–South relations. The Fourth UNCTAD Conference had ended several weeks earlier (May 1976) in Nairobi with its agreement on an Integrated Programme for Commodities and the start-up of negotiations for the creation of a Common Fund. Italy and France favoured the LDCs' approach, while the Americans were much more dubious. The British and the Germans took a flexible stance.

As had been the case at Rambouillet, here too there was little talk of energy, and the gathering did not go beyond urging continuation of the efforts under way for development, conservation and more rational use of energy resources.

The Puerto Rico summit is generally viewed as the least significant of the series. Its treatment by the mass media at the time was unenthusiastic, and the preparations for it were judged inadequate. Many observers began to wonder whether this sort of meeting really made sense; whether there wasn't a risk of needlessly raising the expectations of public opinion, thus creating image problems for the leaders taking part. But despite the poor repute in which it stands, the achievements of the Puerto Rico summit were certainly no worse than those of other gatherings.

London (7–8 May 1977)

The second half of 1976 and the first few months of 1977 helped defuse the optimistic hopes for full recovery of the Western economy. Though there had been progress since 1975, inflation and unemployment were still rising, growth in industrial production and in world trade was slowing, and major balance-of-payments imbalances persisted.

In this anything but encouraging situation, a third meeting of heads of state and government was convened in London. The invitation had originally been made in November 1976 by Japanese Premier Miki, but following pressures from Giscard the United Kingdom was decided on as the site. In January Britain had assumed the presidency of the EC Council of Ministers for the first time, while Roy Jenkins had replaced Ortoli at the head of the Commission.

If there had been no dramatic changes in the economic picture, there were several new elements on the political scene. Jimmy Carter had moved into the White House in January, and the London summit offered him a highly suitable occasion to present himself and his policy on the international stage. Having been a member of the Trilateral Commission, like more than one of his major collaborators, certainly helped make President Carter familiar with the issues he would have to deal with at the summit. His economic preparation, thanks in large measure to his habit of carefully studying the dossiers drawn up for him, exceeded the expectations of the other leaders. Fears of profound differences with Schmidt also turned out to be partly unfounded, and on the whole Carter's image emerged well enough from this first international experience.

Carter brought an expansionist economic strategy, and more than anyone else supported the so-called 'locomotive theory'. This doctrine, to which a restricted group of the OECD's Economic Policy Committee had made a substantial contribution, aimed to counterbalance the negative effects on the Western economic system of deficits in such countries as Italy and Britain by faster growth in the stronger countries. Japan and West Germany were not enthusiastic about the idea, however, and the agreement reached at London did no more than reconfirm the growth targets already established by those nations themselves for 1977 (5.8 percent of GNP for the United States, 6.7 percent for Japan, and 5 percent for Germany), though it did refer to the possibility of further measures should they prove necessary to reach those growth targets. The other governments pledged to pursue stabilising policies.

In practice, of the three countries that were to lead Western economic recovery, only the United States managed to achieve adequate growth in 1977 (5.3 percent). Japan did not go beyond 5.4 percent, and Germany barely reached 2.6 percent, but neither of them adopted any effective measures to respect the pledges made at London.

Besides Carter, the other new participants at the summit were Fukuda and Andreotti. More important, however, was the presence for the first time of the European Community as such, in the person of Commission President Roy Jenkins and Council President Callaghan.

After the Puerto Rico summit, the differences between Giscard (certainly not opposed by Schmidt and Callaghan) and the smaller Community members (led by the Netherlands) had not abated. Despite a vigorious resolution by the European Parliament (22 March 1977), the French President had written to Jenkins confirming his opposition to the Community's participation in a meeting that was supposed to bring together only heads of state and government. It is interesting to note how Giscard — worried that the presence of the Community would inevitably mean broadening the agenda to political issues and faithful to the idea of a gathering limited to a small number of participants — was considerably more rigid on this question than Carter, who was not hostile *a priori* to full representation for the Community.

The dispute was finally settled at the European Council meeting in Rome (25–26 March 1977), exactly twenty years after the signing of the treaties establishing the EEC and Euratom. Finding himself isolated, Giscard had to accept a compromise formula whereby the Community would be represented not only by the President of the European Council but also by the President of the Commission. The latter, however, was to participate only in those discussions concerning matters of exclusive Community competence. This limitation would be gradually done away with in subsequent years, but at the London summit Jenkins was admitted only to the second day's meeting (in which trade policy, energy policy, and relations with the LDCs were discussed), not to the first day's (devoted to economic and monetary policy). Incredible as it sounds, Giscard opted not to attend the inaugural dinner because Jenkins had been invited as well. At any rate, the heads of state and government took scrupulous care (up to the Versailles summit in 1982) to set the dates for their summits in such a way that the country holding the presidency of the European Council was always one of the four European participants.

It certainly cannot be said that the presence of the Community as such has had revolutionary effects on the summit proceedings. Still, in its areas of exclusive competence (essentially trade policy), it has often played a role in encouraging the adoption of a common position by the European participants. Also, the custom of holding the second European Council meeting of the year before and not after the summit has sometimes had significant results (especially in the case of the Tokyo summit, when Community positions on energy carried the day despite American doubts). The importance of this consultation should not however be overestimated, given the numerous other forums in which international negotiation can take place.[15]

The London understandings were more extensive and more detailed than those of the earlier summits, as is witnessed by the length of the final communiqué and the inclusion of a detailed appendix. In addition to agreeing on growth targets for 1977, the seven countries observed that inflation, far from reducing unemployment, is actually one of the principal causes thereof. This acknowledgement, however, was purely formal, since no counter-measures were provided for. The summit endorsed the decision by the Interim Committee of the IMF (April 1977) to approve creation of a new temporary credit facility to help countries in balance-of-payments difficulties.

On trade, given the inability to conclude the Tokyo Round by the deadline recommended at both Rambouillet and San Juan (the end of 1977), the communiqué merely expressed the hope that tangible progress could be made in a number of high-priority areas. However, at the urgings of France and Britain, it also affirmed the right of individual countries to avoid disturbance of their domestic markets, thus implicitly recognising their right to adopt some restrictive measures, in exemption from the OECD Trade Pledge.

For the first time, the final statement included a section devoted to nuclear energy, which in the months leading up to the summit had been the object of strong disagreement between the United States (followed by Canada) and some European nations, led by West Germany. The new American energy strategy, announced by Carter in 1977, put more stress on lowering consumption than on the development of alternative sources. Among potential alternatives, greater emphasis was given to coal, while nuclear energy programmes were drastically cut. At the same time, the US administration insisted that West Germany and France renounce their agreements with Pakistan and Brazil, respectively, for the delivery of new nuclear plants and adhere to new anti-proliferation safeguards. Though they decided to honour their contracts, the two European countries did pledge not to enter into any new ones, but they also warned the United States against instituting a cut-off of uranium supplies to Europe (already enacted by Canada and Australia). At the Downing Street summit there was a certain rapprochement between the two positions, partly because the enthusiasm for nuclear energy that had reigned in previous years had been somewhat doused by a number of objective considerations (doubts on future availability of uranium, opposition from ecological and peace movements, the high initial cost of nuclear power plants) that were valid regardless of the US course change. The difference of opinion over safeguards remained, however, and the problem was put off with the formation of a special International Nuclear Fuel Cycle Evaluation Group, assigned to draw up a study within two months. The inclusion in the communiqué of a paragraph on nuclear energy, which reflected the climate of compromise between the parties, was at any rate useful for some governments (especially Bonn) that were facing considerable domestic difficulties in implementing their nuclear energy programmes.

The Seven also agreed on a new plan for financing the developing countries, comprising in particular the Fifth Replenishment of the IDA. They expressed their willingness to negotiate in UNCTAD for the creation of a common fund for commodities, and they defined the positions they would take at the final session of the Conference on International Economic Cooperation, which would end the following month with uncertain results.

With the London meeting, held in a setting quite different from those of the previous summits (in central London, at Number 10 Downing Street), the practice of annual summits was made official. The sherpas' work was regularised, and their periodic meetings to prepare the issues to be placed on the agenda and to draft a provisional communiqué were supplemented by meetings to monitor adherence to the pledges made at the summit. The personal representatives themselves were in most cases assisted by other officials, generally from the foreign and economic ministries. The 'fireside era' was now definitively over.

Bonn (16–17 July 1978)

The outcome of the understandings reached at London was not encouraging, eliciting the emergence of new disputes among the Western allies. The United States had been the most diligent in respecting the commitments made at the summit, but it now had faster inflation, a greatly devalued dollar, and a growing current accounts deficit due in large measure to an energy policy that had facilitated rising oil import bills. West Germany and Japan, which had failed to reach their growth targets, found themselves with massive payments surpluses and stagnation of production.

This situation resulted in an intensified negotiating effort for the next summit, to be held in Bonn in July with the same participants as the year before. As host, Schmidt wanted the gathering to produce some prestigious achievement, and he was particularly active in the preparatory phase. But it was Callaghan who actually offered the idea which would be the basis of the agreement subsequently reached at the summit: a series of reciprocal concessions among the participant governments in the key sectors of economic cooperation. It was not just a matter of setting growth objectives for the wealthiest countries on the 'locomotive' principle (which had proved inadequate) but of adopting a number of differentiated measures by all the countries concerned, not necessarily in the same area of policy. This 'convoy theory', which had been carefully worked out within the OECD, was adopted by the sherpas in their preparatory meetings and endorsed at Bonn by the heads of state and government. Its fundamental basis was a new agreement among the three leading economic powers on growth, foreign trade, inflation, energy and relations with the LDCs.

In particular, West Germany pledged to submit expansionist measures equivalent to 1 percent of the GNP to the *Bundestag* within six weeks. Japan pledged to increase its real growth by 1.5 percent in 1978 as over 1977, to hold its exports down to their 1977 levels, and to double aid to the LDCs within three years. The United States, in addition to announcing a series of anti-inflation measures, decided on a gradual reduction of oil imports through 1985 and an alignment of domestic oil prices with world prices by the end of 1980. The other countries pledged themselves to reach definite, though more modest objectives, compatible with each one's situation. The European Community, for instance, had just a few days previously (European Council meeting in Bremen, 6–7 July 1978) reached an understanding providing for a 50 percent reduction in Community energy imports by the end of 1985.

The Bonn agreement is considered by a majority of commentators the most successful instance of economic policy harmonisation produced by Western summitry, if not one of the most important achievements in the area of Western economic cooperation since Bretton Woods. The participants managed to negotiate a sufficiently organic and detailed package of reciprocally binding economic measures, despite the fact that a number of them had had to overcome strong domestic opposition.[16] Unlike what had happened after the London summit, all three major economies – United States, West Germany, and Japan – substantially honoured their pledges. For once, the statements of satisfaction by the heads of state and government and the optimism of the final communiqué appeared legitimate.

Subsequently, however, more than one voice has disputed the actual effectiveness of the July 1978 accords. In Germany especially, the worsening of the economy in 1979[17] provoked much criticism of the country's adherence to the Bonn understanding. The doubts expressed by Schmidt himself have nourished the suspicion that the chancellor's acceptance of the 'convoy approach' flowed more from his characteristic concern to avoid isolation on a delicate question than from real belief in its usefulness.[18] Though this is not the place to debate the merits of the issue in full, it should perhaps be observed that the Bonn accords might well have produced more positive and lasting effects had a second oil crisis, in the wake of the Iranian revolution, not broken out just a few months after the summit, convulsing the economy of many industrial nations.

The discussions on this 'package deal' left little time for other topics. On nuclear energy, it was decided to keep on using the studies of the International Nuclear Fuel Cycle Evaluation Group, whose constitution had been fostered by the London summit and which had since been joined by more than sixty countries. As for supply of fissionable fuel, while Australia and Canada had resumed exports,[19] in April 1978 the United States had declared an embargo on uranium shipments to the Community until an agreement with Euratom could be renegotiated. This manoeuvre, which followed the passage of the Nuclear Non-Proliferation Act signed by Carter in March, was subsequently revoked, and at Bonn both Carter and Trudeau pledged to ensure regular uranium supplies.

On trade, a new final date (December 1978) for conclusion of the GATT talks was set, but the fact that 'a number of major problems'[20] remained to be solved made it immediately apparent that this deadline, too, could not be met. In fact the Tokyo Round would end only in April 1979.

The European Community took part in the summit for the second time. Though the final communiqué announced the presence of the Commission president only at 'discussions on matters of Community competence', this time Jenkins was not excluded from any of the meetings. This was due to the fact that monetary policy was recognised as within Community competence, following the presentation of the EMS at the summit.

After the European Council meeting in Copenhagen (7–8 April 1978), at which a political consensus had been reached on the creation of a European exchange system defended by common reserves, the EC's Monetary Committee and the Committee of Central Bank Governors had been charged with drawing up possible monetary schemes to be presented at the next European Council meeting in Bremen (6–7 July 1978) for approval of a European Monetary System. At the same time two sherpas, Horst Schulmann and Bernard Clappier, were preparing a Franco-German project, which was formalised 23 June in Hamburg at a private meeting between Giscard and Schmidt. It was on the basis of this document, which Clappier had illustrated to the other European governments during a tour of EC capitals in late June and early July, that the Bremen discussion was actually conducted. Despite the German and French efforts, however, the European Council failed to furnish a united policy. The scheme was accepted by seven countries, the Netherlands and Ireland adhering in principle, while Britain and Italy expressed substantial reservations.

At the Bonn summit, therefore, Schulmann's and Clappier's creature could not be presented to the Americans as a definitive accord among all Community members. The Carter Administration – and Treasury Secretary Blumenthal in particular – had followed the formation of a European monetary union with growing suspicion, and the United States gave only generic and extremely wary approval to the European proposals. No specific commitment was made to neutralise the fluctuations of the dollar (such measures would be taken only later, on 1 November 1979), just as for their part the Europeans made sure not to be too demanding in their monetary requests. For that matter, the approval with reservations by the Americans was clear in the modest tone of the Bonn final statement, which did no more than take note of the communication, recommending that the Community keep the other governments informed of developments concerning the initiative.

The Bonn summit was the first to make non-economic decisions. A special declaration on air piracy committed the participant governments to halt flights to and from countries that refused to extradite or prosecute hijackers or to return the hijacked aircraft. This was a forerunner of the summits' opening to political issues, confirmed at the Venice meeting in 1980.

Tokyo (28–29 June 1979)

Between the Bonn summit and the one held the following year in To-kyo, world attention was virtually monopolised by the events in Iran and their political and economic effects on the rest of the world. The strike against the Shah in October 1978 had caused a 60 percent drop in Iranian oil exports, which were completely cut off on 26 December and slowly resumed only in March 1979. The revolution that culminated with Reza Pahlevi's ouster in January 1979 and Khomeini's rise to power set off a crisis made all the more acute by a new massive rise in oil prices decided on by OPEC on the very eve of the Tokyo gathering.[21] For in fact Iran was the world's fourth-leading producer and second-leading exporter of oil, as well as an important market outlet for the industrial nations' products and a major recipient of international credit.

The shortage of crude oil on world markets was partially made up for by increased production in other OPEC countries (above all Saudi Arabia and Iraq) and by the oil-consuming countries' resort to oil-company stockpiles and the spot market. Still, it produced a massive drop in crude oil stockpiles and a series of speculative manoeuvres that benefited not only the oil producers but also the major oil companies and certain Western countries, such as the United States and Britain.

The industrial world's response to the second oil crisis, though more determined than in 1973, was inadequate at first and, above all, poorly coordinated. On 2 March 1979, IEA member countries pledged to cut their oil consumption by 5 percent in 1979 and 1980, but each would be left free to adopt what it felt were the most appropriate measures to achieve that objective. This decision was reconfirmed in May in Paris, but just a few days later (25 May) Carter granted a $5.00 a barrel subsidy to US fuel oil importers, showing how slight was his consideration of the collective interest.

Faced with this kind of clash, the European Community managed to agree on a joint long-term strategy to counter US, Japanese and Canadian positions. The European Council meeting in Strasbourg (21–22 June), reconfirming the recommendation put forward in March in Paris, decided to hold overall crude oil imports for 1980–85 to an annual level no higher than that of 1978, although opposition from some member states prevented the setting of individual country import quotas.[22] In addition, it was decided to institute a registry of oil transactions, to facilitate full disclosure of activities in the spot markets of Rotterdam and Genoa.

The Strasbourg decisions remain the Community's greatest contribution to economic summitry to date, and were at the same time an encouraging example of the effect prior European coordination can have on the actions of the other Western partners. The Tokyo summit, which met the following week, in large part accepted the European Community proposals, despite doubts on the part of the United States (whose oil imports were not decreasing), Japan (whose own oil resources were negligible), and Canada (which finally agreed so as to avoid isolation).

As to the individual leaders present, there had been major changes from the previous year. Margaret Thatcher had just begun her term at the helm of the new Conservative government, Masayoshi Ohira had taken Fukuda's place, and Joe Clark had supplanted Trudeau, to whose defeat the economic measures adopted after the Bonn summit had been a contributing factor.

Devoted almost exclusively to energy issues, the gathering in the Japanese capital is perhaps the best example of crisis management summitry. Faced with a crisis that affected all Western nations to a greater or lesser extent, the participants succeeded in reaching a fairly concrete agreement, after intense bargaining that was not confined to the preparatory meetings but continued right up to the end among the heads of state and government themselves.

The compromise reached endorsed the Community's requests with regard to oil-import limitations in return for the adoption of specific country-by-country quotas, on which the Europeans had previously been unable to agree.[23] The Community confirmed the decision to cut oil consumption to 500 million tons in 1979 and to hold annual imports from 1980 through 1985 at the 1978 levels, adding the pledge that each member state's contribution to the achievement of this goal would be specified. The United States, Japan and Canada confirmed the import ceilings already agreed upon within the IEA for 1979 and pledged to hold imports in 1980 at their 1979 levels at most. The import ceilings for 1985 were shared out variously among the individual countries. To ensure regular review of the plan's achievements, a group was formed within the OECD made up of high-level representatives of the participant states and the EC Commission. This group's existence would be prolonged at the Venice summit.

It was also decided, at the European Community's suggestion, to institute a registry of international oil operations, to keep domestic oil prices at world price levels or to raise them to that level as quickly as possible,[24] and to promote greater use of coal and nuclear energy. An International Energy Technology Group was formed, connected with the OECD and the IEA and responsible for coordinating the activities of the participant states in the area of new energy technology.[25] OPEC's decision to raise the price of oil again was condemned in much harsher terms than it had been on previous occasions.

There is reason to think that the pledges made at Tokyo had some effect on the participant governments' energy policies. However, the subsequent developments in the international situation (additional oil price rises, inflation, recession) make an objective appraisal of these policies' practical effectiveness difficult. In any event, the ceilings set for 1979 were substantially respected, and the next year's demand for oil was actually lower than the quotas established.

This emphasis on energy problems did not permit adequate treatment of other economic issues. Still, it is interesting to note that this time economic recovery was not viewed as the top-priority objective, as it had always been in the past. It was acknowledged that inflation, fueled by the oil crisis, had become the main enemy. The final communiqué welcomed the conclusion of the GATT negotiations (April 1979) and the strengthening of the European Monetary System.

Following the example set at the Bonn summit with the statement on air piracy, at Tokyo a similar statement was issued on the plight of the refugees from Vietnam and Cambodia, thus confirming the growing importance that was being accorded to political issues at the summits.

Venice (22–23 June 1980)

The second half of 1979 and the first few months of 1980 were marked by major political events whose gravity had a tangible impact on the very nature of Western summitry. The seizure of the American hostages in Iran (November 1979) and above all the Soviet invasion of Afghanistan (December) put East–West issues back in the spotlight and demonstrated how hard it was at the level of heads of state and government to deal with economic questions separately from political events. Truth to tell, ever since Rambouillet, politics had never been absent from the summits, but political discussion had been limited to the private meetings that always take place between individual participants and strictly excluded from the official sessions, apart from exceptional cases.

A political summit bringing together just the United States, France, the United Kingdom and West Germany had been held in Guadeloupe in January 1979. Formally, the initiative had arisen from President Carter's desire to inform his main allies on the progress of the SALT talks, but the creation of a restricted directorate of the major powers was an objective that France had pursued unflaggingly since the 1950s, and Giscard was quick to take advantage of the situation. Economic issues were also dealt with at Guadeloupe, but the summit focused mainly on political and security problems. The principal topics were East–West relations (the SALT talks and relations with China) and the situation in Turkey, Iran and Afghanistan. The four partners also discussed the possibility of deploying intermediate-range nuclear missiles in some European countries as an answer to the Soviet SS-20s. This was an anticipation of the 'double track' decision made by the NATO countries in December 1979.

The Guadeloupe gathering greatly irritated Japan, Italy and the other EC countries, and French hopes to repeat this kind of meeting periodically were not fulfilled.[26] After the Tokyo interlude, however, the content of Western summits was formally broadened to include the most important political issues of the day, and the addition of *ad hoc* statements to the traditional economic communiqué became a constant feature. To this end, a special meeting among high officials of the various countries was called prior to the Venice summit to settle the top-priority points on which the heads of state and government would concentrate their attention.

On the most important of these – the invasion of Afghanistan and the seizure of American diplomatic personnel in Teheran – the positions were certainly not homogeneous.

Carter's stance towards the Soviet Union (economic sanctions and the boycott of the Moscow Olympics) contrasted with the Europeans' greater flexibility. Giscard had met with Brezhnev in Warsaw in May and again in Vienna the day before the summit, receiving assurances on a partial withdrawal of Soviet troops; and Schmidt had confirmed his intent to visit Moscow at the end of June. Therefore, the statement of the Seven on Afghanistan – similar in content to that adopted a few days earlier by the European Council (Venice, 12–13 June) – did not go beyond calling for the immediate and total withdrawal of the occupying troops and confirming the Olympic boycott by those governments that had already decided on it.

Nor was there a complete identity of views on the hostages. Despite the EC Council of Minister's belated decision (Naples, 17 May 1980) to adopt economic sanctions against Iran, the military rescue mission attempted by the United States in April to free its citizens had been widely criticised as a factor that might aggravate the conflict. The statement issued at Venice made no specific mention of the American prisoners, limiting itself to a condemnation of the seizure of diplomatic personnel as hostages in general and urging the participant states to adhere to the new international convention drafted on this matter.

Two other statements, one on hijacking and one on refugees, reiterated the positions expressed at Bonn and Tokyo respectively. However, no explicit stand was assumed on the Middle East in the wake of the Venice declaration adopted at the recent European Council meeting, which in effect amounted to a call to go beyond the Camp David accords.

The broadening of the Venice summit to non-economic issues made it possible for the first time to involve Japan in a formal process of Western political coordination, overcoming the limitations inherent in that country's absence from NATO and from European Political Cooperation. The full importance of this trend would be revealed three years later at Williamsburg.

There were no major changes in the participants at Venice. The only new face came from the country hosting the summit, where Francesco Cossiga was heading his second government since replacing Giulio Andreotti in August 1979. Trudeau had returned to power in February, after less than nine months in opposition, turning out the Conservative Joe Clark, for whom the Tokyo decision to raise domestic oil prices had proved fatal. Because of Japanese Prime Minister Ohira's death a few days before the summit, Japan was represented by Foreign Minister Okita.

The economic portion of the summit was once again devoted in large part to energy problems,[27] which were viewed in a broader perspective than they had been at Tokyo ('We need to break the present link between economic growth and oil consumption.'). It was thus decided to endorse an IEA resolution (May 1980) that called for a further reduction in global oil imports by some four million barrels a day by 1985. A strategy was adopted to lower the share of oil in the overall energy requirements of the states involved from 53 to 40 percent by 1990, primarily by doubling production and use of coal and stepping up output of nuclear energy. Praise was given to the contributions of the International Nuclear Fuel Cycle Evaluation Group (London, 1977) in the nuclear field and of the International Energy Technology Group (Tokyo, 1979) in the area of new technology.

The Venice decisions on energy, then, were longer-term than those made at Tokyo. Still, it was not possible to set specific commitments country-by-country, partly because most of the leaders attending (including President Carter) were facing elections in the next few months.

In economic policy matters, US–European relations were enjoying a moment of relative calm, after the measures adopted by Carter in November 1979 to help stabilise the dollar. The fight against inflation was once again given top priority, but as before this pronouncement had no concrete follow-up. At the same time, the trade tensions between Europe and Japan were becoming more and more evident.

Development problems were dealt with once again, but no specific commitments were made. A short and perfunctory paragraph was dedicated to the Brandt Report. Mention was made of the possibility of opening an energy affiliate of the World Bank so as to increase loan funds for LDCs in this sector. Significantly, the leaders' personal representatives were given the task of preparing a report for 1981 in which more specific proposals would be drafted.

Ottawa (20–21 July 1981)

In the months leading up to the last of the first round of summits, the Western political scene was rocked by major changes in the leadership of key nations. Ronald Reagan, who had beaten Jimmy Carter in the November elections, moved into the White House on 20 January 1981, simultaneously with the freeing of the US hostages in Teheran. François Mitterrand, with his victory in the French presidential elections in May 1981, formed the first Socialist-Communist government in the history of the European Community, thus putting an end to the reign of the 'spiritual father' of the summits, Giscard d'Estaing. In July 1980, Zenko Suzuki had succeeded Ohira after the crushing electoral confirmation of the Liberal Democratic Party. A few weeks before the summit, Giovanni Spadolini became the first non-Christian-Democratic prime minister after 35 years of DC rule in Italy. The presidency of the European Commission changed, too. In July 1980, Roy Jenkins, who had managed to force through the Community's presence at the summits in much more difficult times, left his position to Gaston Thorn of Luxembourg. The only survivor from Rambouillet was Chancellor Schmidt.

Such far-reaching changes, which altered long-standing equilibria – in Europe especially – could not but affect the very conception of the summit itself. The detailed agenda, the specific agreements, and the lengthy communiqués favoured by Carter were not in Reagan's style. To help orient the new president in the field of international relations, the US side stressed personal contacts and declarations of intent more than the search for concrete policy commitments. Mitterrand soon showed how far removed he was in practice from the idea of informal gatherings that had been so dear to his predecessor. Despite Trudeau's effort to recreate the atmosphere of the early summits, initially hosting the participants in the calm of the Montebello Castle, this return to the past now had a pathetic ring to it. Indeed, in the preparatory meetings the sherpas had been officially accompanied (except for the European Community) by representatives of the foreign and financial ministries, definitively confirming the abandonment of a model that had never really been applied.

Nevertheless, more than any of its predecessors, the Ottawa summit did perform that function – which some consider one of the most important aspects of summitry – of giving the top leaders of the industrialised world the opportunity to get to know one another, thus encouraging a more accurate appraisal of their respective positions.

On paper, before the summit began, the differences between the participants could not have been greater. With regard to economic policy, the American strategy of slow growth of the money supply, based on high interest rates and a strong dollar, had been harshly criticised for its inflationary effects and for the problems it caused for the economic recovery of the other Western nations. Moreover, this was diametrically opposed to the French recipe, which called for fiscal and monetary stimuli to increase consumption. On East–West relations, American positions were rigidly anchored to the doctrine of 'linkage' and the need to consider political behaviour and economic concessions together. North–South relations, too, represented a fairly controversial issue – especially in view of the summit to be held in Cancun in October, the new US administration had forewarned everyone of its much less open policy and its intention thenceforward to emphasise bilateral cooperation at the expense of multilateral, especially in financial matters.

In large part, though not entirely, the summit confirmed the previously existing disagreements. The fight against inflation was again assigned top priority, but this time unemployment was attributed equal importance. The disagreement was over the ways of implementing this generic intention. Slow and stable money-supply growth was deemed essential by the summit, which thus affirmed the correctness of Reagan's position and the wrongness of Mitterrand's. It was acknowledged that interest rates had to play a role in this strategy. But it was also stressed that high interest rates in one country (the United States) could cause big problems for the other economies. This problem continued to poison intra-Western relations in the years that followed and cropped up again in the same terms at the Versailles and Williamsburg summits.

The persistent recession brought protectionism back into the limelight, after its having been neglected the year before at Venice. In fact, the summit agreed to the proposal to call a ministerial-level meeting of GATT in 1982 which had been made earlier by the consultative Group of Eighteen.[28] However, the final communiqué made no specific reference to the more and more serious problems Japan's aggressive trade policy was causing for Europe, although the subject had been discussed at the gathering. For the automobile industry, at any rate, the search for an overall solution covering the entire Community (advocated by the Commission) had already failed, owing to the dogged defence of national interests by the member states in previous weeks, which had essentially played into Japan's hands. After the agreement announced 1 May 1981 by the Tokyo authorities (which provided for a cutback of Japanese car exports to the United States of around 7 percent from 1980 levels), West Germany had sensationally undercut the Commission's efforts, reaching a bilateral agreement that car exports would rise by no more than 10 percent. Similar understandings had been entered into by the Netherlands, Belgium and Luxembourg with the Japanese government. Thus all the members of the Community (except for Denmark and Greece, which have no domestic automobile industry) were covered either by unilateral protectionist measures (Britain, France and Italy) or by bilateral accords.

The Ottawa summit was one of the few to deal at any length with North–South issues. The imminence of the Cancun conference, in which almost all the summiteers would participate, encouraged the inclusion of this topic on the agenda. Trudeau proved especially active on this matter, having been one of the promotors of the Mexican gathering. The differences in approach on this issue emerged primarily with regard to the so-called 'global negotiations', which for the Group of 77 were to be the prime forum for all discussions between North and South, with decision-making powers that would be binding not only for individual states but also for the specialised international agencies. This revolutionary approach was opposed decidedly by the United States and, with minor differences, by some European countries, such as West Germany and Britain. A fragile compromise was worked out at Ottawa, dictated more than anything else by US fears of excessive isolation. Willingness to take part in the preparatory phase of the global negotiations was balanced by the emphasis on private capital, alongside official aid, as an instrument of development cooperation.

Like the Venice gathering a year earlier, the Ottawa summit reserved some space for political issues. Among them, the United States attached by far the greatest importance to East–West relations, viewed from a perspective of indissoluble linkage between politics and economics. The newcomers Reagan and Mitterrand, who differed so widely over macroeconomic policy, revealed an unexpected convergence of positions on this subject, which in the end influenced the definitive drafting of the communiqué.

The participants resolved to consult with one another and if necessary to coordinate their actions in the sphere of East–West relations, to ensure compatibility between economic policy and political and security objectives. This statement reflected American fears over the conclusion of the agreement on the Siberian gas pipeline, which was discussed but of which no explicit trace is to be found in the communiqué. It was also decided to step up monitoring of trade with the Soviet Union in strategic products and the high technology associated therewith. A special section of the political statement expressed concern over the constant build-up of Soviet military strength and reiterated the need to act for effective arms control and for the achievement of disarmament accords, in the framework of linkage between global behaviour and specific negotiations.

The other points of the political statement, expounded publicly by Trudeau, touched on the Middle East (and the situation in Lebanon in particular), the Madrid Conference, Afghanistan, Cambodia, peace and international security, and refugees. A special declaration was issued on terrorism. The foreign ministers of the United States, Britain, France, West Germany and Canada took a position on Namibia.

Part of the press, especially in the US, played up Reagan's success at his first major international appearance, trying to show that the high interest rate policy had been substantially recognised as proper and that the request for firmness towards the Eastern bloc had in fact been adopted. Actually, the chief merit of the Ottawa summit was to make clearer the basic options confronting the new generation of leaders who would dominate the international scene in the years to come. But no particularly important operational decisions were made, and the major differences that emerged continued to mark relations between the Western partners, indeed progressively undermining them.

Versailles (4–6 June 1982)

The second round of summit conferences was inaugurated, like the first, by France, but the differences from seven years previously were only too evident. Giscard's vision of a confidential meeting, as removed as possible from prying eyes, which had been initiated at Rambouillet, had quickly faded with the march of time, and now it was utterly overturned by the spectacular staging desired by Mitterrand. The mass media took on a pre-eminent role, and communication technology was employed as never before.

The leaders who gathered at the Palais de Versailles were the same as the year before, with one significant exception. For the first time the European Community was represented not only by the president of the Commission, Thorn, but also by a president of the Council who was from one of the non-participant nations, Belgian Premier Wilfried Martens. This was no voluntary policy choice, however, but a practical necessity – in fact, even if the summit had been held the following month, the presidency would have been Denmark's.

The same leaders brought with them the same problems, which the year that had gone by had left far from resolved. The Western economy was still mired in persistent recession, US interest rates showed no sign of easing significantly, and the dollar was still extremely high. So monetary policy was included as a top-priority subject on the summit's agenda. In line with the intentions Mitterrand had announced at Ottawa, France had succeeded in boosting consumption by 4 percent in a year, but production had gained only 2 percent, which meant excessive imports and the weakening of the franc. It was only to be expected, then, that there would be a particularly sharp clash between Mitterrand's government, which advocated the need for direct intervention to maintain a regime of stable exchange rates, and the Reagan administration, which favoured floating rates.

In the months before the summit, the finance ministers of the major Western countries concentrated on working out a plan for monetary cooperation. In the course of the preparatory meetings for the summit and in other negotiating forums as well (such as the meeting of the Group of Five held in May in Helsinki in the wings of the IMF Interim Committee's session) a document was drafted defining the commitment to work for more stability in the international monetary system. This compromise was approved at Versailles and appended to the final communiqué as an *ad hoc* statement.

This time, the communiqué contained but few remarks on macroeconomic questions (victory in the battle against inflation as the only way to achieve lasting growth and employment, to bring down 'unacceptably high' interest rates, and to achieve more stable exchange rates). The monetary statement contained elements of considerable interest. In addition to laying down a prohibition against using exchange rates to gain unfair competitive advantage and providing for possible intervention to counter disorder in the foreign exchange markets (as laid down in art. IV of the IMF statutes), it also delegated the five SDR countries[29] to perform a monitoring role in collaboration with the IMF, under an innovative procedure. This agreement was supplemented by the pledge made by the finance ministers − who met separately − to have a study done on the effectiveness of government intervention in exchange markets and to adjust their policies on the basis of the study's findings.

Despite the persistent divergency of approach, then, an effort had been made to encourage Western convergence in the monetary sphere. To this end, the four European countries present at Versailles and the two Community representatives had met prior to the summit to work out a common position.

Where the negotiations were a total failure, by contrast, was in the realm of East−West trade and credit. The American administration's sharp hostility to European participation in the Siberian pipeline project had culminated in December in Reagan's decree of an embargo on materials produced by US companies destined for use in the construction of the pipeline, in the wake of the proclamation of martial law in Poland. This move had caused serious supply problems for the European companies involved in the project, in that many indispensable parts for the construction of the equipment were manufactured in the United States itself. At the same time, the US administration urged its allies to reduce credits to the USSR. To study the matter, a special group composed of high officials of the countries involved met a number of times to try to work out a solution, but none was arrived at before the Versailles summit. Indeed, the inclusion of trade and credit policy towards the East in the agenda for the summit was itself in doubt right up to the last minute, and it was accepted only at Reagan's vehement insistence.

The text of the communiqué on this point reflects the difficulty encountered in trying to reach a compromise. It speaks of a 'prudent and diversified' approach, consistent with the West's political and security interests, through three types of action: monitoring of exports of strategic goods; exchange of information within the OECD on all aspects of economic relations with the East; 'cautious' handling of financial relations, 'including also the need for commercial prudence in limiting export credits'. The progress of these relations was to be subject to periodic review.

Mitterrand's particular activism was manifested in two other areas, apart from the top-priority issues of monetary policy and economic relations with the East. The first concerned relations with the LDCs, which was however accorded less attention than the previous year. The discussion again revolved around the start-up of global negotiations, in favour of which the European Community had long been on record. As at Ottawa, the United States invented a compromise formula to avoid seeming too isolated. It agreed to the commencement of the negotiations 'provided that the independence of the specialised institutions' would be safeguarded. This amounted to saying that the single most innovative feature of the new international negotiating forum (the possibility of orienting and reforming the activities of existing institutions) was to be ruled out from the start.

Also, with a special report read to the participants on the first evening of the gathering, the French president introduced an issue never before touched on at the summits: scientific and technological development, which reflected the importance Paris attached to the computer industry. This initiative did not get an enthusiastic reception from the other leaders, who felt it was excessively oriented to French interests. Still, it was decided to form a working group on the development and use of new technologies, composed of government and European Community representatives. In collaboration with the OECD, this group was to draw up an initial report by the end of 1982, to be examined at the next summit. In Williamsburg, this topic would be barely touched on, but the working group would be renewed.

The Versailles summit was held at a time of tremendous international tension. The Anglo-Argentine war for the Falklands was still going on, and the Israeli invasion of Lebanon was announced to the participants during the summit proceedings. Though the official discussions were monopolised by economic issues, talk of politics was inescapable, and this was done primarily during meals. The Seven issued a generic declaration on the conflict in Lebanon, which did no more than express hope for the cessation of military actions, without making any judgement as to specific responsibilities. The crisis in the South Atlantic, by contrast, was not the subject of any *ad hoc* statement, but there was full confirmation of solidarity with Britain.[30]

The fragility of many of these compromises, especially on monetary matters and East–West relations, was immediately apparent. In their very first statements at the end of the summit, the participants offered contrasting interpretations of the text of the communiqué, each claiming not to have yielded on the key points. The Americans denied that the pledges made at Versailles entailed any change of course on monetary policy. Schmidt and especially Mitterrand declared that they did not feel obliged to cut back credits to the Soviet Union simply because it had been agreed to adopt a 'prudent' attitude.

The weeks that followed were among the most dramatic in the recent history of relations between the United States and Europe. A series of events – not all of which were necessarily interrelated – aggravated the strains in inter-Atlantic relations to such an extent that a profound crisis between the allies was feared. On 11 June the United States decided to impose special duties on steel imported from Europe. On 13 June the Europeans undertook a realignment of the EMS, with a devaluation of the French franc and the lira and a revaluation of the mark and the Dutch guilder. At the same time the French government enacted a number of austerity measures, including a wage and price freeze, and the Federal Reserve Bank intervened with anti-speculative measures to moderate fluctuations on the foreign exchange markets.

The gravest decision though, and one that did flow from the outcome of the summit, was Reagan's announcement on 18 June that the US embargo on exports of high technology material for the Siberian pipeline was thenceforth extended to the foreign affiliates of US companies and to foreign companies that produced under US license. The four European countries with the biggest stake in the construction of the pipeline (West Germany, France, Britain and Italy) responded by instructing their own companies to honour their contracts with the Soviet Union.

This provocative US stance, which was among the reasons for the resignation of Secretary of State Haig the following week, was harshly criticised at the European Council meeting in Brussels on 28–29 June, and cast serious doubts on the usefulness of such encounters as the Versailles summit. It was clear that not only had the summit failed to resolve the long-latent differences among the participants but it had actually aggravated them, revealing itself to be not so much an opportunity for reaching common positions as an alarming instance of inability to communicate.

Williamsburg (28–30 May 1983)

The substantial failure of the Versailles summit and the deep crisis which followed induced the Western allies to try and reach an understanding on the most controversial issues in the second half of 1982.

On 6 August 1982 the EC Commission and the US Department of Commerce reached a preliminary agreement whereby the Europeans agreed to self-limit their steel exports to the United States. The accord was approved by the Community's Council of Ministers on 21 October of the same year.[31]

On 13 November – three days after Brezhnev's death and the day after Andropov was named his successor – the US president decided, after long and difficult negotiations with the Europeans on their trade and credit policies towards the East bloc countries, to lift the sanctions that had been imposed on the supply of equipment for the Siberian gas pipeline. Reagan's decision temporarily put an end to the dispute, which had further strained inter-Atlantic relations in the preceding months, thus making it possible to face with less pessimism the ninth summit of the leaders of the major industrial democracies, which was to be hosted by Reagan himself in the colonial town of Williamsburg, Virginia, at the end of May 1983.

In the meantime, important political changes were taking place in a number of the participating countries. On 1 October 1982 Helmut Kohl became chancellor of the Federal Republic of Germany, bringing to a close the long reign of the Social Democratic Party and its leader Helmut Schmidt, the last survivor of the group that had met for the first summit at Rambouillet in 1975. On 26 November 1982 the new leader of the Liberal Democratic Party, Yasuhiro Nakasone, replaced Suzuki as the head of the Japanese government. On 10 December the Christian Democrats regained the leadership of the Italian government in the person of Amintore Fanfani, after an eighteen-month interval with the Republican Spadolini as prime minister. These changes gave to the Western political scene a more markedly conservative colouring which would to a certain extent influence the preparations for and the course of the ninth summit.

Notwithstanding the scepticism which prevailed on the eve of the summit, extensively reported by the mass media, the Williamsburg meeting distinguished itself from the last few encounters in a number of respects.

First of all, the prospects for economic recovery were decidedly more promising than they had been a year earlier when the world economy was still plagued by stagnation, inflation and high oil prices. The first, though still tenuous, signs of the long awaited recovery had finally appeared.[32] Inflation had slowed down noticeably with respect to the year before in all the participant countries except Italy. The big drop in oil prices, formalised at OPEC's London meeting in March 1983, made it possible to consider the ten-year energy crisis over, even if the new phase would pose different problems, related mainly to the oil producers' indebtedness towards the Western countries. These positive trends were accompanied, however, by a generalised increase in unemployment.

There were also some novel aspects in the way the US administration oriented the preparations for the summit. For the first time it was proposed that meetings of the technical ministers of the seven participating countries be held prior to the summit. The suggestion was received coolly by the other governments, which considered it a useless duplication of the encounters which already took place through a number of multilateral forums. The seven finance and treasury ministers met nevertheless in Washington on 29 April 1983, while at the meeting of foreign trade ministers held in Brussels on the same day the Community participants preferred to be represented by the Commission, justifying their absence with the motivation that the Community was officially responsible for their trade matters.

The biggest surprises came, however, in the contents of the summit itself. On the eve of the gathering, observers almost unanimously agreed that the Williamsburg summit would be dominated by economic questions, with the Reagan administration's fiscal and monetary policies, trade relations with the East bloc, protectionism and Third World indebtedness at the top of the agenda.

Actually, though, not much was decided on these matters. Criticism of the United States' high interest rates and enormous public deficit (the only economic theme on which the Europeans managed to take a common stand) was not as strong as expected and produced no noteworthy results. In fact, in the final communiqué there was no firm commitment on the part of the US to alter its policies.

The expected clash between Mitterrand and Reagan over monetary policy was also not as bitter as predicted. The French president, an advocate of a return to fixed exchange rates, had threatened to desert the summit if US Treasury Secretary Regan's rigidly liberalistic theses were not modified. Mitterrand, backed by the opinions of two 'founding fathers' of the summits, Schmidt and Giscard,[33] had proposed – at a meeting of OECD foreign ministers in Paris on 9 May – that a Bretton Woods-style international monetary conference of heads of government be convened. The other leaders' lukewarm reaction to the idea highlighted France's isolation in holding this position. The Americans, faithful to the principle that direct intervention in the exchange market is useless and convinced that each country must first 'put its own house in order', considered a monetary conference premature at this stage.[34] The response of the other participants, some of whom (Great Britain, Italy and Japan) were preparing for national elections, was also very cautious. France's bargaining power, already weak because of the country's precarious economic conditions,[35] dropped to an even lower level on the eve of the summit. Mitterrand was therefore obliged to backtrack with respect to his initial demands. The confrontation between the French thesis ('everything depends on monetary policy') and the American thesis ('the important thing is to guarantee and expand free trade') was thus resolved in the end with reciprocal verbal concessions of little immediate practical relevance. The final communiqué stated that the seven finance ministers, in consultation with the managing director of the IMF, would define the appropriate means for improving the international monetary system and would 'consider the part which might, in due course, be played in this process by a high-level international monetary conference'.[36] In return, the participants agreed 'to continue consultations on proposals for a new negotiating round in the GATT', after the failure of the November 1982 ministerial conference.

As was to be expected, the study on exchange rate policy commissioned at Versailles was unable to come up with clear-cut proposals. The linguistic ambiguity of the Williamsburg communiqué, like the statement produced at Versailles, reflected the substantial divergence between the US and the other countries on this issue. In the communiqué it is stated that without relinquishing their freedom to operate independently, the seven governments 'are willing to undertake coordinated intervention in exchange markets', but only 'in instances where it is agreed that such intervention would be helpful', which means that each country will continue to act according to its own convictions (and it is common knowledge that the United States considers intervention 'helpful' only in the event of very grave and unexpected developments which threaten to cause sharp oscillations on the exchange markets). The only small step forward was the vague commitment to 'pursue closer consultations'; there is, however, no explicit mention of a formal procedure for coordination among the central banks, which is what the Europeans wanted.

While monetary and fiscal policies were definitely a dominant subject of debate at the summit (even if the results were meagre), the same cannot be said of East–West economic relations.

An agreement on gas imports was reached on 8 May 1983 at an IEA ministerial meeting in Paris. The United States had withdrawn its request for a pledge on the part of the Europeans to limit their imports from the East to no more than 30 percent of national energy needs and had accepted instead a more general commitment to diversify their purchases and avoid excessive dependence on any one supplier.

But this certainly did not put an end to the controversy over East–West trade in general. Reagan had presented to Congress a number of important amendments for the renewal of the Export Administration Act, due to expire on 30 September 1983. One of these gives the president the power to apply sanctions against US subsidiaries or licensees in Europe which sell to the USSR goods whose sale by US firms is forbidden by Washington for 'national security' reasons. The US president's decision came under heavy attack in Europe, especially after it was announced (on 17 May) that negotiations for the export of US grain to the USSR would be resumed.

To avoid the risk of another clash, the subject was taken off the agenda. The final communiqué contains only one cautiously worded paragraph on the matter, whose brevity contrasts with the importance attributed to the problem the year before.

Not much was concluded, once again, with respect to relations with the less developed countries. Apart from a vague declaration of intent by Reagan at the start of the summit, the only novelty written into the communiqué was the 'concern . . . for the debt burdens' of the LDCs. But no mention was made of global negotiations, though a formal wish for the success of the sixth UNCTAD conference, which was to open in Belgrade a few days later, was expressed.

Observers were unanimous in considering the joint declaration on security the most important innovation of the Williamsburg summit. After expressing the hope that 'meaningful arms reductions' would be attained in the framework of the various international negotiations under way, the document turns to the subject of intermediate-range nuclear forces, inviting the USSR to constructively contribute to the success of the INF negotiations and reiterating that the French and British deterrent forces are to be excluded from the bargaining. If an agreement on medium-range missiles is reached, 'the negotiations will determine the level of deployment'; otherwise 'the countries concerned will proceed, at the end of 1983, with the planned deployment'. It was at this point that the governments represented at the summit decided to insert the most significant phrase: 'the security of our countries is indivisible and must be approached on a global basis.'

The importance of the document lies not so much in its contents (the concepts had already been expressed many times in other forums) as in the fact that it was adhered to by France, which is a member of the Atlantic Alliance but not of its integrated military structure and hence did not take part in the Euromissile decision, and by Japan, which is not even a member of the Alliance.

Unlike the economic document, whose general features had been established during the preparatory meetings of the sherpas and finance ministers, the political declaration can be considered in large part an original product of the summit itself. True, the subject had been discussed earlier by the leaders' personal representatives. But the general impression given before the summit was that the heads of state and government would limit themselves to discussing the subject informally over meals, as they had done on other occasions. The decision to issue an *ad hoc* statement on security, proposed by Reagan and received not without objections on the part of the other leaders,[37] matured in a relatively short space of time, and for understandable reasons.

First of all, the United States wanted the Europeans to formally reconfirm their commitment to install the Euromissiles starting at the end of 1983 if the INF negotiations under way in Geneva failed to produce positive results. Second, it was undoubtedly easier for the countries present to adhere to a document reaffirming the 'double-track' strategy than it was to reach an agreement on economic issues which presented much greater obstacles. On security, in effect, the Seven gave a noteworthy show of cohesion. It may also be that the emphasis on security matters was favoured by the cultural backgrounds of the leaders present, none of whom can be considered an expert in economics and hence especially attached to the summit model invented eight years earlier by the 'economists' Giscard and Schmidt.

Two other factors which emerged just before the summit opened also made the strategic declaration of highly topical interest. On 24 and 25 May the US House and Senate had approved an appropriation of 625 million dollars for the development and testing of the first MX missiles, reversing the negative vote expressed on 20 December 1982. On 28 May, just as the summit opened, the Soviet government issued a formal statement reiterating the threat of countermeasures if NATO did not revoke its decision to install the Euromissiles and if the United States did not adopt a more constructive posture at the Geneva negotiations.

But, above all, the declaration responded to the common need of the Europeans and Japanese to prevent the deployment of Soviet SS-20s in either Europe or Asia. After NATO's abandonment of the 'zero option' and in the absence of a Soviet commitment to destroy its missiles, Tokyo feared that the missiles targeted on Europe might simply be moved to the vicinity of its own borders. In this context, the US attempt to bring the Europeans and Japanese together met with success, materialising in an unprecedented assumption of joint responsibility. The strategic declaration provoked critical reactions in many countries, however. The opposition in Japan, Germany and Italy denounced the apparent extension of the NATO 'umbrella', and in France the governing coalition was split by serious contrasts.[38]

All considered, the Williamsburg summit closed with less negative results than had been feared before it started. If nothing else, the Western countries managed to avoid the traumatic rift experienced the year before by leaving aside the problem of economic relations with the East and by giving a show of unity on the less controversial terrain of security. In this sense, Reagan's augmented ability to conduct a meeting at the highest level was recognised by all. The president got the confirmation he wanted on deployment of the Euro-missiles and conceded nothing at the economic level, even if his hope of a fuller recognition of the certainty of a recovery was not fulfilled.

Those who wanted to see progress in the field of economic cooperation were instead completely deluded. The most tangible results of the summit were another big surge in the value of the dollar and the concrete possibility of a new increase in US interest rates; the exact opposite of what all had hoped for. Irritation over this outcome was clearly expressed by both Chancellor Kohl and President Mitterrand. The latter went so far as to question France's participation in the next summit, to be held in Great Britain in 1984.[39]

Notes

1. Such gatherings as the North–South summit in Cancun (October 1981) are irregular and atypical.

2. The original participants (United States, Japan, Federal Republic of Germany, France, United Kingdom and Italy) were joined by Canada in 1976 and by the European Community in 1977.

3. Between 6 Oct. and 22 Dec. 1973, the posted price of crude was raised from $3.01 to $11.65 a barrel.

4. H. Kissinger, *Years of Upheaval* (Little Brown, Boston, 1982), p. 934.

5. Actually, the decision was made in two informal meetings of the Group of Five and Group of Ten: the first aboard the US presidential yacht, the evening before, and the second just a few hours before the Interim Committee meeting. In addition to eliminating the official price for gold, the agreement laid down that the total gold holdings of the IMF and the central banks could not be increased, that the parties could not unilaterally modify the understandings concluded, and that the Bank for International Settlements should be authorised to oversee respect of the agreements.

6. So named because one of its earliest meetings was held in the White House library. On the origins of the Library Group, see Putnam, chapter 2 in this volume.

7. What the American founders of the Trilateral Commission actually had in mind was a series of regular, structured, and widely publicised meetings. On this, see Z. Brzezinski, 'U.S. Foreign Policy: The Search for Focus', *Foreign Affairs*, July 1973; and H. Owen, 'Summitry Revisited', *The Atlantic Monthly*, March 1973.

8. Among these advisers, who would play a fundamental part in the summit process, was George Schultz, who as treasury secretary under Nixon had been a member of the Library Group. For his part, Giscard named Raymond Barre, later to become prime minister of France.

9. Obviously, this justification no longer held the following year, without the issue of Community participation as such being resolved.

10. This amendment did not go into effect until April 1978, after the requisite ratification by 60% of the member countries representing an 80% majority of the votes.

11. On this point, Wilson demanded a British presence separate from the rest of

the Community, justifying his stance by reference to the fact that his country was about to become a major oil producer and would have a special role to play on all the other questions to be discussed. The polemics over Community participation at the Conference on International Economic Cooperation continued at the European Council meeting in Rome (1–2 December 1975) and ended with a compromise granting Britain the right to make statements in its own name, provided they were cleared in advance with the other partners.

12. See Bank for International Settlements, *Annual Report* (Basel, 1976).

13. In particular, the Italian government had taken a series of measures in the first five months of 1976 to stop the fall of the lira, which had been devalued by some 25% against the dollar between 20 January and the beginning of May. The value of the pound sterling had fallen under $2.00 for the first time. Some responsibility for the French franc's difficulties should perhaps be attributed to the results of the first ballot in the cantonal elections, which saw major gains for the parties of the left.

14. On 26 July 1976, the Commission – its hand strengthened by a previous opinion by the Court of Justice (no. 1/75, 22 November 1975) – initiated legal proceedings against West Germany, France, Italy, and Britain for violation of art. 69 of the EEC Treaty.

15. Moreover, the tradition of holding the European Council meeting before the summit was broken with Versailles (1982) and Williamsburg (1983).

16. The National Energy Act presented by Carter in April 1977 got a rather cool reception, and was passed – with substantial amendments – only in October 1978. The decision to raise domestic oil prices had given rise to dissent within the administration itself. In West Germany, the adoption of expansionary measures was opposed by some members of the government as well as by the banks.

17. In 1979, West Germany ran its first current accounts deficit since 1962, and the inflation rate climbed over 5%.

18. However, some recent statements by Horst Schulmann, Schmidt's chief economic adviser and his personal representative from the Bonn summit on, underscore the importance of the 'convoy theory' in 1978 and suggest an updated version thereof (with Britain taking the place of the United States in the lead group) as a remedy for the current international recession. (See *La Repubblica*, 8 February 1983, p. 9.)

19. In July 1977 and January 1978, respectively.

20. This quote from the summit communiqué and the others that appear in this chapter are taken from the relevant issues of the *Department of State Bulletin* (Washington D.C.).

21. Through December 1978 oil prices had seen a period of relative stability, holding at the price of $12.70 a barrel for Arabian Light decided on at the OPEC summit in Doha in December 1976. The Abu Dhabi summit (December 1978) had decided on a 10% rise for 1979, but a subsequent extraordinary OPEC conference (Geneva, March 1979) left cartel members free to add whatever surcharge they managed to get. In April and May, therefore, a series of indiscriminate price hikes had vastly widened the range of prices. The next OPEC summit in Geneva (27–28 June 1979) partly succeeded in containing the range, limiting it to $5.50. On the other hand, the price of crude was raised to $18 (Arabian Light), nearly 50% higher than in December 1978.

22. The main protagonists of the dispute were France, which favoured specific commitments, and West Germany, which preferred not to go beyond the setting of an overall figure for the Community.

23. The agreement on national quotas was reached on the last day, after frenetic negotiations among the leaders of the major countries. In view of Italy's particularly

severe dependence on imports, it was conceded an *ad hoc* clause whereby the pledge to hold oil imports to the 1978 level was accepted 'in the context of the overall commitment of the European Community'. This would enable Italy to take advantage of a possible greater-than-pledged reduction in the other European countries' imports and of possible new production from British North Sea wells.

24. This was particularly important for the United States inasmuch as it artificially lowered its domestic energy prices below world levels.

25. This group was short-lived, however; it was not renewed the next year.

26. Still, there was no lack of efforts by Giscard, as is witnessed by his autumn 1980 project of convening a new restricted summit in Martinique, which Schmidt rejected. A subsequent report by four international studies institutes in New York, Paris, Bonn and London also suggested a similar solution to the problem of Western coordination on security policy. See K. Kaiser, T. de Montbrial, W. Lord, and D. Watt, *Western Security: What Has Changed? What Should Be Done?* (Royal Institute of International Affairs, London, 1981).

27. Between July 1979 and May 1980 oil prices had seen another increase, of around 50% (the price of Arabian Light rose from $18 to $28 a barrel).

28. The meeting was actually held in Geneva, 24–29 November 1982, but the results were very poor.

29. The dollar, the yen, the German mark, the pound sterling, and the French franc.

30. In the wake of the Argentine invasion of the islands, the European Community, together with the United States, Canada and Australia, had taken two measures against Argentina: an embargo on arms exports and a block on all Community imports of Argentine products. These sanctions were lifted on 21 June, a few days after the end of the conflict.

31. The agreement is for the period from 1 November 1982 to 31 December 1985 and foresees a reduction of 9% in Community steel exports to the United States by means of a contraction from 6.4 to 5.75% of the Community's quota for ten groups of speciality products.

32. The IMF had projected a GDP growth in 1983 of 2.8% in Japan, 2.4% in the United States, 1.7% in Canada and 1.5% in Great Britain, while it was expected that France and Italy would have to wait until 1984.

33. For their opinions, see *The Economist*, 26 February and 21 May 1983.

34. Even though Treasury Secretary Regan had mentioned a similar possibility in December 1982.

35. On 21 March 1983 the franc was devalued for the third time and a rigid austerity programme was consequently drawn up by the French Finance Minister Delors. On 16 May the EC finance ministers approved France's request for a Community loan of 30 billion francs, which followed other loans raised in the preceding months by the French government on the international market and from Saudi Arabia. Even though the rate had dropped sharply compared to the year before, France's inflation was still much higher than the average for all the other EC countries, excluding Italy.

36. On the basis of what US Treasury Secretary Regan said at a press conference at the end of the summit, it seems that only the finance ministers of the five SDR countries will be involved. In the annex to the declaration, moreover, the procedure of joint monitoring of monetary stability by the SDR countries and the IMF, decided at the Versailles summit, is confirmed.

37. France's objections regarded the opportunity of issuing a declaration on defence and security problems at a summit formally dedicated to economic issues. Ac-

tually, Mitterrand was afraid of being associated with an easily criticisable solidarity commitment. Canada and Germany instead worked to obtain a more flexible version of the original text (which referred to the 'zero option') and succeeded in overcoming the resistance of the United States and Britain.

38. The contents of the document were in any case confirmed by the NATO defence ministers who met in Brussels on 1–2 June, notwithstanding the formal reservations expressed by Greece, Spain and Denmark on the installation of the Euromissiles.

39. In an interview for French television which was printed on 9 June 1983 in the daily *Le Figaro*, Mitterrand stated: 'I have doubts on the usefulness of these annual summits, at least in their present form . . . and I do not want France to participate again, unless the method is changed radically.'

2 THE WESTERN ECONOMIC SUMMITS: A POLITICAL INTERPRETATION

Robert Putnam

'Nothing could be more fatal than the habit (the at present fatal and pernicious habit) of personal contact between the statesmen of the world.' This classic critique of summitry by the British diplomat Sir Harold Nicolson was aptly recalled by David Watt on the eve of the 1977 gathering in Downing Street of the leaders of the seven major industrial democracies.[1] At first glance, the record left by the ensuing seven summits (London, Bonn, Tokyo, Venice, Ottawa, Versailles and Williamsburg), as well as the two earlier ones (Rambouillet and Puerto Rico), might appear to sustain this negative judgement. Economically, the 'discomfort index' of inflation and unemployment in the summit countries had risen inexorably during this period, and the international climate between the Europeans and the Americans, and between both and the Japanese, has chilled almost as markedly. To be sure, no estimate of the effects of summitry can be fully persuasive, based as it must be on counterfactual comparison – who knows what things would have been like without the summits? Yet the public record apparently does little to dispel the sceptics' view that summitry creates problems rather than solving them. What, then, explains this fashion for regular meetings among heads of government?

One important answer was offered by Watt himself: 'Nicolson, writing in the 1920s, did not make allowance for what has become a more and more critical factor in the conduct of foreign relations – namely, the existence in all the Western countries of a powerful public opinion sufficiently sophisticated to perceive a connection between international events and its own well-being.'[2] He might have added that well-established trends in international economic interdependence have made this connection between international affairs and domestic prosperity so firm that governments would need to worry about the linkage even if it were not apparent to their constituents. As Richard N. Cooper pointed out a decade ago, 'increased economic interdependence, by joining national markets, erodes the effectiveness of [national economic] policies and hence threatens national autonomy in the determination and pursuit of economic objectives . . . The growing interdependence of the world economy creates pressures for common policies, and hence for procedures whereby countries discuss and coordinate actions that hitherto were regarded as being of domestic concern exclusively.'[3] For a chief executive whose political fate hung on his electorate's economic well-being, international economics by the mid-1970s could no longer be considered 'low politics', left to bloodless diplomats, to cunning central bankers, to distant international organisations, or to the haphazards of the market.

This domestic political resonance of international economics would probably suffice to explain the emergence of contemporary summitry, but in the early 1970s a second factor became relevant: the waning of the American hegemony that had undergirded the post-war international economic regime, a development symbolised by the collapse of the Bretton Woods monetary order, followed almost immediately by the first oil shock and the worst downturn in economic activity since the 1930s. The collective clipper of the Western economies had suddenly entered stormy seas, the captain had disappeared, and the ship's mates scuttled around the helm in wary confusion. In place of the hegemonic stability that American predominance had assured for a quarter-century, a new system of collective leadership for the world economy would need to be jury-rigged. For a generation of leaders who had themselves come of age during the Great Depression, the risks of a return to an alluring, but ultimately catastrophic economic nationalism were vivid. As we shall see a bit later, it was natural that the particular men in power in key countries in the mid-1970s would turn to summitry as a means for reasserting collective leadership; but given the political stakes, it was probably inevitable that chief executives themselves would confront the task of re-establishing a new world economic equilibrium.

In this chapter, I shall set forth a political interpretation of the Western economic summit process, trying to understand the multiple motives of the participants and how they are addressed in the context of summitry. In order to do so, I offer first some notes towards a political theory of international economic cooperation, drawing on the theory of games and bargaining.[4] Second, I shall describe the actual process of negotiations behind the Western economic summits of the last nine years, including a word or two about the immediate historical antecedents of this summitry and some discussion of the preparations undertaken by each of the participants.

Finally, I shall offer some speculations about the actual consequences of this summit process. My concern throughout will be the entire summit process, including the extensive preparations and follow-up meetings that often span much of the year; the encounter among the heads of government themselves is obviously the highpoint of the process, but it is by no means the only element of interest.

The description and speculation that follow derive from confidential interviews with approximately 150 participants and close observers of summitry in Washington, London, Bonn, Ottawa, Tokyo, Paris, Rome and Brussels. Included among these interviews were encounters with a dozen past and present heads of government and cabinet members, more than two dozen 'personal representatives' (those all-important 'sherpas', in the jargon of summitry, who conduct the international summit preparations on behalf of the heads of government), half a dozen central bank governors and deputy governors, and scores of senior diplomats, civil servants, political advisers, members of parliament, businessmen, journalists, trade unionists, and officials of international organisations. Given the sensitivity of the events and topics I was probing, it was necessary to assure anonymity to all of my interlocutors. Consequently, my accounts here will lack the savour and rigor of full citation. However, I used triangulation extensively to assure myself of the accuracy of the reports I received.

A Political Approach to International Economic Cooperation

Nearly two decades ago Richard E. Walton and Robert B. McKersie offered a 'behavioural theory' of social negotiations that is strikingly applicable to international economic cooperation.[5] They sought to understand the range of behaviour exhibited when two parties enter negotiations aimed at reaching agreement about common activities; labour-management negotiations was the case that specifically concerned them. Their theoretical approach assumes, first, that the agenda for the negotiations contains a mix of conflictful and collaborative items, so that the parties must simultaneously defend self-interest and engage in joint action. Second, because the relationship between the parties is a continuing one, involving more than the items under negotiation at any point in time, the negotiators are concerned about the overall tone of their relationship as well as the immediate outcome. Third, the negotiations of interest 'involve com-

plex social units in which the constituent members are very interest-
ed in what goes on at the bargaining table and have some influence
over the negotiators'.[6] Under these circumstances, Walton and Mc-
Kersie suggest, negotiations between the parties can be decomposed
analytically into four sub-processes.

Distributive Bargaining

These activities involve the strategies and tactics of each party to
achieve its goals when they are in basic conflict with the goals of the
other. Distributive bargaining arises in 'fixed-sum' games, that is,
when one party's gain inherently involves a loss to the other. Below
some point each party may simply prefer a breakdown in the negotiations, but typically there is some overlap between the minimally
acceptable outcomes of the two parties, and the issue is who will appropriate these 'gains from agreement'. A wide range of tactics for
distributive bargaining is familiar from game theory and from ordinary experience — from dissembling about one's own utilities ('bluffing') to attempting to modify one's opponent's perceptions of his
utilities ('arguing'). Wage bargaining is the classic example of distributive bargaining from labour–management relations. Assuming
that the summit countries have agreed to limit their collective consumption of petroleum to some fixed quantity — which was approximately true in Tokyo in 1979 — their haggling over national quotas
involves distributive bargaining.

Integrative Bargaining

In some circumstances the achievement of one party's goals need not
require equivalent sacrifice by the other, because their objectives are
not in fundamental conflict and can thus be 'integrated'. In such
'variable-sum' games, the negotiators can be said to be engaged in
integrative bargaining or joint problem-solving, trying to maximise
their joint gains. Jean Monnet had precisely this type of activity in
mind when he spoke of lining up all the negotiators on one side of
the table and their problems on the other. A typical example from
labour–management relations involves the search for changes in
working conditions that might increase productivity, while reducing
worker discomfort. Examples from recent Western summitry might
include the 1978 discussion of air hijacking and the 1982 discussion
of the future of technology. Whereas the archetypical outcome to

distributive bargaining is a 'compromise', the archetypical outcome of integrative bargaining is a 'solution'.

Virtually any real-world agenda item can give rise to both distributive and integrative bargaining. The hard-fought struggles of distributive bargaining generate incentives for the negotiators to find ways to increase the available pie, and in the typical case it will seem likely, though not certain, that they can find ways to do so, if they are clever enough. (If the United States would expand coal production, might that mean more energy all around?) On the other hand, once additional gains are in sight, the question of distribution of those gains arises once again. (New technologies, cooperatively developed, may raise productivity throughout the West, but where will the new industries be based?)

Virtually all social interactions involve some mixture of motives: there are distributive elements even in marriage and integrative elements even in war. The fundamental dilemma of games in which the mix is more even − such as labour-management relations and international political economy − is that strategies appropriate for distributive bargaining (such as concealing one's real priorities, firmness in stating one's proposals, setting time deadlines) are directed contrary to the requisites of integrative bargaining (such as candor, openmindedness, and a longer time horizon) Negotiators concentrating on distributive bargaining may forego opportunities for joint gain, but a negotiator who adopts a singlemindedly integrative approach may well find himself badly exploited by a more distributive-minded competitor, at least in the short run.

Attitudinal Structuring

In any enduring and multifaceted social relationship, negotiators are inevitably and quite sensibly concerned not merely with the immediate content of the bargaining, but with the overall relations of trust or hostility, cooperativeness or competitiveness between the parties. This broader question of tone has practical implications both for the implementation of bargains once struck and for future bargaining agendas and outcomes. In the labour−management context, for example, strategies can be influenced by the desire to maintain friendship or mutual confidence − 'good labour relations' − quite apart from the content of a specific contract. In international political economy, many summiteers speak of the importance of maintaining 'Western solidarity' or of establishing personal rapport, 'so you can more easily pick up the phone'.

Intraorganisational Bargaining

The simplifying assumption of much of the theory of games and negotiations is that of a 'unitary actor', but both labour bargainers and international negotiators know that that assumption is false. In the first place, the negotiator himself is often caught between the realities of the negotiation and the higher expectations of his principals, and he must worry about achieving 'ratification' of any bargain that is struck. Secondly, his principals themselves may not be of one mind about their objectives; older workers are more concerned about pension rights, while younger ones worry about take-home pay. One of the most novel and enlightening features of Walton and McKersie's approach to negotiation is their analysis of the strategies open to negotiators for achieving internal consensus and of the interplay between integrative and distributive strategies 'across the table' and intraorganisational strategies 'behind one's chair'. One common pattern, of course, is the emergence of tacit or even explicit cooperation between the negotiators in dealing with their respective intraorganisational problems.

For several reasons, intraorganisational bargaining is an even more prominent and intractable element in international political economic negotiation than in labour–management relations. First, the costs of failure to reach agreement internationally are likely to be more obscure to most constituents than the costs of rejecting a contract are to most workers, so the 'strike threshold' is probably lower in the case of international political economy. Second, and even more important, in any modern society the diversity of interests that are affected by international economic trends is immensely greater than the diversity of interests within a single union or firm.

Indeed, the politics of international economic coordination can usefully be conceived as a two-level game. At the national level, domestic groups seek to maximise their interests by pressuring the government to adopt favourable policies, and politicians seek power by constructing coalitions among those groups. At the international level, national governments seek to maximise their own freedom to satisfy domestic pressures, while minimising the adverse consequences of foreign developments. (Governments may also pursue certain 'state' interests, such as prestige or security, that are only indirectly related to pressure from their domestic constituencies.)

These two games are played simultaneously, so that national policies are in some sense the resultant of both the domestic and the international parallelograms of forces. Neither of the two games can be ignored by policy-makers, so long as their countries remain interdependent, yet sovereign democracies. A national political leader appears at both game boards. Across the international table sit his foreign counterparts, and at his elbows sit diplomats and other international advisers. Around the domestic table behind him sit party and parliamentary figures, spokesmen for the great domestic ministries, representatives of key domestic interest groups, and the leader's own political advisers. (Domestic interest groups may be 'players' not because of their direct lobbying, but because of their anticipated reactions to possible moves, as interpreted by their bureaucratic patrons or by the leader's political counsellors. The absence of overt party or interest group involvement in international economic coordination by no means proves that the interests and preferences of those groups are irrelevant to the process.)

The special complexity of this two-level game is that moves that are rational for a player at one board (such as raising energy prices or limiting auto imports) may be quite irrational for that same player at the other board. Nevertheless, there are powerful incentives for consistency between the two games. Players (and kibitzers) will tolerate some differences in rhetoric between the two games — which is why each summiteer gives his own news conference after the summit — but in the end, either energy prices rise or they don't, either auto imports fall or they don't. Moreover, rhetoric intended for one set of players may upset bargains struck at the other table; as we shall see, this is essentially what happened in the aftermath of the Versailles summit, causing the basic bargain on East–West trade issues to come unstuck.

It is natural to think that the conflicts in this process pit domestic interests against international pressures; most Americans (and most Japanese) want their national quota for petroleum imports to be as high as possible, and both steel workers and steel management in Pittsburgh (or Lille) urge their government to defend 'American' (or 'French') interests against foreign competition. On the other hand, economic interdependence and domestic diversity can sometimes produce powerful interests within each country that point in the same direction as certain international pressures. German trade unions might welcome foreign pressure on the Federal Government to carry out a more expansive fiscal policy, and Italian bankers might welcome international demands for a more austere Italian monetary policy. Thus, at least in principle, one might discover transnational alliances, tacit or explicit, in which domestic interests pressure their respective governments to adopt mutually supportive policies, a pattern of bargaining that is virtually unheard of in labour—management negotiations and that therefore is not discussed by Walton and McKersie.

The political complexities for the players in this two-level game are staggering, quite apart from the technical-economic complexities. Any key player at the international table who is dissatisfied with the outcome may upset the game board, and conversely, any national leader who fails to satisfy an adequate number of his fellow players at the domestic table risks being evicted from his seat. Moreover, each national leader already has made a substantial investment in building a particular coalition at the domestic board, and he will be loathe to try to construct a different coalition simply to sustain an alternative policy mix that might be more acceptable internationally. Economic adversity further complicates the game, by making it more nearly zero-sum and by reducing the policy 'gains from trade' that might allow side-payments to disaffected participants. Even in theory there is no guarantee that any solution exists that will simultaneously satisfy the needs of the key players, and if such a solution exists in principle, the uncertainties of practical politics — the counterpart of Clausewitz's 'fog of battle' — may prevent the players from reaching it.

Virtually any aspect of international negotiation could be analysed in terms of these four processes: distributive bargaining, integrative bargaining, attitudinal structuring, and intraorganisational bargaining. Walton and McKersie, for example, offer an illustrative analysis of the Cuban missile crisis in these terms. But Western summitry is likely to differ in several ways from the negotiations embedded in normal international power politics. First, the topics addressed in the economic summits are more likely to be variable-sum in nature, involving more nearly shared interests, so that integrative bargaining should be relatively more prominent in summitry, although we would not expect distributive bargaining to be absent. (On the other hand, as we shall discuss later, the episodic and non-technical nature of the summit discussions means that many of the preconditions for effective integrative bargaining are absent from summitry, by comparison with the OECD, the IMF, or other international organisations.) Second, because the summit participants are long-standing allies with many shared interests not explicitly on the agenda itself (such as national security, for example), we would expect 'attitudinal structuring' – that is, the maintenance of mutual trust – to be more important than, say, in the SALT negotiations. Third, because the summits concern topics that have a major significance in domestic policies, from the price of oil to the jobless rate, and because the chief negotiators are themselves primarily domestic politicians, we would expect intraorganisational bargaining and multilevel games to be relatively more important.

In analysing summitry from the point of view of international political economy, we must keep in mind that the summits themselves are merely one moment in a continuous flow of domestic and international discussion and bargaining about these issues. As a foreign policy aide to one European premier warned me, 'You cannot understand the summits without taking account of all the other ongoing international meetings. When we set out to influence another government – and I presume the same is true of anyone trying to influence us – we say, "We'll start off at the OECD ministerials in May, follow up at the summit, and then hit them again at the IMF in September".' Similarly, virtually all the items under discussion at the summit – from interest rates to East–West relations and from oil supplies to overseas development assistance – are the subject of continuing debate within the domestic arena. Consultation with business, bankers, unions, and other interest groups is rarely, if ever, an important part of the national preparations for the summit, because, as I was told repeatedly, 'We already know what they think about these subjects; we're talking about them all the time anyway.' The strategems and ploys, the convergences and divergences, the decisions and non-decisions, that are visible within the summit process itself cannot be interpreted in isolation from this wider context. On the other hand, just as a cloud chamber filled with saturated water vapor allows physics students to detect charged particles whose passage all around us ordinarily goes unnoticed, so the summit process condenses features of international political economy that are otherwise easier to overlook.

A last, related misunderstanding of summitry must be mentioned. The popular press, encouraged by over-enthusiastic government press agents, sometimes has cast the summit as a kind of grand assize of the Western world, a supranational forum in which decisions on the great problems facing the industrial democracies are collectively rendered by the world's leaders. This image evokes a unity of purpose and a decisiveness of collective action that is inappropriate for this or any other international forum. 'You can't expect spectacular decisions from a meeting like that,' said one of the original sherpas. 'It's naive to believe that that is possible.' One of the most distinguished summiteers added frankly, 'You don't go to the summit with the idea of "making policy", or usually of reaching any great conclusions about world economic problems. Every nation goes there, first of all, to explain its own problems, and secondly, to see how far it can get others to help it with its own problems. I doubt if many of us go there saying, "Here is the central problem of world economic strategy. What measures should we all take to improve it?" We are all convinced of the value of an international trading system, so there is some attempt to take the world view, but basically we are most concerned about our own domestic problems.'

On the other hand, summits at their most effective have represented precisely the recognition by heads of state and government that they cannot solve their own problems without attending to world problems – in short, their recognition that they must play at both game tables, unless they wish to retreat to economic autarky. In the 1980s growing world economic integration has created an ever-sharper dilemma for democratic political leaders, who must respond to narrower national or sectional constituencies. The fate of a congressman from Youngstown depends on decisions taken in Brussels or Tokyo. The *projet* of a French socialist president is constrained by decisions of American monetary authorities. The trade-off for price stability in Hamburg may be unemployment in Harlem. In such predicaments politicians must choose some mix of two broad strategies, one nationalist, one internationalist. They may try to gain control over their own destiny, by re-erecting protectionist barriers to international commerce and finance, risking the broader benefits that derive from integrated markets. Or they may seek instead to co-operate with their counterparts abroad in an effort to manage politically the mutual interference that is the price of interdependence.[7]

Thus, economic interdependence is not an unalterable fact of life, immune from politics. Indeed, a precondition for the maintenance of a relatively open world economy is some degree of international coordination of policies once considered purely domestic. 'International policy coordination' sounds technically neat and politically antiseptic. But to suggest, as do some analysts, that only 'political will' is needed for governments to coordinate their policies internationally is disconcertingly like Moliere's suggestion that all that is needed to cure sleeplessness is a 'dormitive potion'. The real question is this: Under what circumstances and through what mechanisms is the requisite 'political will' likely to emerge? An interpretation that begins with the multiple and primarily domestically oriented goals of the participants will most likely lead to a better understanding of the practice and the limitations of summitry and other forms of international economic cooperation.

The Prehistory of the Western Summits

When, over lunch at the British Embassy in Helsinki in July 1975, Valéry Giscard d'Estaing first broached to Helmut Schmidt, Harold Wilson, Gerald Ford, and their foreign ministers the idea of a summit meeting later that fall (to include also the Japanese Prime Minister Takeo Miki) at which monetary and other economic issues would be discussed, he did not have in mind the institutionalisation of annual summitry. Rather, he was drawing upon a little-known practice of confidential meetings among finance ministers that had grown up in the aftermath of the collapse of the Bretton Woods monetary system. A word or two about this series of meetings will help clarify the genetics of Western summitry.

During the monetary crisis of February–March 1973, leading towards the eventual adoption of a generalised flexible exchange rate regime, the finance ministers of the United States, Britain, France, and Germany began what was to become a series of informal, initially secret meetings, generally on the margins of meetings of larger international bodies, such as the Group of 10 and the Committee of 20. Accompanied only by one senior aide each (and occasionally by their respective central bank governors), the ministers insisted on a minimum of protocol and a maximum of discretion, partly because of the ever-present danger of protests from excluded countries and partly because of their own sense that in a turbulent and threatening world they needed to close ranks as political leaders, escaping from the technical pettifoggery of bureaucrats.

Nicknamed 'the Library Group', after the site of one of their earliest meetings in the library of the White House, the group initially gave priority to sorting out international monetary questions in the uncharted waters of floating exchange rates. Even in their earliest sessions, however, their discussions ranged across the spectrum of international and domestic political economy, including macroeconomic policy and (with some prescience) international oil prices. In these relaxed meetings, free from the normal constraints of international negotiations and domestic rivalries, a climate of personal camaraderie and mutual trust developed, along with a remarkable frankness in expressing frustrations with political and bureaucratic adversaries back home. It was for most participants an experience unique in their official lives. 'We became friends for life,' recalls one. Over the course of the next year or so, the group expanded slightly, as first the Japanese and then the Italians could no longer be excluded. Nevertheless, nearly a decade later, participants in these meetings would still recall with nostalgia their sense of exclusiveness, solidarity, and shared power, sitting together at the central panel of the world economy.

Personally, the key figures in this group were remarkable leaders, and it was hardly surprising when in 1974 two of the participants, Helmut Schmidt and Valéry Giscard d'Estaing, ascended to the positions of Chancellor and President, respectively. Nor was it surprising that they should wish to carry to their new responsibilities the idea of confidential and informal conversations among the West's key political leaders. Thus, Schmidt supported Giscard's initiative over lunch in Helsinki with alacrity. He insisted that in the preparation of the proposed summit, as in the earlier meeting of the Library Group, the bureaucracy should be excluded. It was decided that each chief executive should appoint one personal representative to prepare the agenda. 'Otherwise, it will become a negotiation, with bargaining and so on,' Schmidt is reported to have said. 'We want very private, informal meetings of those who really matter in the world.'

The initial choices of personal representatives to prepare the Rambouillet summit reveal the degree to which it was hoped to retain the earlier sense of a fireside chat among friends, disconnected from the official apparatus of government. Schmidt chose Wilfried Guth, a leading German banker whom Schmidt admired personally, Giscard's selection was Raymond Barre, an ex-European Commissioner, but in 1975 an economics professor with no official post, and Ford, reportedly at Schmidt's suggestion, selected George Shultz, a founding member of the Library Group as Treasury Secretary, but by now back in private life. Apparently after some consideration of appointing a non-official as his representative, Wilson eventually settled on Sir John Hunt, who, as Cabinet Secretary, was close to the Prime Minister and somewhat above the departmental fray. The Japanese prime minister was represented by former Ambassador

Nobuhiko Ushiba, joined in time by Rinaldo Ossola, Director General of the Bank of Italy, on behalf of the Italian premier, although neither apparently played a significant role in the preparatory discussions.[8]

The image of Western summits as a friendly fireside chat, 'prepared' as informally as possible, is thus traceable historically to the casual conclaves of the Library Group. This interpretation of summits continued to be espoused with special force by Schmidt and Giscard, whose friendship had germinated in the Library Group and had flourished when they ascended to their new posts. This image fit their personalities and their perspectives on economics and foreign affairs: both were supremely confident of their own economic expertise, both were sceptical of bureaucracy, both preferred tightly held international discussions.

As we shall see later, the Library Group image does highlight certain aspects of summit meetings, and it has a continuing attraction for leaders as diverse as Ronald Reagan and François Mitterrand. But it is definitely not an adequate and comprehensive account of the evolving reality of summitry. Indeed, Rambouillet, which has entered the lore of summitry as the purest case of a 'fireside chat', was not really faithful to its Library Group antecedents. The notion of casual, unofficial preparations did not last out even this first round of official summitry. For example, after the very first meeting of the personal representatives, Guth was succeeded as Schmidt's representative by Karl Otto Pohl, State Secretary at the Finance Ministry. Moreover, as one participant recalls, 'I learned very soon that it was not possible to act entirely on my own. Too many ministries were involved and too many subjects on which I was not expert, and I began to coordinate my activities with the regular departments – that's always a delicate thing in government.'

The major item on the agenda for Rambouillet was the still unresolved controversy between France and the United States about the shape of the future international monetary system. Parallel to the sessions of the personal representatives, negotiations aimed at narrowing the differences continued between top officials of the various finance ministries. Eventually a delicate agreement was hammered out (the metaphor is not inapt) in marathon transatlantic negotiations between Edwin Yeo of the US Treasury and his French counterpart, Jacques de Larosière. It was this accord that was unveiled at Rambouillet and later ratified in the Jamaica agreement of January 1976.

'Heads of state and government', as they are officially termed, cannot divorce themselves from their official machinery, nor can most hope to range widely across complex problems in 48 hours without detailed preparation. Most of the Library Group, after all, had been trained as economists, but it was unlikely that all of the world's leaders would be so trained, or that the untutored among them would forego systematic preparation and simply sit quietly at the feet of their more expert brethren. Secret encounters, possible for a handful of finance ministers, are impossible for the most visible leaders of the world. Already at Rambouillet, despite its 'country house' setting, the summiteers were accompanied by tiers of officials, advance guards, as it were, for the legions that would throng subsequent summits. The political pressure to achieve visible 'results' from such a prominent world rendezvous almost inevitably inclines most summiteers to wish some public statement of 'agreements' reached. Moreover, the hope of some of the founders to avoid 'negotiating' and 'bargaining' was also illusory, although the hope itself bespoke a striking commitment to what Walton and McKersie term 'integrative bargaining', that is, joint problem-solving. The centrepiece of Rambouillet, the US—French monetary accord, emerged not from the fireside chats, but from hardheaded bargaining among key bureaucrats. The original concept of a Library Group for the leaders of the world, noted one nostalgic alumnus, had already proved naive and unrealistic.

The deliberations of the Library Group appear to have been very unusual and perhaps unique among international meetings at a ministerial level in the degree to which 'integrative bargaining' and 'attitudinal structuring' dominated 'distributive bargaining', and in the degree to which the participants frankly shared information about their respective 'intraorganisational bargaining' at home. Something of this climate continues to pervade the meetings of the sherpas who today prepare the summits, as we shall note in a moment. Nevertheless, the summits themselves are no longer — and probably never were — the 'openhearted gossip among friends' that one summiteer recalls intending they should be.

The Summit Process

Key to the preparations of the summits today, as in the beginning, are the meetings of personal representatives or 'sherpas'. (Credit for

coining this convenient label is generally given to Sir Kenneth Cou-
zens, one of the British participants.) Although by now so many persons have served in this group that Mitterrand is said to have expressed the fear that the summiteers would soon be faced with demands from 'a union of retired sherpas', the unique sense of camaraderie and frankness bequeathed from the Library Group has been
remarkably persistent. One sherpa recalls that in his first meeting
with the group he felt very distinctly the 'new boy' entering an inti-
mate club, and another reports occasionally feeling a sense of loyalty to this anomolous international institution overriding his national
loyalty. Though doubtless none can forget for long that he is present
as a representative of his nation's highest authority, with the official
obligations that necessarily follow, by most accounts the climate in
the sherpas group is rather unusual in international negotiations.[9]
Key to the special character of the group is a climate of sufficient
mutual trust that each participant can be frank about pressures and
divergences of view within his own government, reasonably certain
that the others will not abuse or exploit these confidences. This atmosphere is crucial to any successful resolution of two-level, domestic-international games.

Although the practice of using non-governmental figures as sherpas disappeared after the first summit, for the most part the notion
has persisted that the personal representatives should be 'personal',
that is very senior policy makers close to the head of state or government. One experienced sherpa notes that 'it is important that the
people around the table are not diplomats, but senior domestic officials, there because of their relationship with the chief executive, not
because of any connection to the foreign ministry. The discussion is
very frank, including our discussions about domestic politics, because we are closer to domestic politics than most diplomats.'

In fact, however, not all of the sherpas fit this description equally
well. The German sherpa from 1978 to 1982 was Horst Schulmann;
a close aide of Schmidt, Schulmann retained his role as personal representative when he moved in 1981 from the *Bundeskanzleramt* to
the number two post in the Finance Ministry. On the other hand,
Helmut Kohl designated Hans Tietmeyer, Schulmann's successor in
the Finance Ministry, as his sherpa, implying a more constitutional
criterion for selection. Barre's successor under Giscard, Bernard
Clappier, the head of the central bank, did not have easy access to
the President, but Mitterrand's sherpa has been Jacques Attali, the
President's chief of staff and closest personal adviser. The British

sherpa – there have only been two so far – has always been the Cabinet Secretary, sometimes called 'The Prime Minister's Permanent Secretary'. Ambassador Henry Owen, Jimmy Carter's sherpa, had close access to the President and devoted virtually full time to coordinating the administration's international economic policymaking. The chef du cabinet of the President of the European Commission has always served as his sherpa. On the other hand, in the cases of Canada, Italy, Japan, and (under the Reagan administration) the United States, the role of sherpa has become linked to a specific post with diplomatic responsibilities, typically the top official responsible for economic affairs in the foreign ministry.

All the sherpas are reasonably well 'plugged into' domestic political realities in their respective capitals, but one can detect something of a trend towards 'depersonalisation' of the role, particularly as compared to the initial pattern for Rambouillet, a trend most marked in the case of the United States.

As the agenda of the summits became more regularised and the topics diversified, the sherpa meetings expanded from one-a-side, so that by 1977 the typical pattern came to be for each nation to send three representatives to the preparatory meetings, typically adding a senior official from the foreign ministry and one from the finance ministry, although in some cases the third member of the troika represented another economics ministry. Formally speaking, this expansion corresponded to the fact that the foreign and finance ministers had become part of the official delegation to the summit itself. More practically, the expansion reflected the increasing 'bite' of summitry into matters traditionally in the departmental preserves and the consequent desire of those departments to keep a close watch on negotiations that might affect their interests. (Significantly, this expansion is said to have been sparked by the Americans and the Japanese, the two countries in which bureaucratic rivalries are most well-developed. Consistent with their status as second-class citizens in the summit context, the European Commission has generally been restricted to a single sherpa.) In an attempt to curb the growing 'bureaucratisation' of the sherpa process, the French chairman in 1982 convened a number of sherpa meetings restricted to one-a-side. However, as we shall see, this practice did not reverse the tendency towards greater and more regularised involvement of representatives from various ministries in summit preparations.

The sherpas typically meet three or four weekends a year, once in the winter to review the aftermath of the previous summit and to conduct an initial *tour d'horizon* for the next, and then roughly monthly from March until the summit itself in June or July. After 1977, five topics became standard agenda items: macroeconomics, monetary issues, trade, energy, and North–South issues. International political and security issues have always figured in the informal 'dinner' discussions among the summiteers, but beginning with the Venice summit, these issues have been increasingly accepted as part of the standard fare, and at Williamsburg a joint statement on defence and disarmament became the very centrepiece of the summit.

During the sherpas' first meeting of the new year, agreement is generally reached on which agenda items will merit high priority (for example, monetary affairs in 1982 and 1983), and which can be dismissed with less attention (for example, energy in 1982 and 1983). Often one or two summit nations will urge that attention be given to some special theme, and the inclusion of these novel items is sometimes a matter of some controversy. For example, the Americans pressed very hard for East–West economic relations to be included on the agenda for Versailles in 1982, but the French vigorously resisted this proposal until the eve of the summit itself, even though lively discussions about the topic among the summit nations continued throughout the spring. On the other hand, hoping to strike an upbeat note for the summit that would be useful both internationally and domestically, the French successfully pressed for the inclusion in the 1982 agenda of a special discussion on the future of technology. Most of the other summiteers were sceptical about the French proposals, but deferred to the host's prerogative.

At least until 1983 the preparatory discussions were centred on thematic papers drafted on the personal responsibility of one or another sherpa. Assignment of these papers was sometimes a subject of genteel jockeying. In 1982, for example, the macroeconomic paper, traditionally produced by the Americans, was assigned instead to the less ideologically rigid British. The initial paper on trade problems in 1982 was offered by the Japanese, but it provoked a counter-draft from the European Commission. The Italians produced a paper on North–South issues in 1982, a modest effort following a very ambitious collaborative seven-nation paper on those topics prepared for the Ottawa summit. Finally, the Americans produced a paper on East–West trade in 1982, but this draft was allegedly more one-sided than is typically expected of these papers, and it did not play a major role in the collective discussions.

The preliminary papers served to focus the sherpas' discussions, and those discussions merged imperceptibly into the negotiations about the wording of the final communiqué. (One participant offered a useful simile, comparing the discussion papers to disposable stages in rocketry which fall away as the vehicle gathers speed.) The significance of the negotiations about communiqué language has been itself a matter of some dispute among participants. Some dismiss communiqué-writing as the least productive part of the summit exercise, vitiating the advantages of frank, private discussion. Particularly as the positions of governments on the fundamental issues of macroeconomics have drifted apart, the communiqués have tended to become what one participant termed 'tossed salad' documents in which each summiteer could find a sentence or two endorsing his own policies. (A Japanese participant used a different culinary metaphor, speaking of the sherpas as producing different frostings that could be applied to the summit cake, according to taste.) On the other hand, other experienced sherpas report that the preparatory give-and-take becomes substantively focused and rigorous only when participants are forced to confront language encapsulating alternative approaches to the underlying problems, so that communiqué-drafting (in this view) becomes a vehicle for policy coordination. (As will be noted further on, the 1983 preparation followed a somewhat different path.)

'Integrative bargaining' is clearly an important element in these preparatory discussions, as the sherpas and their collaborators seek to refine problems, clarify points of view, and conceive new approaches that can reconcile apparently divergent interests. The summit-linked discussions of energy in 1979 and 1980, for example, did yield new ways of addressing problems of conservation and alternative energy sources that moved beyond the earlier, more sterile confrontation over allocation of oil shortages. 'We are always pushing for the "highest common factor",' said one participant. On the other hand, what one sherpa refers to as 'distilled differences' remain. On these questions, sherpas engage in all the well-known strategems of good, tough 'distributive bargainers', from bluffing to genteel blackmail. In 1978, for example, the Americans delayed a firm commitment to attend Helmut Schmidt's summit until they had some assurance that Schmidt would be responsive to the American demand for additional German fiscal stimulus, and Schmidt in turn withheld his final concession until he was sure that Carter would agree to satisfactory language on US energy policy.

One common rule of thumb is that virtually everyone seeks to avoid being left in a minority of one on any important issue. Formally speaking, any summit conclusion must be unanimous, so there is no reason why any outvoted participant should not simply dig in his heels, and that does sometimes happen, of course. However, participants often appear to adjust their positions, sometimes even in advance of the meeting itself, in order to avoid complete isolation. Examples of this dynamic include the German position on the locomotive issue in 1978, the Canadian position on energy in 1979, the US position on North–South issues in 1981 and 1982 and on East–West trade in 1983, and the Japanese position on trade in several years. Some sherpas report that the pressure to make key concessions to achieve unanimity is especially great on the host government, for whom the 'success' or 'failure' of the conference has a special domestic political resonance. (How substantial these adjustments are in practical terms is a question addressed in the final section of this chapter.)

One significant development in the preparatory process has been the use of subsidiary forums to work on specific subjects. Often these specialised discussions are carried on in connection with existing international agencies. For example, in some years the paper on macroeconomics has been produced and debated in the context of the so-called 'bureau' of the OECD Economic Policy Committee, an *ad hoc* group consisting of the Committee representatives of the summit countries, presided over by the Chairman of the American Council of Economic Advisers. From 1977 through 1981 this venue allowed the OECD staff to play an important, though informal role in the summit deliberations on macroeconomics. For example, the OECD staff made a significant contribution to the evolution of the proposal for coordinated reflation put forward at the London and Bonn summits in 1977 and 1978. Recently, however, this linkage has been greatly attenuated, at least in part because of the disaffection of some key policy-makers with what they see as the 'unreconstructed Keynesianism' of the OECD staff.

On energy, the 1979 Tokyo summit established a special 'high level monitoring group' consisting of the chief energy policy-makers from the summit countries, and this group meets in cooperation with the International Energy Agency to prepare the summit energy deliberations, typically on the basis of a paper drafted by the head of the IEA. In 1982 the controversial subject of East–West trade and credit was debated in an *ad hoc* group of specialists, and the failure of this group to resolve the (perhaps unresolvable) dispute between the United States and the Europeans foreshadowed the failure of the summiteers themselves to reach agreement. In 1983 this subject was addressed in a variety of institutional forums, including the OECD and COCOM, and differences between the Americans and their partners were successfully subdued.

The summit talks on international political issues are normally preceded by a meeting of senior foreign ministry officials, who simply exchange notes on what topics their principals are likely to want to discuss. Without more detailed preparations, the agenda for this section of the summit has usually been determined by the previous weeks' headlines: South-East Asian 'boat people', Lebanon, the Falklands War. In 1983, to the surprise of many observers (and several participants), political issues came to dominate the summit discussions, in the form of a spirited and apparently spontaneous day-long debate among the summiteers on defence, arms control, and the Euromissile issue. The divergent views were eventually reconciled in a joint public statement, but whether future summiteers will want to follow this precedent for intensive, 'non-pre-cooked' political discussions is still uncertain.

The 1982 preparatory deliberations on monetary matters usefully illustrates how the summit is enmeshed in the broader fabric of international meetings and bilateral contacts. The early sparring between the French, who argued for more extensive intervention to maintain exchange rate stability, and the Americans, who defended a fully free market in currencies, peaked in an intense debate in the April sherpas' meeting. At the conclusion of that debate a possible compromise was articulated by the spokesman from the French Finance Ministry and tentatively accepted by the representative from the American Treasury. This formulation was further refined in a meeting of the Group of Five finance ministers and central bank governors on the margins of the May IMF Interim Committee meetings in Helsinki, and that proposal was then fed back into the next meeting of the sherpas. Accepted with little debate by the summiteers themselves at Versailles, the proposal was further elaborated in extensive discussions among finance ministry officials who were part of the official delegations to the summit. Follow-up of these deliberations was then scheduled to coincide with the annual meeting of the IMF and World Bank in Toronto in September, in a meeting between the Group of Five finance ministers, working from a paper prepared by the IMF Managing Director. This new 'G-5 + IMF' forum was reconfirmed at Williamsburg. The interweaving of these different institutional contexts is greatly eased by the fact that in many cases the key national representatives are in fact the same in each forum, so that viewed in terms of process rather than institution, the discussion is carried forward by mostly the same people, merely meeting under different rubrics.

This review of summit preparations makes clear how embedded the summit has become in the multifaceted array of continuing international economic negotiations. As the one time each year during which national bureaucracies can all be certain of gaining the attention of their chief executives, the summit preparations exert a gravitational pull on virtually all ongoing discussions of any significant international issue. Most of this ancillary negotiation never reaches the actual summit table, and a good portion would continue virtually unaffected if the summits were to disappear. This fact makes it difficult to assess the 'product' of the summit itself. Nevertheless, as we shall discuss later, the potential involvement by the highest authorities in each government does serve to energise these ongoing negotiations and, in certain crucial instances, to influence their outcome.

This account of the preparatory process also makes clear just how far summitry has come from the Library Group ideal of 'an openhearted gossip among friends'. Despite repeated resolves to limit the summit machinery, hundreds of officials are involved by now in the substantive preparations, not to speak of the cast of thousands working on logistics, ceremony, and press-agentry. Little wonder that 'over-preparation' has become a standard complaint of a number of summiteers themselves.

In some respects, the plenary sessions of the summit itself appear somewhat anticlimactic, for the meetings are usually too brief for sustained discussion of any single issue. The first session is given over to formal statements of national positions, and the final meeting is typically consumed in a hectic redrafting of a few controversial sections of the communiqué. Thus, no more than three to five hours are left for plenary give-and-take, and this give-and-take is further limited by the linguistic barriers that have increasingly divided the summiteers. (All of the Library Group and most of the summiteers until 1981 were competent in English, but of the Williamsburg summiteers, only the English, American and Canadian participants speak English easily.)

What *can* be accomplished in the plenary sessions – and even more in the many informal corridor and mealtime conversations – is for these fellow politicians to exchange moods, to take one another's measure, and to compare notes on broad issues of political and economic strategy. Those closest to the summiteers themselves emphasise the importance of the multiple bilateral conversations that can conveniently be held around the edges of the main sessions. Typically, the main substantive issues have been actually resolved outside the conference chamber itself, and the occasional exceptions (for example, the 1979 Tokyo plenary discussions of oil import quotas and the 1982 Versailles confrontation about East–West trade) were deemed unproductive by most participants. Often the summit has seemed to resemble a doughnut, with a tasty and satisfying perimeter, but an empty core. This pattern is probably inevitable if the summit process is to embody detailed policy negotiations, but it has increasingly irritated those summiteers fond of the Library Group image of summitry, who vigorously object to 'pre-negotiated' communiqués.

The American hosts approached Williamsburg in 1983 determined to prune the preparatory process drastically, but with the significant exception of the political discussions (mentioned above), most of the key economic issues on the Williamsburg agenda were in fact worked out in advance by the sherpas and relevant ministers from the participating countries. The final communiqué was not drafted until the summit itself, but behind the scenes the several sherpas are said to have worked on language that was likely to be acceptable to their leaders. Whether a pure 'Library Group' summit is actually feasible or even desirable remains to be seen.

The National Preparations[10]

The special role of sherpas in organising the summit has imparted a basic similarity to the preparatory process within each national capital. In all cases the principal responsibility for coordinating preparations lies with the personal representative, even in administrative systems where such 'one-man shows' are not traditional. Everywhere, participants report that as compared to the normal policy-making processes, summit preparations are more personalised, more centralised, more tightly held, and less bound by conventions of bureaucratic clearance. 'What counts in the preparation for the summit,' ran one typical account, 'is more the person and his relationship to the chief executive and less his job title.'

On the other hand, in every capital the unusual character of summit preparations has become more and more attenuated over the years, as the process has become institutionalised and assimilated to the normal practices of the administration. At the top, as one of the early sherpas told me, 'We were originally all mavericks, but over the years the mavericks have lost the battles with the regular bureaucracy.' To some degree this trend reflects the greater range and complexity of the issues handled within the summit context, for sherpas everywhere have recognised their need to draw on the expertise − and to maintain the goodwill − of the great ministries of state. In most countries a summit 'team' or 'task force' has been established under the direction of the personal representative, often in collaboration with several 'deputy sherpas'. The most common pattern is a 'troika', usually consisting of one person from the central executive agency (the White House, the Cabinet Office, the *Bundeskanzleramt*, and so on), one from the foreign ministry, and one from the ministry of finance, but frequently other economics ministries are also represented.

The relative weight of these different agencies varies a good deal from country to country. Where a central executive agency is well-established, its role in summit preparations is always quite important. In Britain, Germany, and France, for example, the Cabinet Office, the *Bundeskanzleramt*, and the Elysee exercise a degree of initiative on summit matters greater than would be characteristic of ordinary policy-making, and, of course, the White House staff dominate the American preparations. In Japan and Italy, on the other hand, the office of the prime minister is institutionally weaker, and more of the substantive preparations for the summit are handled elsewhere.

The foreign ministry is always included in the core task force, but it is rarely in a dominant position. In Japan, however, the sherpa is always located in the foreign ministry, and he typically clears his work within the ministry before widening the circle of consultation to include bureaucratic rivals from MITI and the Ministry of Finance. (The general institutional position of the *Gaimusho* seems to have slipped in recent years, and well-placed Japanese participants describe control of the summit preparations as 'the last trump' the foreign ministry still holds.) At the other extreme, the *Auswärtiges Amt* plays a relatively subordinate role in German summit preparations, except on international political questions. Generally speaking, the more the personnel and the activities of the major domestic ministries have become 'internationalised', the less prominent is the role played by the foreign ministry.

Given the historical antecedents of the summits, it is not surprising that representatives from the ministry of finance are always in the inner circle for summit preparations. On the other hand, except on money matters, the finance ministry is almost never the lead agency. The top officials responsible for international finance in these countries comprise a kind of informal international 'money mafia', and from time to time they use independent channels of communication to exchange views about summit matters among themselves. These finance officials are often slightly uneasy about the risk that the summit process will undermine their institutional authority, by bringing outsiders into the act, particularly from the foreign ministry.

The role of the central banks in summit preparations varies widely. Officials from the Banca d'Italia play a leading role in substantive summit preparations in Rome, although procedurally and politically, responsibility for coordination lies with the Prime Minister's diplomatic adviser, a career diplomat. (Strikingly, the regular financial and economic ministries in Rome appear to have played little part in summit preparations until recently, when certain key posts in these ministries were assumed by ex-officials from the Banca d'Italia.) The Bundesbank has played an important secondary role in German preparation, in part through representation on the interagency task force, but primarily because of personal ties between Helmut Schmidt and the top leadership of the Bank. In the three English-speaking countries, central bankers are occasionally consulted informally by the sherpas on monetary issues. Finally, at the other extreme, the central banks in France and Japan have no autonomous role in summit preparations at all, for these banks are institutionally subordinate to the finance ministries.

The remaining economic ministries generally provide 'backstopping' without direct involvement in summit preparations. The ministries of trade or energy, for example, provide briefing papers on specific subjects, but officials from those departments are rarely involved in broader discussions of summit strategy and tactics. The two important exceptions to this generalisation are in Germany and Japan. Below the Chancellor's personal representative, most of the key officials involved in summitry in Bonn are in the Economics Ministry. In part, this fact has reflected a need for political balance, since both the Chancellor and the Finance Minister have been drawn from the senior coalition party (the SDP or the CDU), whereas the Economics Ministry has been led by a Free Democrat. Moreover, the officials responsible for trade, energy, and macroeconomic planning in the Economics Ministry have through long experience acquired international reputations for expertise and good judgement. In Tokyo MITI has waged a long and partially successful struggle for a greater share of the status and influence that accompany involvement in summit preparations. In recent years MITI has become a basically 'internationalist' force in Japanese policy-making, but ironically, this shift closer to the foreign ministry's position on substance appears to have intensified the two ministries' rivalries over bureaucratic turf.

This rapid survey of summit preparations in the seven capitals has highlighted the role of government officials, for 'outsiders' have surprisingly little direct involvement. Despite pro-forma consultation with business and union leaders in a few countries, interest group activity on summit matters is rare everywhere, and officials privately discount the significance of most of those few contacts that do occur. For example, a delegation of union leaders from the seven nations traditionally meets with the summit host just prior to the summit itself, but these encounters are dismissed by insiders as insignificant.

Summits rarely deal with sectoral issues that might arouse real interest among business or labour groups. 'Only if the summits began to touch on particular sectoral interests would these groups become active and possibly influential,' said one sherpa. The rare instances of interest group activity prove this general rule. In 1982, for example, the German Chamber of Commerce made strong public and private representations to the Chancellor, urging that he stand firm against American pressure to restrain trade with Eastern Europe, and in 1979 Prime Minister Ohira consulted with business leaders before agreeing to unexpectedly stringent oil import targets. Even in this latter case, however, the really decisive debate about whether to accept the targets reportedly took place within the bureaucracy.

Parliamentary and party involvement in summit preparations is equally scant. Apart from a handful of parliamentary questions and a prime ministerial statement following the summit itself, neither oppositions nor government backbenchers have shown much interest in summitry. Two exceptions illustrate the sorts of issue that can arouse greater interest among politicians. Following the 1978 summit agreement by Chancellor Schmidt to introduce an additional one percent fiscal stimulus package, a lively debate preceded parliamentary approval. Also LDP politicians from rural constituencies took a strong interest in the proposed liberalisation of Japan's agricultural imports prior to the 1982 summit. For the most part, however, the political classes of the seven nations have been content to leave summit deliberations to the governments.

As a consequence, the controversies that have arisen in the course of national summit preparations are almost always structured along bureaucratic lines rather than along conventional political cleavages. Of course, this fact does not mean that conventional domestic politics is irrelevant to summit discussions, for senior bureaucrats usually play by what Carl Friedrich once termed 'the rule of anticipated reactions', that is, they take into account the probable reactions of other key actors to proposed courses of action, particularly when those actors represent the special constituency of a given department. Officials are well aware of interest groups' positions on the broad topics that appear on the summit agenda. 'We don't need to be told that the unions favour reducing unemployment, or that bankers are concerned about inflation,' pointed out one sherpa. Ordinarily, a government's stance on such issues reflects a fairly stable equilibrium among the diverse groups within a government's supporting coalition. On the other hand, as we shall see later, when this domestic equilibrium is unstable because of strong internal divisions, then the play at the domestic game board becomes more lively and its connection with the international game becomes more visible.

The most common kind of dispute in summit preparations divides the foreign ministry from domestic departments, with the diplomats favouring a 'softer' line in the international negotiations. In 1982, for example, the State Department was closer to the Europeans' stance on East-West trade and credits than most other American participants, including President Reagan, and the Quai d'Orsay expressed more understanding for the American position than any of the other French participants, including President Mitterrand. This pattern, of course, represents a classic case of intraorganisational bargaining, as analysed by Walton and McKersie, in which each negotiator finds himself caught between his opposite number and his own principals.

If legislative politicians are largely absent from summit preparations, what about departmental ministers? The answer, strikingly similar in most countries, is that the key officials keep their ministers informed about the progress of preparations, but that the ministers themselves are seldom directly involved. (In 1983 the Americans tried to arouse interest in the idea of using a joint meeting of trade and finance ministers from the Seven to help prepare the summit, but most of the other participants objected, and this innovation is not likely to be repeated.) Sometimes the prime minister or president will consult directly with a few of his senior colleagues, often the foreign minister or the minister of finance, but cabinet discussion of the summit preparations is at best brief and perfunctory everywhere. (The 1978 German stimulus package is a significant exception here.)

This description of the respective roles of politicians and bureaucrats belies the hopes of some of the founding generation of summiteers to perpetuate the anti-bureaucratic tenor of the Library Group. The evidence should not be interpreted to mean that the bureaucrats have escaped from political control. Officials rightly protest that they would be caught up short if they were to deviate substantially from the main lines of their minister's policies. However, the picture I have sketched does imply that if political initiative is to be imparted to the national summit preparations, that impulse must come from the head of government himself and his personal political advisers.

The intensity of direct involvement of the chief executive himself and his top political aides in the substance, strategy, and tactics of summitry has varied widely. Not surprisingly, the host summiteer and his closest aides generally are deeply involved in the preparations, not least because the domestic political risks and resonances are much greater for him than for any of his colleagues. This pattern aside, recent summiteers have tended to devote less of their own energies and that of their closest collaborators to summit preparations than their predecessors.

The founding fathers of Western summitry continued to hold a conception of the institution that reflected its Library Group origins, and their personal involvement in summit preparations was correspondingly intense. President Giscard, for example, disparaged elaborate preparations. What counted for him were direct contacts among heads of state, and even his personal representative was kept at arms length. Under Helmut Schmidt, despite increasing involvement by the ministerial bureaucracy in the detailed preparation of the German position, major strategic decisions were held within a narrow circle of Schmidt's most senior advisers and colleagues, including several senior ministers, a handful of aides in the *Bundeskanzleramt*, and several trusted outside confidents, particularly in the world of banking. James Callaghan was convinced of a direct connection between his domestic political concerns and his relations with his foreign counterparts, and he too invested a good deal of personal energy in summit preparations. Distrustful of the regular civil service, especially in the Treasury, he relied heavily on his Cabinet Secretary and the staff of the Prime Minister's Office.

The successor generation of summiteers have been more inclined to leave summit preparations in the hands of the official machine. Drafting of position papers has been pushed out of the office of the chief executive and down into ordinary administrative channels. In terms of substance, as opposed to appearance, the successor generation tend to take summits less seriously. This seems to be true of Reagan as compared to Carter, of Thatcher as compared to Callaghan, of Kohl as compared to Schmidt, and perhaps even of Thorn at the European Commission as compared to Jenkins. (Mitterrand in 1982 held the preparations as close to the Elysee as Giscard had done, but that may have reflected his special responsibilities as host. Turnover among Japanese and Italian summiteers is too great for any simple trend to appear. Only Trudeau remains from the founding generation.) All these trends are particularly marked in the United States. In 1982, for example, the American sherpa was an Assistant Secretary of State, separated from the president by several layers of bureaucracy and apparently more respected abroad than in the Reagan White House.

If the attention of summiteers to the substantive preparations has diminished, however, their attention to the media has not. To be sure, summit publicity does provide a kind of international education for the broader publics. (Europeans who object to the massive American and Japanese press contingents may be overlooking this latent function.) For the more peripheral nations, such as Italy, Canada, and even Japan, merely 'being there' may be the most important fact about the summits. This international recognition of their status as members of the Western club probably increases the readiness of these societies to share broader burdens, including security burdens.

On the other hand, even as the press has become more sceptical about the efficacy of summits, the concern of government publicists to present their own principals in a favourable light has intensified. Official press agentry has increasingly presented the summit as a kind of international jousting match, and the summiteer as a national paladin, vigorously and victoriously defending national interests against obtuse and even malevolent foreigners. In 1981, for example, a leading international newspaper offered 'An Ottawa Scorecard' to help the reader 'to see who is scoring which points against whom', and an American spokesman concluded that President Reagan 'walked away with most of the prizes'.[11] Such imagery hardly contributes to better mutual understanding among Western publics, and it can erode the effectiveness of the summit itself.

Both excessive publicity and inadequate preparation at the top contributed centrally to the disastrous aftermath of the Versailles summit in 1982. On the eve of the conference itself no clear resolution had been reached on one of the two central issues, the American demand for restrictions on East–West trade. (A tentative compromise had been reached on the second issue, the French demand for greater management of exchange rates.) After chaotic consultations, including intensive bargaining in the plenary session itself, a fragile agreement was reached on communiqué language that appeared to meet the minimal political requirements of the Reagan and Mitterrand administrations. Meanwhile, however, the American Secretary of the Treasury was giving a press conference that appeared to dismiss the monetary accord as insignificant. Outraged, the French president responded with a post-summit press conference of his own, in which he minimised the importance of the agreement on East–West commerce and credit. Back in Washington, presidential aides who had been sceptical all along about the language on East–West issues cited the Mitterrand comments to convince Reagan that the French had been duplicitous, and, in retaliation, US sanctions on European participation in the Soviet gas pipeline project were tightened.

In the 'global village', rhetoric intended primarily for internal consumption can bring international complications. Six months of careful diplomacy by the new Secretary of State, both inside the administration and with the allies, were required merely to clear the post-summit debris and reconstruct the same tenuous deal that had been struck at Versailles. Animosity between the White House and the Elysee remained. The first rule of summitry has always been 'no failures', but as one senior British official noted, Versailles was the first summit which left relations among the participants worse than before. As a consequence, preparations for the 1983 summit were expressly designed to lower press expectations and to minimise divergent national press briefings, in short, a kind of conspiracy to avoid catastrophe. Measured against these lowered expectations, Williamsburg was generally seen as more successful.

Nevertheless, the evidence of a general decline in the special character of Western summitry cannot be ignored. What can explain this institutional decay? One answer might be that the economic challenges facing Western leaders have grown, but it would be difficult to sustain the argument that the economic outlook in 1975 was substantially brighter than today. Changes in the summit process itself and in perspectives of the participants are probably more relevant. As we have seen, the summit process has become more bureaucratic over time, following a kind of Parkinson's law of administrative entropy. The founding generation of summiteers were participating in the creative stage of summitry, whereas their successors inherited an established institution, where personal intervention has less scope. Fundamentally, it is not an institution built to their specifications. Moreover, the current Western leaders as a group seem personally more insular and nationalistic than their predecessors. In virtually every major summit country, government successions in recent years have seen more internationally-minded leaders replaced by more domestically-oriented ones. (This trend itself may have been fostered by continuing economic adversity.) Finally, the ideological climate of the 1980s, with its heavy emphasis on free enterprise monetarism, may be less congenial to the sort of collective economic management that so closely linked domestic and international macroeconomic decisions in the earlier years. Whatever the correct explanatory mix, this tendency towards estrangement of summiteers from the substance of summitry − if confirmed in the years ahead − will have important implications for the character and consequences of summitry as a technique for sustaining international economic cooperation.

Consequences

Any student of the Western economic summits is bound to ask 'So what?' Yet assessing the consequences of summitry is frustrating for three reasons.

1. As history is not an experimental science, we cannot be sure how governments' attitudes and policies would have evolved in the absence of summitry.

2. As the summit is merely one event in a continuing stream of multilateral and bilateral exchanges, its specific effects are hard to disentangle from the effects of other international contacts.

3. As governments are *national* governments and summiteers *national* politicians, the effects of international discussions are almost always secondary to domestic pressures. As I have argued earlier, the summit should not be seen as a kind of supranational institution, and the summit communiqué should not be read as a kind of treaty to be implemented. Summits have seldom witnessed definitive decisions on fundamental issues of trade, energy, macroeconomics, and so on. Those seeking realistically to understand the consequences of summitry must look primarily for indirect effects of the summit process, especially within the domestic arena.[12]

These three factors are necessary qualifications to the following reflections.

Fostering Personal Understanding

Personal acquaintance with their fellow leaders is the effect of summitry most often stressed by summiteers themselves and their closest aides. Unlike bureaucrats (and academics), who are typically 'paper-readers', politicians are typically 'people-readers', for whom face-to-face exchanges are important. 'The summits were for us — for the people who went,' said one. 'I got an understanding of you and what your real problem was — as distinct from what your State Department said to the foreign ministry — and what domestic troubles you had in formulating an agreement. Heads of government share a certain sense of the loneliness of our position, and in some ways we could talk to each other more frankly than to our colleagues at home.'

Such personal ties can lubricate international relations. Many sherpas and summiteers note the utility of 'being able to pick up the phone' and talk to a well-placed friend and colleague in another capital. Occasionally, personal rapport can have practical significance. For example, Helmut Schmidt is said to have influenced the last Labour Government's economic policies through his personal relations with James Callaghan, and several participants claim that Prime Minister Fukuda's impressive personal performance at the London summit forestalled planned complaints by others about Japanese trade practices.

Summiteers note that personal amity — and the knowledge that one would have to face one's colleagues again next year — can have a 'shaming' effect, inhibiting unilateral national policies.[13] Said one British minister, 'You would think twice about taking actions against a friend.' 'It is like a schoolboys' club,' noted one of his French counterparts, 'and you would not like to violate the rules of the game.' When Germany failed to meet the growth targets agreed at the London summit, Helmut Schmidt was said to be personally embarrassed; 'I have been made to look ridiculous [*blamiert*],' he told associates at home. Fear of having their prime minister put in 'the pillory' or 'the prisoner's dock' has induced the Japanese to make anticipatory trade concessions just prior to several summits. In discussions within the last Labour Cabinet about selective protectionist measures, Callaghan's disinclination towards a protectionist strategy were strengthened by his international contacts, and he in turn used that line with his colleagues to some effect. 'This would embarrass me at the next summit,' he would say. Or, 'I've just been talking to Helmut [or Jimmy], and I think we should avoid that sort of thing now.' On the other hand, the moral suasion derived from summit-engendered personal relations can be important only at the margins. It can strengthen prior convictions, perhaps, but, for example, neither Callaghan nor his protectionist colleagues thought that the internationalist argument would have carried the day in the face of strong contrary currents in domestic politics.

Meeting their colleagues can also have an educational effect on the participants. The prospect of the summit forces the chief executive to do his homework on foreign economic policy and to focus on the international dimensions of the problems he has been grappling with domestically. Moreover, face-to-face encounters convey the international constraints more vividly than dry diplomatic cables. 'Any meeting of the head of government with foreign counterparts shows him that it's all more complicated than he thought,' explained one slightly jaded official. A summiteer agreed: 'The main point is to learn how the others see the problems.'

This educational effect is especially important for politicians whose background is more insular, a category that includes a growing number of Western leaders. The Italians have a word for it; well-placed observers there say that the single most important effect of the summits has been to *sprovincializzare* [de-provincialise] Italian leaders, a phenomenon paralleled in other summit countries. The summits have provided a kind of 'culture-shock' for Japanese politicians; Prime Minister Ohira recalled after the Tokyo summit, 'I felt naked – like a little child.' The Ottawa summit was used both by Europeans and by some Americans to begin the education of Ronald Reagan in the realities of international economic relations and to induce his recognition of the *acquis* of international cooperation, such as the International Energy Programme. From the perspective of one seasoned European diplomat, 'summits introduce politicians whose primary experience has been domestic to the long-running serial of international collaboration: "New readers begin here".'

Energising the Policy Process

Summits engage the prestige and the power of the highest authorities in each country. Consequently, summits energise the policy process, allowing central executives to overcome bureaucratic and political obstacles that would be more obdurate under normal circumstances. For example, in countries as diverse as the United States, Italy, and Canada, the pressures of summit preparation have been used by some officials to increase the low priority normally attached to North–South issues. Some people in Brussels believe that the advent of the summit encourages the Europeans to move more quickly towards common positions on such issues as international monetary questions or trade with Japan. During the final stages of the Tokyo Round, both the American and European chief negotiators found it useful to cite the London and Bonn summit commitments to a prompt and successful conclusion of the negotiations. By engaging the international and domestic credibility of the heads of government, these public statements of intent reduced the ability of narrower interests to resist concessions that the respective negotiators knew were necessary to complete the deal.

This energising effect of summits is most marked in Japan, where traditional consensus-building seems interminable. The characteristic reluctance of Japanese leaders to override strongly held differences of opinion and to dictate policy is, in the context of the summit preparations, somewhat offset by the equally characteristic fear that the prime minister may 'lose face' internationally unless a more defensible policy can be agreed upon within the government. For example, during the 1982 summit preparations Chief Cabinet Secretary Miyazawa is said to have demanded with 'un-Japanese' bluntness that the various ministries concerned with trade issues resolve their differences. 'I understand your problems,' he reportedly told recalcitrant bureaucrats, 'but I must have a decision now.' The summit deadline seems to have become an integral part of Japanese policy-making. 'We should finish this matter "by the summit"' is said to be an increasingly common comment.

Justifying Internationally Desirable Policies

As a rule, national leaders go to summits to get international legitimation for their existing policies, not to discuss changing those policies. The ideal for every summiteer was represented by an American
newspaper headline following the Puerto Rico summit: 'Summit
Leaders Endorse Ford's Economic Policy.' Much of the communiqué negotiation involves efforts by each participant to obtain as
ringing an affirmation of his programme as possible. (Of course this
tendency is even greater when the summit coincides with a national
electoral campaign, as in the case of Ford in 1976 or Thatcher in
1983.) Both government and opposition politicians in many of these
countries believe that this international endorsement has real impact
in domestic politics, and conversely, that communiqué language
contrary to the thrust of a government's current policy could be used
profitably by opponents.

Sometimes the search for 'helpful' language is intended to fore-
stall any weakening of the government's own commitment to a given
policy. Italian officials favouring a stringent economic line are said
to 'relish' the inclusion of language emphasising the need for austerity, and elsewhere, too, the summits' stress on fighting inflation
strengthened the government's resistance to demands for fiscal and
monetary relaxation. Giscard found the Rambouillet accord useful
in fending off Gaullist critics within his own majority who opposed
compromise with the United States on international monetary questions. Similarly, statements on the importance of nuclear energy
have been inserted in successive communiqués at the request of the
German and British governments, seeking international reinforcement for domestically controversial programmes.

By definition, this sort of 'policy justification' does not involve
government's pursuing policies that they would not otherwise wish
to pursue, but it can help them to pursue policies that would otherwise be more difficult to pursue domestically. As the chief political
aide to one summiteer put it, 'The summit can give us a tailwind in
domestic politics.' On the other hand, international legitimation is
not necessarily sufficient to save a government that is pursuing internationally desirable, but domestically unpopular policies. Canadian
Prime Minister Joe Clark lost office in 1979, in part over his policy
of raising oil prices, despite international encouragement of that
policy at the Tokyo summit a few months earlier.

If the communiqués were pure 'tossed salad' documents, with no concern whatever for internal consistency, policy justification would have no impact on international policy coordination. In fact, however, the practice of policy justification marginally encourages policy moderation around the international median. As a leading international banker noted, 'It is harder to put forward some lunatic domestic proposition in an international forum, so summits and other such meetings tend to moderate doctrinaire points of view.' A central banker close to summitry added that in recent years domestic politics in a number of countries have thrown up unusually ideological governments, probably more than offsetting the moderating impact of summitry. Without such international confrontation of views, the tendency towards divergent national dogmatisms might have been even more destabilising.

Accommodating Divergent Policies

Flexible exchange rates were supposed to free national policymakers from the need to follow international policy fashions slavishly. However, the 1970s showed that international money markets react so sharply to national policy divergences that most deviants are forced back towards the international median policy mix. The cases of Britain in 1976, the US in 1978, and France in 1982 show that this effect applies even to the major countries, although less immediately than to smaller, highly open economies.

The summit process mirrors this economic tendency in political terms. The paper on macroeconomics prepared for the sherpas in 1982 illustrates the point. After reviewing the monetary and fiscal policy mixes of the participating governments, it suggested that the two most deviant were the US and Japan. The US was urged to tighten fiscal policy and loosen monetary policy, while the prescription for the Japanese was the reverse.

The most powerful countries can try to adapt to this 'regression towards the mean' by using the summit process itself to shift the international climate of opinion in the direction of their preferred policy mix. For example, this was in part the strategy of the Carter administration in 1977–78 and (with a different set of policy preferences) the Reagan administration in 1981–82. Large countries are in that sense 'policy-makers', just as large producers and large suppliers in commodity markets are 'price-makers'.

Smaller countries, on the other hand, are essentially 'policy-takers'. For them, the summit process offers an important opportunity for learning the likely future of the international policy marketplace. 'When we are deciding on our policies,' said a key Italian economic official, 'we need to know where the others are headed, and we cannot simply wait until the exchange markets show us we are out of line. That's why the sherpa meetings and the summit itself are so important for us.' A Canadian participant (and football enthusiast) referred to the importance of 'getting on side' in policy terms, and recalled that when Prime Minister Trudeau realised during one summit that the international policy climate was moving in a restrictive direction, he returned home to propose an austerity package to parliament. (That this package contributed to his subsequent electoral defeat only confirms the difficulty of the clash between international economics and domestic politics.)

One experienced participant in summit preparations put the point vividly: 'The lemmings need to get together each year to tell each other where they are going.' One of his less cynical colleagues explained that 'you return from the summit feeling more secure that you know the general drift of the others' policies, so that at least you know where the problems are going to arise.' In theoretical terms, this phenomenon of 'policy-taking' is the exact opposite of the 'free-rider' problem; perhaps it should be termed the 'forced-rider' problem. Although I have phrased the point as if all countries were either pure policy-makers or pure policy-takers, it would be more accurate to say that countries follow strategies composed of different mixes of policy-making and policy-taking.

Even the most powerful participants have been led on occasion by the summit process towards mutual accommodation. For example, discussions in connection with the London summit appreciably narrowed differences over President Carter's initial tough line on nuclear energy and nonproliferation. On North–South issues, the summit-linked discussions in 1981 and 1982 reduced the gap between the Reagan administration and the Europeans; the Americans were induced to adopt a more open-minded position on the so-called 'global negotiations', while Europeans came gradually to appreciate Reagan's emphasis on the role of private enterprise in development. Similarly, a certain rapprochement between the Reaganites and the other participants on East–West economic relations and international monetary policy was generated during the run-up to the Williamsburg summit.

In some cases, mutual accommodation reflects simply a political process of 'splitting the difference', but in other instances, accommodation is based on 'integrative bargaining', in which participants gradually come to understand better the priorities and the logic of the opposing positions. For example, some participants report that from Ottawa to Versailles one could see a growth in mutual understanding on macroeconomic and monetary issues, leading to a less simplistic confrontation about US interest rates and to a procedural agreement to study the effects of exchange rate interventions, a typical device in integrative bargaining.

None of these instances of mutual accommodation eliminated national divergences completely, but as one summiteer pointed out, 'It is the cumulative effect of the summits that counts.' Of course, mutual accommodation is the bread-and-butter of everyday diplomacy, but the summit process plays a special role in encouraging movement when (as in the instances cited) the chief executive has been identified personally with the policy in question.

Typically, the accommodative effects of the summit process operate primarily by increasing (if only marginally) the weight of dissidents from the official line within each of the contending governments. Generally speaking, the advent of the summit strengthens the hands of the more internationalist factions within each government. 'Let's avoid a row on this at the summit if we can,' is usually a useful argument in intramural debates. Conversely, domestic advisers in more than one government have been known to castigate the summit process in general, and the sherpas in particular, as a kind of 'internationalist conspiracy'. This view was as common among domestically-oriented liberal Democrats in the Carter White House as it appears to be among conservative Reaganauts.

Resolving Prisoners' Dilemmas

Summits may also facilitate international cooperation in the context of 'prisoners'-dilemma' problems, in which each participant would be better off if collective action were taken, but in which each, individually, has powerful incentives to defect from the collective action and become a 'free rider'. For example, in the face of the OPEC challenge of 1979, it was clear that Western consumers would be better off if all could agree to reduce their demand for imported oil. On the other hand, for any single country, the ideal outcome would be for all the others to limit demand, while its own consumption remained unconstrained. The logic of collective action in such a situation requires that the major countries each make a credible, mutually binding commitment to reduce consumption, which was the result achieved at the Tokyo summit. Officials in all the participating countries, as well as impartial observers at the International Energy Agency, agree that the Tokyo targets did have a significant impact on national energy policies, strengthening the hand of conservationists. (On the other hand, government policies were probably less important in accounting for the subsequent reduction in demand than the direct effects of price rises and the subsequent world recession.) North–South issues may be another case in point, since development in the Third World is a public good for the West as a whole (greater world demand; possibly increased political stability), but development aid typically ranks much lower on national and bilateral agendas.

The summit is a particularly useful venue for addressing such public-good or prisoners'-dilemma problems. First, all the major countries whose involvement is necessary are present, and yet their number is sufficiently limited for the responsibility of each to be clear.[14] Second, the visibility and authority of the summiteers make their mutual commitments more credible, for it is costly to renege on a commitment made by the head of state or government. This, too, is the significance of the repetition of the 1974 OECD Trade Pledge in successive summit communiqués. Such commitments can be used in subsequent domestic debates. One American summit participant, recalling internal debates about proposed restrictions on shoe imports, noted: 'If a president commits himself to something at a summit, and you can cite that in a meeting, that's a damn powerful argument. The rest of the government may not always be impressed, but the president is.'

The Bonn Summit: Policy Coordination, Linkage, and Divided Governments

The discussion of the last few pages has illustrated how summits can marginally improve international policy coordination. By all odds, however, the high point of summit efforts at policy coordination came in 1978. Since early 1977 the Carter administration had sought in vain to have the Germans (and the Japanese) match America's reflationary measures, following the so-called 'locomotive' strategy for world economic recovery.[15] In the absence of such coordination, the dollar had fallen precipitously. Some advocates of flexible exchange rates had earlier supposed that floating would obviate the need for international coordination, but by mid-1978 it was becoming clear that massive exchange rate adjustments had very damaging side effects. With support from the sidelines from the smaller European countries and the OECD, the Americans in 1978 renewed their pressure for more German domestic stimulus. For their part, the Germans (again, with the quiet support of the other summit countries), sought a substantial reduction in American oil imports, which they saw as a continuing threat to international economic stability.

After extensive negotiation in a variety of forums throughout the spring of 1978, agreement on a package deal was reached at the Bonn summit. Helmut Schmidt agreed to additional fiscal stimulus, amounting to one percent of GNP, and Jimmy Carter committed himself to decontrol of domestic oil prices before the end of 1980. Secondary elements in the Bonn accord included a Japanese commitment on import growth and export restraint and a renewed undertaking to improve domestic growth, an American undertaking to give priority to fighting inflation, and French acquiescence to progress in the multilateral trade negotiations. All in all, the Bonn summit produced a balanced agreement of unparalleled specificity, and rather remarkably, virtually all parts of the package were actually implemented at the national level.

In retrospect, opinions differ on the substantive economic merits of this deal. Many Germans and Japanese (though not all) believe that their stimulus measures contributed to subsequent budget deficits and inflation, whereas many Americans and other Europeans continue to believe that additional stimulus was the right medicine in June 1978 and attribute the subsequent inflation to exogenous factors, especially the Iranian revolution and the second oil crisis. (All agree that oil price decontrol in the US was a success.) This is not the place to resolve these questions of retrospective economic assessment. For present purposes, it is important to note two crucial features of this rare case of genuine international policy coordination.

First, the Bonn package deal involved a linkage between different sectors − particularly energy and fiscal policy − a linkage that was fundamentally political, so to speak, and not functional. Because in the modern state such distinct sectors normally are handled by different bureaucracies and respond to different domestic constituencies, cross-sector trades rarely can be accomplished without the active involvement of the chief executive. Only he has the authority to compel one sector to make what is, for it, an uncompensated concession, and only he can balance those costs against the benefits that will (presumably) flow to his nation from the counterpart concession by the other party. Without such cross-sector trades, important positive-sum international games may never be concluded. For example, there was no possible German concession within the energy field that could have induced the American energy concession.

Summitry encourages governments to address linkages and priorities among issues traditionally handled by separate networks of specialists. As one sherpa explains, 'In working out an agreement, I might say to my fellow sherpas, for example, "I know that's what my development aid specialist said, but there are more important things than that".' Some sectors of international economics, such as trade and monetary affairs, have historically been handled by independent networks of specialists in the various governments, but today's problems often cut across these sectoral boundaries. Assuming adequate attention to sectorally-relevant detail, the involvement of chief executives and their staffs in summit preparations makes it easier to overcome the centrifugal effects of sectoral 'sub-governments' and to strike mutually beneficial deals.

A second feature of the politics of the Bonn accord is even more revealing: agreement was reached only because within each of the key governments a powerful faction actually favoured the policy being demanded internationally. On the American side, oil price decontrol was strongly (but not loudly) urged as in the American national interest by a coalition of the President's international and economic advisers, in opposition to his domestic political aides and key Congressmen. On the German side, certain officials in the *Bundeskanzleramt* and the Economics Ministry, as well as leaders in the Social Democratic Party and trade unions, argued privately in early 1978 that further stimulus was domestically necessary. Opposition came from some in the Finance Ministry and the banking community, especially the leadership of the Bundesbank. Helmut Schmidt's public posture was one of firm opposition, too, but some people close to him suspect that he privately welcomed being pushed onto a more expansionist course. Although public mythology in Germany now holds that the stimulus package was forced on a reluctant Germany by foreign pressure, most participants in the 1978 process (including many opponents of the package) say privately that the domestic pressure for expansion was also essential. Indeed, many believe that even without foreign pressure, a somewhat smaller stimulus package would have been produced later in the year. On the

American side, the summit commitment played a crucial role in the subsequent, heated intramural debate about the administration's energy policy, and was probably crucial in the final decontrol decision.

Ironically, in the climactic negotiations between the German and American sherpas, each negotiator privately favoured the policy being pressed on his government by the other. Elsewhere during the summit preparations the transnational alliance of convenience that underlay the final deal occasionally became explicit. At least one American official urged his German counterparts to put more pressure on the American government to reduce oil imports. Conversely, German expansionists arranged the timing of the summit to maximise the impact of foreign pressure. A similar analysis applies to the politics of the Japanese contribution to the 'locomotive' agreement, as pro-stimulus Japanese officials welcomed additional US pressure as a way of overcoming objections from the Ministry of Finance.[16] The conjunction between distributive bargaining and intraorganisational bargaining was crucial to the success of the deal.

In short, international coordination is most likely when governments are deeply divided, that is, when powerful factions within each government already favour the desired policy change. Dieter Hiss, the 1978 German sherpa, later wrote that summits are likely to effect changes in national policy 'only insofar as they mobilise and/or change public opinion . . . and the attitude of political groups . . . Often that is enough, if the balance of opinion is shifted . . . providing a bare majority for the previously stymied actions of a strong minority.'[17] The reshuffle of alignments at the domestic game board thus permits a deal to be struck at the international table.

This favourable constellation of circumstances is not common in international political economy. Other potential summit packages have failed because of the absence of the appropriate domestic reinforcement. For example, during 1982 some participants spoke about a summit package in which the Europeans would agree to restrictions on East–West trade and credit in return for American concessions on monetary or North–South issues. However, supporters (even tacit ones) of reduced trade with the East were very rare within European governments, and conversely, very few Reagan administration officials favoured significant exchange rate intervention or global negotiations.

Generally speaking, a government's policies reflect a fairly stable coalition of domestic interests. To change those policies for the sake of better international coordination would often require a significant readjustment of the government's base of support and offend the personal convictions of key government leaders. Thus, the potential gains from the international game must be quite large to offset the domestic costs of coordination, particularly given the high uncertainty surrounding the international game.

Moreover, even when transnational coalitions are in principle possible, their construction is impeded by the reluctance of most officials to search for potential allies among dissidents within foreign governments. Intraorganisational bargaining is more often seen as an obstacle, rather than as an aid, to efficient international negotiation. Even when the respective negotiators are aware of internal divergences across the table, the obstacles to transnational coordination and the risks of failure are high. During the Library Group meetings, for example, Helmut Schmidt himself once urged his foreign counterparts to call publicly for a more expansionary German policy, but when the call was issued, the instigator joined his compatriots in complaining about 'foreign interference'. Academic theorists of transnational politics may have underestimated the resilience of the norms of state unity and sovereignty.

What the Summits Can and Cannot Accomplish

It would be wrong to see summitry as a substitute for other international contacts, or as a process that must inevitably circumvent and undermine existing international organisations, such as the OECD, the GATT, the IMF, or the IEA.[18] In theory, summitry and these institutions represent complementary, not competitive, approaches to international economic cooperation. As we have seen, the organisations have several inherent weaknesses that summitry tends to offset. The size of the organisations tempts free-riding and reduces intimacy, making it harder for them to address prisoners' dilemmas. The less intense involvement of national politicians, particularly heads of government, in the activities of the organisations makes it somewhat harder for them to foster resolutions of domestic-international political dilemmas, to address cross-sectoral trade-offs, and to elicit credible national commitments. On the other hand, compared to chief executives and even sherpas, participants in the organisations are generally more expert in technical terms and enjoy greater continuity. These characteristics mean that the organisations are likely to be better at 'integrative bargaining', that is, joint problem-solving.

For the most part, those involved in summitry have been sensitive to the need to coordinate their activities with the ongoing work of the international organisations. Informal collaboration with the OECD worked fairly well until recently, and relations with the IEA continue to be satisfactory. The initiative for the 1982 GATT ministerial meeting emerged from the summit process, and the failure of that session can hardly be attributed to summitry as such. The 1982 Versailles monetary accord actually increased coordination between the summit process and the IMF, by involving the IMF Managing Director in continuing discussions among the summit countries on monetary and macroeconomic issues. It may perhaps be true that the effectiveness of the international organisations has in some measure declined since the 1960s, but if so, summitry is not to blame. More important factors have been the waning of American leadership and the devisive impact of domestic politics, and, as I have argued, summitry itself is a response to precisely those problems. Improving the effectiveness of summitry and reinvigorating the organisations are complementary, not alternative tasks.

Amidst the uncertainties of conjectural history and counterfactual comparison, the summits appear to have produced some modest achievements. From time to time, the process has contributed to the resolution of policy differences among the summit countries and has served as a prophylaxis for the health of the international trading system. Hiss states the case this way:

> Of special interest is the question whether governments ever undertook any measures, occasioned by the summit, which they would not have undertaken without the summit. The answer is clear. No country violates its own interests. But certainly the definition of its interests can change through a summit with its possible trade-offs and give-and-take . . . It was always clear that the orientations achieved at the summit could not have the character of common resolutions about definitive measures . . . However, the results of the summit meetings, inserted efficaciously into the domestic decision process, make it easier to steer this process in a direction which produces positive results not only from the narrower national point of view, but also in the international context, [so that] the potential for international cooperation grows and the

potential for serious international economic, monetary, or trade policy conflicts and beggar-thy-neighbour policies declines.[19]

What counts in successful cases of international coordination is less the official communiqué itself than the effects that summitry induces within the domestic arena, strengthening the hands of the more internationalistic contenders in the policy process. If no significant domestic pressure for an internationally cooperative line of policy exists, summitry cannot create it, but where such pressure exists, the summit process can amplify its effectiveness.

However, summitry has been no cure-all. The experience of the last nine summits has made clear just how difficult international policy coordination really is, not only in economic terms, but also in political terms. Moreover, summitry as an institution has tended to deteriorate in effectiveness in recent years, as the preparations have drifted further from the direct purview of the chief executives, and as public relations have come increasingly to outweigh substance in the approach taken by key participants. If the Library Group image of summitry was symbolised by the summiteers' retreats to Rambouillet and Puerto Rico, and if the 'results-oriented' interpretation emphasised during the Carter years was linked to the more work-a-day sites of London, Bonn, and Tokyo, the more recent fashion for photogenic eighteenth-century places in Versailles and Williamsburg (prefigured, perhaps, by the sixteenth-century palaces of Venice) might seem to herald a third image: the summit as 'world spectacle'.

Ironically, both Mitterrand and Reagan, hosts for the last two years, are said to believe that the ills of summitry could be cured by reducing the scale of summit institutionalisation and turning the summits into small seminars. In my view, however, this position confuses pomp (which is antithetical to effective summitry) with preparation (which is actually vital for effective summitry). Beginning with Rambouillet, successful summits have required careful preparation. Even in the case of the avowedly more 'spontaneous' Williamsburg summit, much of the apparent convergence on such issues as East–West trade and international monetary policy emerged in extensive prior consultations during the spring of 1983. Inadequately prepared summits are unlikely to engage the really difficult and complex problems posed by economic interdependence, and are more likely to degenerate into shouting matches. But in the final analysis, since only the most authoritative national politicians can credibly aggregate domestic interests in a broader international context, a world without summits would be a less stable world.

Notes

Acknowledgements: For support in the research reported here, I am grateful to the Center for International Affairs at Harvard, to the Deutsche Gesellschaft für Auswärtige Politik, to the Japan Foundation, to the Royal Institute of International Affairs, and to the Social Science Research Council. Naturally, I am especially grateful to all those persons in the seven summit nations and the European Commission who graciously agreed to talk with me about their experiences and perspectives. For comments on this chapter, I want to express my special thanks to the participants in the Maastricht conference, as well as to Robert Axelrod, Nicholas Bayne, Richard Cooper, John Goodman, Jeffrey Hart and Sir Michael Palliser. Naturally, none of these individuals or institutions is responsible for errors of fact or interpretation that remain.

1. David Watt, 'Pros and Cons of Political Summitry', *Financial Times* (London), 29 April 1977.
2. *Ibid.*
3. Richard N. Cooper, 'Economic Interdependence and Foreign Policy in the Seventies', *World Politics*, January 1972, pp. 164, 179.
4. Economists have recently begun to apply game theoretic approaches to this same set of issues. See, for example, Ralph C. Bryant, *Money and Monetary Policy in Interdependent Nations* (Brookings Institution, Washington D.C., 1980), esp. pp. 453–481; Richard N. Cooper, 'Economic Interdependence and Coordination of Economic Policies', in Ronald Jones and Peter B. Kenen (eds.), *Handbook for International Economy* (North Holland, 1984, forthcoming), and the works cited therein.
5. Richard E. Walton and Robert B. McKersie, *A Behavioral Theory of Labor Negotiations: An Analysis of a Social Interaction System* (McGraw-Hill, New York, 1965).
6. *Ibid.*, p. 3.
7. At one time it was theorised that flexible exchange rates might offer a simple way of insulating national economic autonomy without forgoing the benefits of international commerce, but the last decade has shown that we cannot float off the horns of the sovereignty–interdependence dilemma so easily.
8. One of the rare published accounts of some of these events that I have discovered is George P. Shultz and Kenneth W. Dam, *Economic Policy Beyond the Headlines* (Norton, New York, 1977), pp. 12–13. For brevity's sake, I pass over the involved story of how Japan, Italy, Canada, and subsequently the European Community were added to the list of participants in the Western summits. The overall tone of the meetings and of the preparations continue to be set primarily by the original four participants, even though on many specific issues and in specific instances, the others often play important roles.
9. Some participants report a similar climate in other small international committees that meet frequently, such as the COREPER (Council of Permanent Representatives) of the European Community.
10. I leave aside here the role of the European Community in coordinating the

positions of the European participants in the summit, because that topic is treated elsewhere. There has been some convergence of European positions on summit matters over the years, and participants from the Commission are inclined to attribute that convergence to Community activities. On the other hand, participants in the preparations within the four European capitals discount completely the significance of Community coordination as a factor in their decisions, except in the case of trade, where the Commission has powers granted by the Treaty of Rome. Whatever European convergence has occurred, they say, is due to more fundamental changes in economic interests. Bilateral European contacts, especially between Bonn and Paris, have been important in summit preparations.

11. *International Herald Tribune* (Paris), 23 July 1981; *Financial Times* (London), 23 July 1981.

12. For an alternative view on this point, see Pelkmans' chapter in this volume.

13. Writing in the tradition of formal game theory, Robert Axelrod has shown that the likelihood of cooperation between competitors is increased when they expect to encounter one another again. This logic, which applies both to individual leaders and to nations, is probably an important underlying element in international policy coordination. Robert Axelrod, 'The Emergence of Cooperation Among Egoists', *American Political Science Review*, vol. 75, no. 2 (June 1981).

14. For an explanation of why smaller groups find it easier to solve public-good problems than larger ones, see Mancur Olson, *The Rise and Decline of Nations* (Yale University Press, 1982).

15. Mr. Randall Henning of Tufts University is now completing a doctoral thesis on the world reflation controversy of 1977–78. I am grateful for several extended discussions of these events with Mr. Henning.

16. See I.M. Destler and Hisao Mitsuyu, 'Locomotives on Different Tracks: Macroeconomic Diplomacy, 1977–1979', in I.M. Destler and Hideo Sato (eds.), *Coping with U.S.–Japanese Economic Conflicts* (D.C. Heath, 1982).

17. Dieter Hiss, 'Weltwirtschaftsgipfel: Betrachtungen eines Insiders', in Joachim Frohn and Reiner Stäglin (eds.), *Empirische Wirtschaftsforschung* (Duncker and Humblot, 1980), pp. 286–287 (my translation).

18. For a critical view of the impact of summitry on traditional international institutions, see J. Robert Schaetzel and H.B. Malmgren, 'Talking Heads', *Foreign Policy*, Summer 1980, pp. 130–142.

19. Hiss, 'Weltwirtschaftsgipfel', pp. 282–284.

3 COLLECTIVE MANAGEMENT AND ECONOMIC COOPERATION

Jacques Pelkmans

Why Are Summits Economic?

Gatherings of heads of state and government were quite rare until 1975. Nonetheless, they were certainly not unique as is exemplified by such notorious cases as the Vienna Congress and the Conference of Yalta. What is conspicuous, is that they are a recurrent phenomenon and that they deal predominantly with economic issues. Their being repetitive is only new, however, for the Western developed world as a whole (but not for the European Community) since the Warsaw Pact/Comecon countries as well as such congregations as the Organisation for African Unity and the non-aligned countries have been organising summits for decades. Rather, the striking property of Western summitry since 1975 is its economic character.

It is possible to explain this property by the economic, political and uniquely personal circumstances prevailing at the time of the first summit meetings. A later tendency to include security and traditional foreign policy discussions is little more than a return to normalcy; yet, it is consistent with the reasons for the original economic focus as those factors weakened considerably over time.

The economic circumstances of the five years preceding the Rambouillet summit (November 1975) were surely very worrying. Due to a most unusual synchronisation of business cycle peaks throughout the developed market economy, some commodity speculation and a few bad harvests, a commodity boom and food shortage arose in 1972/73, culminating in hesitant increases in the price of oil. Inflation in the early 1970s was rampant. The international monetary system underwent severe shocks such as the devaluation of the US dollar (preceded by a temporary 10 percent surcharge on all US imports), repeated closures of the foreign exchange markets due to the unbearable pressures of 'hot money' flows against the untenable parities of certain currencies, an EC 'snake' that lost three participants within the first nine months of its existence, and, finally, the definitive collapse of the Bretton Woods system in February 1973.

Pressures for protectionism started to build up: in the US Congress the Burtke-Hart Bill remained a protectionist threat for three consecutive years and the first Multi-Fibre Agreement covered all textiles (and clothing), rather than merely cotton textiles (as its predecessor had).

It is against this background that the reactions on the October War in the Middle East have to be understood. Helped by structural excess demand for oil, ever since OPEC was founded (1960), a decision was taken not to repeat hesitant price increases, but, rather, to exploit market power in a truly oligopolistic fashion by quadrupling the price. A convenient political side-show consisted in the oilembargo against the US and the Netherlands that revealed a vulnerability not hitherto realised.

Accommodative financing of the inevitable addition to inflation, as well as the relatively low capacity of OPEC countries to absorb the new incomes (hence, increasing savings, thereby withdrawing effective demand for Western production) led to huge balance-of-payments deficits, in turn leading to even greater volatility of exchange rates than witnessed in the first three years of the decade. Strong disagreements arose among Western countries over how to react appropriately to OPEC: although a US attempt to construct an oil monopsony (the West as a collective buyer monopoly) was shot down by the Europeans and the Japanese, the International Energy Agency (IEA) was founded at last, but without French membership.

In the course of 1975 France started to reconsider its position. Its 'special relationship' with the Arab world had yielded little else than the same long-term supply contracts the Japanese got, except for some extra arms sales. Unemployment started to rise rapidly and a recession announced itself. France had been forced to leave the 'snake' in 1974. Though it had re-entered in 1975, the franc's position was anything but secure every time a dollar decrease led to upward pressure on the Deutsche Mark. This led to great sensitivity about the US stance of 'benign neglect' of its exchange rate.

Therefore, lots of sound economic reasons can be found which make Giscard's summit initiative look sensible. Of course, economic summitry itself was rather unique in the developed West at large, but had already become institutionalised in the form of the 'European Council' in the realm of the European Community. To countries such as Japan and the US, accustomed as they had become to long-standing Western economic cooperation in many domains, the summit could credibly be presented as a political forum of last resort to restore some international economic stability upon the remnants of the old economic order. The summit could set out to achieve a minimum of short-term economic policy coordination as well as a joint formulation of policy rules, so badly lacking in the international monetary non-system of the day. Realising that the refusal of international economic cooperation had been a major cause of the Great Depression being so deep and so prolonged, participation in an exercise of joint economic leadership was difficult to decline.

The summits being economic, however, can also be explained politically. With the Vietnam and Yom Kippur wars over, and the Helsinki Agreement signed, the worries of political leaders shifted to the stagnant world economy and less cooperative attitudes in foreign economic policy. But such a complete neglection of politics could, of course, only be shortlived. The prejudice seems to be confirmed by the steadily rising importance of the summits' political discussions since the Bonn summit of 1978. There is a convenient complement to this position in that Japan is not, and France is half-heartedly, part of the NATO structure which renders a formal summit on security politically difficult. Pursuing the idea not only imposes an entirely informal setting for the debate on security but also requires a credible smoke screen of pressing items warranting legitimate cooperation. An economic summit offered the latter while providing plenty of opportunities in the 'corridor', during meals and around the fire-place to exchange views on security and traditional foreign policy issues without worrying about public expectations and press communiqués. The political explanation is therefore entirely consistent with, and complementary to, the economic justification.

Finally, the year of Rambouillet witnessed an entirely accidental group of political leaders, many well-versed in matters of economic and financial policy, some of whom were accustomed to highly informal and frank discussions among policy-makers of a few core countries. I refer to what has sometimes been called the 'Library Group'[1] of finance ministers and, occasionally, central bankers of the US, Japan, France, the United Kingdom and West Germany. Giscard d'Estaing and Schmidt were members of the Library Group before rising to the highest political post in their countries and were known to display great enthusiasm for its modes of operation. Giscard's proposal to hold an economic summit might be viewed as a longing for open economic policy debates at the highest political level. At the same time, however, can it be viewed as a revival of de

Gaulle's idea (in 1958) of replacing US leadership by a 'directorate' of core countries.[2] Giscard's personal blend rendered this idea more attractive by emphasising the economic contents and the informal nature of the summit.

Summitry and International Economic Organisations

Economic summitry for a core group raises questions about the role of international economic organisations such as the GATT, IMF, OECD and IEA. These institutions have a much wider, or worldwide, membership and their policies can be discussed and co-decided by all country participants in accordance with international treaties. This is not to say that all have equal decision- or policy-making power. In the IMF voting takes place with a complex formula of weights, reflecting the financial importance of each country; furthermore, the SDR-unit consists of only five core currencies and the informal Group of Ten plays a crucial role in short-term swaps for balance-of-payments purposes. Also the GATT trade negotiations are traditionally dominated by practices of commercial diplomacy that put 'principal suppliers' and large trading powers in a leading position. However, the sense of belonging, the right to be informed, to lobby or organise interests jointly with other (small) powers, as well as the occasional possibility of mediating are extremely worthwhile accomplishments for many countries. Would economic summits subordinate or 'marginalise' the existing economic organisations?

The post-war Western economic order was based on the principles of automaticity (under a common rule of law) and hegemony, with an occasional element of negotiation.[3] But with the hegemony of the US declining and no adequate substitute leadership in sight, the rule of international economic law became more and more difficult to enforce while bilateral and multilateral negotiation – imposed by increasing domestic political pressures calling for more national policy discretion – started to carve out exceptions to the accomplishments of previous decades. According to several economists, leadership is a necessary condition for international economic stability under capitalism and a lack of it cannot normally be remedied by other means, including negotiation.[4] The reasons lay in the capacity of getting around the free-rider problem for countries with domestically-oriented politicians, taking rules and events in the world economy more or less as exogenous whilst forging short-run tactics maximising the expected probability of getting (re-)elected at home (see also the section 'Towards a System of Trade Negotiation'). Proposed solutions included a German–US 'bigemony', trilateralism between the US, Japan and a vague entity called Western Europe and other variants of hierarchical economic policy cooperation.

Given this view, one is tempted to suggest that the summits of the Seven-Plus[5] constitute a remarkable attempt to restore leadership by exercising it jointly. The interpretation does not carry us very far, however, with respect to the first nine summits held. Although the joint communiqués are not without value, they always contain a number of diplomatic compromises cloaked in generalities that are inoperational for guidance in actual policy decisions. Apart from a few conspicuous instances, they are not strictly intended as policy guidance, let alone that they be binding. The function exercised is therefore one of patient persuasion, with a better understanding of one another's domestic economic politics as the indispensable by-product. Since economic interdependence within the core group is generally well understood, the summits tend to prevent a mutual misreading of policy signals, akin to the *ex ante* concertation of price changes in a mature oligopoly in order to avoid price wars. To call that 'leadership', however, seems misleading because it implies an incomparably weaker capacity to pre-empt or suppress free riding than under a single country's hegemony.

A more realistic view is that the summits, despite their theoretical potential to function as the highest resort of Western economic co-operation, in fact pursue the worthwhile but modest objective of confidence building. It may be argued that clear directives or de-tailed institutional initiatives with respect to existing international economic institutions would bring those bodies under the tutelage of a big power directorate, undermining fundamental principles of in-ternational (economic) law. Political subjection of the actual opera-tion of the GATT and the IMF to the Seven-Plus would indeed se-riously weaken these organisations. However, no such attempts have been undertaken. At any rate, such world organisations deal with problems that can no longer be 'internalised' by the leading Western developed countries. This is only possible with issues the OECD and the IEA deal with, but in these cases the political willing-ness to cooperate has never been impressive, even at the time of US leadership.[6] Common OECD positions are rarely formulated in operational ways. Its Codes on Invisible Trade and on Capital

Movements are unenforceable, if only because of long lists of exceptions that take the teeth out of the agreements. Its Code on Multinational Enterprises is not only voluntary but highly general, having little or no impact. The OECD recommendations on 'positive adjustment' to changes in technology and comparative advantages (1978–79) as well as the Interfutures exercise (1979) have certainly spread an awareness of the structural consequences of numerous defensive government interventions, including protection and propping up ailing enterprises. They have cleared the way for a new look at the supply side in the mixed economy, ranging from a drastic deregulation in some countries to more sensible industrial policies in others. But the OECD's role in 'positive adjustment' should not be overplayed since the GATT, to a lesser extent the IMF, and, above all, the (Competition Reports of the) EC Commission, as well as certain countries individually had been arguing for years in a similar fashion.

The summits have not, or at best have marginally 'guided' the OECD in these matters. On the contrary, the sherpas have repeatedly relied on certain studies or policy papers from the OECD secretariat when preparing the agenda and the draft communiqués. A conspicuous example is the adoption of the 'locomotive theory' at the London summit and the 'convoy commitment' in Bonn.

As a confidence-building act, the (Ministerial) Trade Pledges of the OECD have been supported by the summits from Rambouillet onwards. As I shall set out later, the actual significance both of the Pledges and of the summiteers' support is at best dubious.

The summits have been slightly more assertive in matters concerning the IMF. Indeed, by the time the reform proposals of the Committee of Twenty (1974) failed to make any impact, IMF rules had become largely irrelevant and a dangerous legal vacuum arose. Adjustable but pegged exchange rates were unilaterally installed by large groups of countries in currency blocs, but these blocs (except the 'snake') had no rules: hence, sudden discrete changes remained possible. Other countries advocated (and claimed to practice) truly flexible exchange rates; however, some of them really conducted a 'dirty float' (i.e. with recurrent intervention) while others saw their experiment frustrated by the very fact that the large majority of countries did 'manage' their rates in one form or another, hence influencing the market rates of 'freely floating' currencies too. These inconsistencies, in a time of high, yet differential inflation, pronounced the impact of 'hot money' flows. Short-term capital flows had swollen to huge amounts due, first, to the dollar overhang generated in 1970 and 1971, and its amplification in the Euro-dollar market and, second, to the sudden boost of OPEC incomes in 1974 that could not immediately be absorbed in local development programmes.

The Rambouillet summit was organised around a compromise between France and the US, meant to recognise the virtues of exchange rate flexibility (by France) and to underwrite the need to combat 'erratic' fluctuations of a currency rate (by the US). One could therefore argue that the first summit yielded a breakthrough, leading to the Jamaica rewrite (January 1976) of art. IV of the IMF rules. Although this argument is formally correct, the summit was neither a necessary nor a sufficient condition to alter the IMF in a meaningful way. It was not sufficient since Jamaica essentially codified a non-system permitting virtually any thinkable variant of exchange rate rules. The only commitment was to stick to the prohibition of aggressive competitive depreciation, but the 'Guidelines for floating' (1977), specifying a possible IMF 'surveillance' have never led to anything. Before Versailles (1982), the summits had never called for specific, in contrast to general, endorsement of IMF surveillance of exchange rate policies. The Swedish devaluation of 16 percent (September 1982), widely regarded as a competitive depreciation, received some criticism but went essentially unpunished. It is most unlikely that a summit would call for IMF sanctions to enforce the avoidance of competitive depreciation.

Rambouillet was also not necessary for the Jamaica rewrite to come about. The compromise between Giscard and Ford exemplifies the classic case for bilateral diplomacy, perhaps facilitated by high IMF officials or by the services of a third country (say, Germany).

In Versailles (1982) a separate declaration on stability in the international monetary system was issued. Five summit conferences offered to begin building a 'quintal key currency system' by attempting to stabilise the SDR, in turn facilitating the 'firm surveillance' of the IMF. It is probably too early (in the fight against inflation) for this idea to become operational and its long-run requirements, moreover, are rather demanding. It is too early since the French are not ready for it and the Japanese capacity to stabilise the yen (with their truncated openness in financial capital markets) seems insufficient, irrespective of the rate of inflation. It is demanding because, if it truly became a key currency system via SDR-trading, monetary policy would come to be geared to external constraints once again (as under the gold standard and the Bretton Woods system), except perhaps for a modest crawling peg. As the Annex to the Williamsburg (1983) declaration shows, the continuing consultations refer more and more to 'policies designed to bring about greater convergence of economic performance' in seeking 'non-inflationary growth of income and employment', a laudable objective that, however, has no direct impact on the IMF as such. At the same time it should be observed that the Williamsburg communiqué invites the 'ministries of finance, in consultation with the managing director of the IMF, to define the conditions for improving the international monetary system and to consider the part which might, in due course, be played in this process by a high-level international monetary conference.'

It is certainly gratifying to note the officially expressed dissatisfaction with today's international monetary non-system. And it is appropriate that seven countries with enormous voting strength in the IMF take the lead, explicitly recognising the IMF's role. On the other hand, the cautious phrasing conceals significant differences of opinion on what the new system should look like.

The connection between the Western economic summits and the GATT is feeble. Besides endorsing the (OECD) Trade Pledges, not to revert to new protection, the summit communiqués have set (shifting) deadlines for the Tokyo Round to be completed. These deadlines had neither legal nor material significance and were not comparable with the deadline of the Kennedy Round, imposed by the US Congress (in the 1962 Trade Expansion Act) through the five-year mandate to the president to conduct trade negotiations.[7] In Ottawa (1981) the summiteers endorsed the 18-countries initiative to convene a GATT meeting at ministerial level in November 1982. Again, this amounted to a passive act of support, since no further initiative was taken to improve the chances for the GATT meeting. As is known, it proved to be a total failure: the conference had to be extended merely to soothe disputes, so that at least a joint communiqué could be issued.[8] At Williamsburg (1983) the summiteers committed themselves 'to halt protectionism . . . and actively pursue the current work programmes in the GATT.' In the sections 'The Entropy of the Free Trade System' and 'Towards a System of Permanent Trade Negotiations' I shall explain why such declarations are, though necessary, grossly insufficient.

The summits did play an exceptional and important role in amplifying the International Energy Agency's policy recommendations. Since France is not a member of the IEA, its energy policies can only be coordinated with other Western countries within the European Community or, indeed, in the summits. Galvanised into action by an unfolding second oil shock, in mid-1979, the European Council in Strasbourg agreed (under Giscard's presidency!) to quantitative oil import ceilings for 1980–1985 (fixed at the 1979 import volumes) and to an immediate freezing of EC oil consumption at 500 million tons. In Tokyo (1979), the EC asked the US to commit itself to comparable measures of quantitative reduction as well as abolition of its import subsidy scheme that kept oil (and gas) prices below world price levels (and hence discouraged domestic production whilst increasing demand pressures on OPEC oil). The upshot was a courageous (and successful) attempt by the four major EC countries (and the president of the EC Commission) to 'impose' individual country oil import and oil consumption targets on their Community partners. At the Venice summit (1980), a medium-term strategy, first formulated and agreed under IEA auspices, was endorsed. Hence the Western summit operated as a mechanism to have France subscribe to and participate in the strategy of an international organisation, the major goals of which it claimed not to endorse. The French position is especially interesting since its original objection to the IEA was that it might develop into a monopsony (buyer cartel) directed against the Arab part of OPEC. Presumably it has less serious objections to the 'sharing out' mechanism that the IEA would apply in the case of crisis or boycott. Yet, in fact, the Tokyo-Venice commitments are a (weak, but unmistakable) manifestation of buyers' collusion. All the same, France continues to refuse IEA membership.

For the US, the pressure from the summits in Tokyo and Venice to alter its domestic energy pricing policy was formally rejected as a matter of supply security for the American hemisphere; yet, there were clear indications that President Carter's U-turn in phasing out the subsidisation could be better 'sold' to the American voters by pointing to the international political and economic frictions the old policy generated, up to the highest level of policy-making.

It follows that the connection between Western economic summitry and international economic institutions is generally weak. With the conspicuous exception of the two 'energy' summits, the recommendations or appeals with respect to international economic organisations are overly general and anything but emphatic. The locomotive and convoy attempts at macroeconomic coordination were very much inspired by the OECD secretariat, backed up (in London at least) by President Carter's firm desire to get the US economy growing again.

The remainder of this essay will study the effectiveness of economic summitry by addressing the main issues of international economic cooperation directly, rather than the institutions formally entrusted with these domains. In particular, I shall deal with protectionism, macroeconomic coordination (including monetary issues) and, briefly, energy. A few suggestions for improvements will be made as well.

Other essays in this volume provide some interesting alternative justifications for the activity of summiteers. They include a desire to improve mutual understanding of domestic political constraints and establish better personal relationships, so as to enable direct contact in the event of a need for conflict management.

Protectionism

The Entropy of a Free Trade System

Protectionism is a political attitude. It purports to provide artificial advantages to resident producers (i.e. advantages not deriving from the firm's present economic performance) and thereby to discourage or prevent import competition. The General Agreement on Tariffs and Trade of 1947, and especially the amendments of 1955, its Codes and seven Rounds of tariff reduction have severely reduced the instrumental options of protectionism in Western countries. The formal strength of the GATT is that, in principle, previous tariff reductions (or removal of quotas) cannot be undone, although there is no obligation to dismantle border protection in the first place. The GATT formula has a ratchet effect: the trick is to overcome or preempt 'free riding', whereafter no back-pedalling is permitted. Of course, the material strength of the GATT depends on its enforcement capacity, which, in turn, is a function both of the willingness of the larger trading partners to accept the transaction costs of system maintenance and of the would-be sinner's fear of retaliation. Transaction costs include, first of all, the domestic political costs of forgoing free riding; in addition, the estimated diplomatic and domestic costs of the risk of being drawn into a trade war with a country that is 'opting out' (as GATT rules provide for common sanctions) and the diplomatic investment as well as the costs of domestic political rigidity to fight entropy resulting from the cumulative employment of substitutive instruments of protection.

But, once a system of relatively free trade has established itself, there are significant advantages in maintaining it, although they tend to be less susceptible to political articulation. Import competition exerts a continuous pressure upon all domestic industries that produce goods similar to imports to maintain competitiveness vis-à-vis the most efficient producers in countries with a most-favoured-nations treatment. In sectors that enjoy or could come to enjoy comparative advantages, permanent effort with respect to cost efficiency and product improvement (if not innovation) is required to encroach upon foreign markets and retain worthwhile market shares. The beneficial impact of the free trade system is therefore twofold: first, its establishment removes the inefficiencies in the importables sector and the inhibitions for the exportables sector (a static, once-for-all effect, that causes the degree of economic openness to rise substantially), and, second, system maintenance imposes a permanent drive to uphold competitiveness for all industries that are directly or indirectly exposed to the world economy (representing a much higher share of national economic activity than the share of exports and imports together!).

In recessionary circumstances the temptation to indulge in schizophrenic trade policy is very great. The general adherence to the GATT principles, certainly among Western countries, is maintained, since every single country has a vital interest in avoiding difficulties for its exportables sector, but small, highly specific exceptions on the import side are formulated that reduce the domestic political transaction costs of system maintenance in the face of well-organised pressure groups, whilst tailoring country discrimination in such a way that the diplomatic costs are negligible.

Over a period of one and a half decades, the sophistication in the art of 'free riding' has achieved an admirable level. Public coverage of losses of public firms, both in the importables and exportables sectors, various direct subsidies, special energy tariff rates, ingenious technical specifications, voluntary export restraints (whether published or secret; between industries, or governments, monitored or not; organised with informal GATT collaboration or not), trigger prices, dumping litigation with dubious 'injury' clauses, export credit subsidies, public procurement policies (especially in advanced industries) and special tax breaks for specialised exporters (DISC) are all expressions of a political attitude to buy off domestic political pressure while claiming to support a system of open access for trade. This is not to say that protectionism is necessarily illegitimate or irrational: the objectives sought are usually legitimate aims of a modern mixed economy and the governments of the day − responsive as they are and, in some measure, ought to be to pressures in a democratic society − may act rationally in a domestic political sense when agreeing to protectionist exceptions.

The schizophrenia of today's protectionism consists in the dichotomised view on trade policy: the public good of the international trade order should be maintained in general but rarely in particular. The implicit assumption that 'atomistic' decisions on products of the six-digit SITC[9] level of disaggregation, preferably geared to a few target countries only, can be piled up indefinitely without eventually undermining the 'system' itself is simply untenable. Moreover, what is an atomistic decision in the first instance tends to spread to closely related products both because the investment in pressure group politics is shown to be profitable (under certain conditions, the rents from protectionism at the product level can be captured by the entrepreneurs, and possibly also by the workers, in the product sector) and because foreign exporters tend to respond to higher barriers in one product by heightening competitive pressures in substitutes or functionally related goods that require few additional skills, investment or marketing knowledge. Since protection is hardly ever conditional upon restructuring of domestic production, political responses to import competition tend to take over from economic responses more and more. The upshot is that the level of product aggregation susceptible to protection tends to increase over the years virtually independent of whether left or right is in government. The process can only be stopped politically. But nitty-gritty incrementalism in hundreds of highly specific products does not easily reach those policy-makers and political leaders that speak out in favour of system maintenance in general terms. This is how entropy sets in.

Domestic counterpressures are notoriously weak: for consumers, the ratio of the transaction costs of effective lobbying to the benefit of free trade in a single product is rarely such as to expect vigorous political pressure; for exporters and consumers, there is also a monitoring problem since information of incrementalist protection is hard to obtain and to assess. The incentive for exporters, finally, is largely the fear of retaliation and since the latter will probably be very specific as well, exporters do not get beyond generalities by genuinely investing in lobbying.

There is a further element to the question of size, namely country size. What is a small move for a big trading country, might cause big ripples for several modest traders, whilst audacious protectionist measures by a small trading country might pass unnoticed but to some individual exporters.

Towards a System of Permanent Trade Negotiation

The post-war international trade system gradually changed from one characterised by automaticity-cum-hegemony to one of near-permanent negotiation. Reliance on automaticity alone is a naive though long-time favourite among economists, precisely because it is apolitical and avoids discretion. When negative international economic cooperation is accepted in all its domestic consequences, automaticity under a well-defined set of common rules is surely a theoretically attractive idea. It would effectively block incremental protectionism by outlawing it, whilst making exceptions subject to common judicial review, on the basis of the (common international trade) law.

This is roughly the system of the Internal Market of the European Community. Although this system is imperfect, the differences with respect to the present GATT/OECD system of trade liberalisation are fundamental. First, the surveillance and monitoring of the EC system is in the hands of a neutral Commission with at least some independent authority and the right to sue member states in a European Court. Second, the EC Court is independent, has been endowed with substantial powers, has been enmeshed into the national legal systems by a linkage procedure (which solves a part of its enforcement problems) and has acquired legitimacy and authority that is but occasionally defied. The GATT's surveillance system is based on country complaints, mere (diplomatic) consultation, and ultimately perhaps some sort of political review, if any. There is no court, although expert panels and legal procedures are employed.

The institutional differences are paralleled by an appreciable disparity in mutual trading interests. Every EC member country always has a larger, usually much larger, stake in maintaining the intra-EC market open than virtually any Contracting Party in GATT with any other one (with the exception of Canada's stake in keeping the US market open — but that is likely to be so, independent of GATT), as is indicated in Table 3.1. Altogether, a reliance on automaticity under common rules seems most improbable in the Western economy, given the desire of mixed economies with representative government to dispose of an autonomous external trade policy and of discretion to employ internal substitutes.

But automaticity can be combined with hegemony, up to a point. A hegemonial power could supply the leverage for rules to be accepted and for the system to be maintained. The property of hegemony could be attributed to a country if it could offer sufficient tangible benefits for other countries to forgo free riding and help construct the public good of the international trade order, whilst, at the same time, wielding sufficient sanction power vis-à-vis individual countries to generate multilateral enforcement. It is not necessary that tangible benefits be solely in trade policy; they could include a security alliance, be monetary or relate to long-term supply security of oil or minerals. Of course, the hegemonial country ought not to be 'all-out dominant' as this would reduce the negotiating power of the trading partners to such an extent that hegemonial discretion would become too great to be subject to rule-making, while enforcement would hinge on the politics of the day (that is, automaticity would be lost). On the other hand, the stability of an automaticity-cum-hegemony system depends crucially on the retention of the hegemony over time. If the hegemonial power is seen to enjoy prerogatives, they ought to be perceived as proportional (in some political sense) to the transaction costs of producing the international public good and the risks of initiating costly sanctions. When prerogatives degenerate into violations of automaticity, especially in trade relations with notorious 'free riders' that have been persuaded after all to subscribe to the world trade order, the credibility of the enforcer is severely damaged (cf. the invention of 'voluntary export restraint' by the USA in 1957, vis-à-vis Japanese textile and clothing exporters, leading to the Short Term Arrangement on Cotton Textiles, then to the aberration of the Long Term Arrangement). The upshot might be that entire sectors will be carved out of the system's coverage (indeed, the Multi-Fibre Arrangements have become increasingly comprehensive in terms of product and country coverage, in a sector representing 9 percent of world trade in manufactures).

The US certainly approximated to a hegemonial role, as defined here, in initiating a world trade order during the first decades after World War II.[10] But its support as well as actual trade policy be-

Table 3.1: Three Largest Export Markets of the Seven in 1980 (Shares as Percentage of Total Exports)

Country	Largest		Second		Third		EC
	Country	% share	Country	% share	Country	% share	% share
USA	Canada	15.6	Japan	9.5	Mexico	6.9	23.8
Canada	USA	63.1	Japan	5.9	UK	4.0	12.5
France	FRG	16.1	Italy	12.5	BLEU*	9.4	51.0
UK	FRG	10.4	USA	9.5	Neth.s	7.8	42.2
Italy	FRG	18.3	France	15.1	UK	6.1	47.5
F.R. Germany	France	13.4	Neth.s	9.5	Italy	8.6	48.1
Japan	USA	24.4	FRG	4.4	S. Korea	4.1	12.8

* BLEU = Belgium, Luxembourg Economic Union
Source: *UN Yearbook of International Trade Statistics*, Volume I (Trade by Country)

haviour grew more and more conditional. Hence, its claim to exceptions[11] undermined the determination of other countries not to opt for free riding. When voluntary export restraints were imposed by the US upon EC exporters of steel in the late 1960s and the Mills Bill and Burtke-Hart Bill nearly made it in Congress, US leadership in the maintenance of the trade order was over. In August 1971 it employed a temporary, across-the-board tariff in order to enforce 'the right to devalue the dollar'. In 1974 an ingenious mixture of cooperative trade policy and semi-automatic procedures for protection was inserted in the Trade Act, with the president being entrusted the ultimate political discretion to act.

Henceforth, system maintenance had to be guaranteed by cumbersome mechanisms of informal conflict management between the EC, the US and Japan, as well as by a set of new GATT Codes – to be agreed in the Tokyo Round – that cloaked trade policy disagreement with diplomatic language, unfit for private traders desiring reasonably secure access to markets. As pointed out earlier, incremental protection and bureaucratic ingenuity took on a life of their own, with no authoritative surveillance available. The management of trade policy conflicts quickly grew into a permanent exercise and negotiation became the mode of preventing retaliation. Meanwhile, large sectors rather than single products had become the subject of conflict management: synthetic fibres, automobiles, shipbuilding, steel and leather products. Negotiation under mutual threat became the rule, rather than automaticity, with the inevitable result that the trade wars had to be prevented at the highest political level.

Changing to a setting of permanent negotiation, it is the rules of politics that take over from the rule of law. Hence, there will be a drift towards hierarchical organisation. There are at least two possibilities. One is to assume collectively the surveillance of trade order that was hitherto exercised predominantly by the US. For collective leadership to be effective, the required properties of predominance are no different than under a hegemonial system, only much more difficult to realise and maintain. Not a single country of the Seven has the capacity to absorb sufficient transaction costs (i.e. concessions to others in order to have them forego free riding) or to accept the risk of waging a trade war for the sake of discipline in the system. But six of them, at least, do possess sufficient trading power to destabilise multilateral trade. Perhaps the trade power structure is better viewed as a triopoly, with Canada having some room for free (protectionist) riding on the fringe. The triopoly EC–Japan–US is ineffective as a guardian, first, because it has no appropriate mechanism for trade policy conflicts within the group (other than informal 'management', meant to soothe disputes before they flare up into damaging and antagonistic domestic pressures), and, second, because trade with third countries has widely disparate effects on each of them.

The second possibility is to structure the non-system of permanent negotiation by installing a two-tier management of trade conflicts: the higher tier consists of the Seven-Plus, which, *de facto*, boils down to the EC–Japan–US triopoly, while the lower tier consists of the EFTA, some Mediterranean countries, Australia, New Zealand and perhaps a few others. The second tier is permitted to be more protectionist vis-à-vis third countries as long as they comply reasonably well with the (low) common denominator set at the higher tier.

Even the unambitious objective of this loosely structured decision-making runs the serious danger of not being accomplished since it hinges on the effectiveness of the higher tier to contain incremental protection. In a setting of permanent negotiation, threats of retaliation will only be credible if they are occasionally tried out and if they are both limited and tangible. Only then can they become sufficiently politicised to reach the highest echelons of politics without, however, losing all possibilities of containment. Precisely such a noisy policy of retaliatory deterrence leaves plenty of room for 'atomistic' trade measures on miniscule product groups, whether through voluntary export restraints, anti-dumping or countervailing duties, 'new' technical or health requirements or other ingenuities.

Summitry's Role in Trade Matters

The clearest signal that the Western countries witnessed an erosion of the international rule of trade law consisted in the annual OECD Trade Pledge at the ministerial level (since 1974). With hegemony waned, no appropriate judicial review in sight and no reliable means of enforcement available, general support for the maintenance of intra-OECD free trade was formulated by the same high-level politicians that acquiesce to incremental protectionism in their daily work at home. The summits have pushed these expressions of general support to the highest plane of political review, already beginning one year after the First Pledge was made at ministerial level. At Rambouillet the summiteers proclaimed that 'in a period where pressures are developing for a return to protectionism, it is essential for the main trading nations to confirm their commitment to the principles of the OECD pledge and to avoid resorting to measures by which they could try to solve their problems at the expense of others.'

In an interdependent system with permanent negotiation on the permissible extent of protectionism, major changes of protectionism are next to impossible. It is incremental protectionism that one has to cope with. The summits' contribution of raising the trade pledge to an even higher plitical level of support does not seem helpful in this respect. Of course, negotiation under mutual threat is delicate enough to underpin it with enouncements of a general willingness to forgo protection. It provides a minimum of confidence, so that the diplomats can contain individual trade policy conflicts, as they emerge in the course of the year. But can one continue to assume forever that trade policy conflicts will be contained as watertight, small problem cases, not inflicting upon the system at large? In 1976, the Seven merely repeated what they had said in 1975. The language was perhaps even slightly weaker: 'wherever departures from the policy set forth in the recently renewed OECD trade pledge occur, elimination of those restrictions involved is essential and urgent.' No assignment to trade ministers is provided; no method is indicated.

At the same time, however, the summiteers explicitly endorsed an important effort in commercial diplomacy: the Tokyo Round. Both in 1975 and 1976 there was an explicit commitment to complete the Round before the end of 1977, although, to little avail. When in 1977 it became clear that the many specifics of tariff reduction and new GATT Codes would swamp the generalities of the summiteers' endorsement, prudency crept in: 'We will give a new impetus to the Tokyo Round of Multilateral Trade Negotiations. Our objective is to make substantive progress in key areas in 1977.' No deadline was set, deadlines that had helped the Kennedy and Dillon Rounds to finally get over the stumbling blocks. In addition, the serious problem arose that the Seven-Plus could not claim jurisdiction over one of the central, and eventually unsolved, issues — whether safeguard clauses in cases of market disruption (like art. 19, GATT) could be applied discriminatorily. The economic openness of the Western economy to the NICs and new textile exporters had increased so much that the Western summit could not 'internalise' the problem. The cryptic phrase in London was: in matters of trade, 'structural changes in the world economy must be taken into consideration', which can be interpreted as a call to open up markets for the NICs, but equally well (and closer to political reality) a call to rewrite art. 19 in a discriminatory fashion.[12] On the generalities the London summit employed fierce language: 'We will provide strong political leadership to expand opportunities for trade to strengthen the open international trading system . . . . We reject protectionism.' Essentially the same language appeared in the Bonn communiqué of 1978, that is, vague on safeguards and other specific problems of trade policy and firm on generalities, the latter including a call for 'positive adjustment' policies and the facilitation of structural change. However, the six and the EC were successful in pressing Japan to announce 'various efforts to facilitate imports' and 'moderation in exports', adding the exact 'aim of keeping the total volume of Japan's exports for . . . 1978 at or below the level of . . . 1977.' An important example of an outcome of negotiation under threat, without the (GATT) rules or hegemony being of any influence. But Japanese diplomacy masterly manoeuvred a possible check-and-sanction follow-up to a secondary plane at the Tokyo summit of 1979, helped by alarming price jumps of oil: Japan was not even mentioned in the brief section on trade.[13]

On the Tokyo Round, Bonn had shifted the deadline to 15 December, 1978, but it was only partially finished by the time of the Tokyo summit (and safeguards have remained unresolved in a legal sense). The notion that the summits can accelerate a GATT Round and bridge cleavages by political compromise at the highest level, ignoring technical details and conflicts among specialists, does not seem tenable.

The Venice summit was very disappointing on protectionism. It did not get beyond a brief synopsis of all previous, general statements on the strengthening of an open system and the commitment to an 'early and effective' implementation of the results of the Tokyo Round. Japan escaped a 'good brush' because Prime Minister Ohira died shortly before the summit. In Ottawa (1981) the political leaders clearly sought and found international backing to resist rising domestic pressures for protection, whether 'overt or hidden trade restrictions or in the form of subsidies to prop up declining industries'. They endorsed the initiative, taken in the GATT by a much larger group of 18 countries, to convene a GATT meeting at ministerial level in November 1982, but did not specify any particular goal. The Reagan administration's concern about incremental protectionism popped up in a curious paragraph: 'We will keep under close review the role played by our countries in the smooth functioning of the multilateral trading system with a view to ensuring maximum openness of our markets in a spirit of reciprocity.' This was a prelude to the US debate on 'reciprocity' in late 1981 and early 1982, an extremely dangerous undercurrent that would throw the management of Western trading back to the pre-GATT period.[14] After the firm denial by Brock and Baldridge in March 1982 that a unilateral evaluation of 'reciprocity' should be the basis for the continuation of most-favoured nation treatment by the US, the phrase was dropped in the Versailles declaration.[15] A Japan debate in Ottawa was prevented by a conciliatory trip of Prime Minister Suzuki, and later MITI Minister Tanaka, to all six capitals of summit partners as well as to the Benelux. One concrete 'result' was a voluntary car export restraint of the Japanese to the USA, Benelux, UK and Germany. The Versailles summit too was uninteresting in this respect, dominated as it was by the economically relatively unimportant issue of East–West trade, and its proper instrumental value for security and high politics.

After the Versailles summit, a few conspicuous examples of further erosion of the world trading system caused increasing alarm. To mention just two: in the early autumn of 1982 the EC had to agree to a 'voluntary export restraint' of steel to the US in order to ensure that its market share would remain close to 5.6 percent of the US market; in February 1983 Japan had to agree to a comprehensive list of export restraints (or warnings to that effect) with respect to the EC market, with a detailed, three-year arrangement for videorecorders as the hard core of the package. Furthermore, the GATT conference — endorsed in the Versailles communiqué for the purpose of 'concrete progress' — that took place in November 1982 brought little else than controversy. In the course of the inter-summit period, the agricultural trade dispute between the US and the EC also became more acrimonious as the US started to counter the EC's subsidised exports by retaliatory export subsidies on its own surpluses. No wonder that ex-Chancellor Helmut Schmidt called for 'at the very least . . . binding commitments (of the Seven) not to introduce any further obstacles to trade with each other or with third countries in the next two years.'[16]

Yet Williamsburg (1983) hardly differed from previous declarations. Although the Seven-Plus emphasised the expansion of trade with developing countries, their actual attitude during UNCTAD VI in Belgrade, only a little later, was uncompromising. There are references in the communiqué to the liberalisation of trade in services and high-technology products but without a sense of commitment. And what the agreement 'to continue consultations on proposals for a new negotiating round in the GATT' amounts to is unclear but certainly not very promising.

Altogether, the Seven-Plus have relied on a sort of declamatory politics in matters of trade and protectionism, the effectiveness of which may only be appreciated in terms of vague notions of mutual confidence. At no summit have the leaders taken truly political decisions that materially aided the functioning of the GATT, the implementation of the new Codes or the containment of incremental protectionism. Behind the scenes, or on the fringes, certain bilateral trade conflicts were resolved or reduced to manageable proportions (especially vis-à-vis Japan). It seems to be a policy of the Japanese to avoid being solemnly proclaimed the culprit of the difficulties in Western foreign trade. Although this provides summitry with some leverage, it is subsidiary to the bilateral trade negotiations under threat.

Macroeconomic Coordination

Towards International Macroeconomic Conflict

In the post-war heydays of demand management, international economic cooperation was implicitly based on a distinction between expenditure-switching and expenditure-level policies. In a world of pegged (but adjustable) exchange rates and little or no financial capital movements, putting a brake on domestic expenditure (having caused an external deficit) had, of course, a negative effect on trading partners. The latters' exporters would suffer a setback but only because the importing country had temporarily lived beyond its means. For the maintenance of the exchange rate, adjustment of export demand (along with other components of the level of overall expenditure) was considered inevitable: after all, by far the largest burden of adjustment would fall on the overspending country itself.[17]

Expenditure-switching, on the other hand, would alter the composition of a given level of expenditure by changing the relative price of products of foreign origin to those of domestic origin. Expenditure on foreign goods could be partly switched to domestically produced goods by devaluation or by (raising) protection. It was thought indispensable for the construction of a stable world economy that countries would tie their hands in employing devaluation only as a means of *last* resort – and with IMF agreement, based on rules of thumb, to prevent aggressive depreciation – and in committing themselves *never to raise* or reinstall protection, once removed.[18]

Thus, 'beggar-thy-neighbour' policies were outlawed, so that, for a given level of Western expenditure, no country could employ the means to artificially direct a larger part of a given level of spending towards its own production. In this simple world economy, with employment as the only serious policy objective, no further cooperation was required: macroeconomic coordination through the mutual influence on the level of expenditure was superfluous as expansive domestic policies spilled over to trade partners through the foreign trade multiplier, in turn yielding beneficial repercussions back home.

The character of today's world economy is very different and it warrants a renewed look at the need for macroeconomic coordination. Important differences with the period 1949–1969 include exchange rate flexibility, short-term capital mobility, inflation and the demonetarisation of gold.

When the US in 1968 effectively separated the gold/dollar price for central banks from that in private gold markets, the gold-exchange standard ceased to exist and a dollar standard came into being. But there were no rules for a dollar standard, not even self-imposed rules. A basic rule of such a standard could be price stability in the country issuing the dollar, as this would impose medium- to long-term price stability on other countries wishing to acquire dollars. Macroeconomic coordination would then become 'automatic' according to the following assignments: the US would abstain from a balance-of-payments policy but would assign monetary policy to domestic price stability; other countries would conduct a balance-of-payments policy in such a way that their preference to accumulate dollars over time would be commensurate to the growth of international exchange.

There are severe dangers in this approach. One is that, having cut the link with gold, there is no disciplinary force monitoring and correcting the issuer of dollars. The combination of a particular domestic political economy (Johnson's Great Society) and a perceived necessity to contain the spread of communism, seen as a threat to Western security (Vietnam), led the US to incur accelerated inflation and very large balance-of-payments deficits, in turn rendering two devaluations and later flexibility of the dollar inevitable. A second danger is a scramble for dollars by attempting to run balance-of-payments surpluses. Indeed, *assuming* stable prices in the US, other countries would have to deflate or the dollars would have to appreciate along a crawling peg before external dollar cumulation would be possible on a large scale. SDRs were created to deal with this problem precisely when the US laid the basis for a huge dollar overhang around 1970/71, that still has not been removed.

One way of looking at Reaganomics is that it reflects the firm intention to restore stability to the issuer of dollars. However, this in itself would not remove the dollar overhang; neither is there any guarantee that price stability will stay given the rather capricious conduct of American domestic politics.

The drastic difference with the pre-1969 period, however, is the combination of exchange rate flexibility, inflation and financial capital mobility. In such an international economy, it is no longer true that domestic stabilisation policies will be internationally supportive (when expansionary), or that they will marginally adjust export demand (when contractionary). In what now amounts to a massive theoretical literature virtually any possibility can be found, dependent on specific assumptions.[19] Nonetheless, a few rules of thumb have emerged that could be employed for Western macroeconomic coordination.

Deriving Rules of Thumb

When discussing the international effects of domestic stabilisation, it is useful to remember that, until around 1970, unemployment rather than inflation was the highest ranking priority. In the course of the 1970s, countries became concerned more and more with the possible importation of inflation. Initially, this concern arose from rampant inflation in the US, transmitted via less and less firmly pegged exchange rates until early 1973. A second impulse was the simultaneity of business cycle peaks in 1972/73 throughout the Western economy (a rare phenomenon) concurrent with an exceptional boom in commodity prices. The oil shock and accommodative financing pushed average OECD inflation into the two-digit range. Henceforth, 'disturbances' from abroad could be inimical to domestic expenditure (i.e. employment) but equally well to domestic price stability (with both monetary causes and 'real' ones like the terms of trade deterioration due to oil price hikes).

Now, in a *non*-inflationary economy with high financial capital mobility over frontiers and a flexible exchange rate, a fall (or rise) in foreign expenditure is transmitted to the domestic economy. The reasoning is as follows: the fall in foreign expenditure (say, because of contractionary fiscal policy) causes an incipient trade surplus for the foreign 'economy' and a deficit for the 'home' country, without the latter having pursued any concurrent policy; if international capital mobility is high, the exchange rate will hardly adjust because bonds will flow out from the home country (bought by foreigners) as foreigners will substitute foreign assets, that are expected to carry a declining interest rate, by 'home' assets; high capital mobility assures that the interest rate will, in fact, not fall, but 'home' exports will, and hence 'home' employment.

One might object that this outcome is similar in kind to that under pegged exchange rates without capital mobility – which is correct. But there is a cardinal political difference: under the old system the presumption was that a policy-induced fall in foreign expenditure would only be prompted by currency stability considerations, agreed to by all, whereas, under flexible exchange rates, national stabilisation policy has no such system-wide rationale! It was thought, for some time, that flexible rates would make macroeconomic coordination superfluous as they would 'insulate' economies from one another. The point above consists precisely in showing that this is incorrect.

But there is more than this. Suppose the contractionary policy is brought about through restrictive monetary policy 'abroad'. This causes an incipient rise in the foreign interest rate, inducing immediate flows of 'home' financial capital to the 'foreign' economy. This will push up the exchange rate and cause a trade deficit (in contrast to a surplus in the case without capital mobility) and a 'home' trade surplus, hence a *beneficial* effect on 'home' employment: the exchange rate effects, due to capital mobility, swamp the spending effect on the trade balance, i.e. on employment.

Matters become a good deal more complicated if we explicitly account for inflation, inflation differentials and inflation expectations at different moments in time. When inflation rates differ among countries as they did among Western countries throughout the 1970s and early 1980s, the rates of return on financial assets will differ for two reasons (even if everything else would remain constant, and exert no influence). One is the wedge between nominal and real rates of return, expressed in the currency in which the asset is denominated; the other is the exchange rate risk, when converting the yield into another currency, preferred by the portfolio holder. Domestic macroeconomic policies influence both factors, while macroeconomic policies of, say, the other summit countries may also have some impact on the risk of exchange rate changes. The effects of financial capital mobility in this world are determined by expectations of private portfolio holders and differential speeds of adjustment to (expected or current) exchange rates.

In general, capital markets are not impressed by vague political intentions and campaign speeches to 'beat' inflation but react independently. To understand capital mobility, therefore, we have to understand how expectations are formed in the minds of portfolio holders and to what extent portfolio holders consider financial assets from different countries as (im-)perfect substitutes. If there are differences in the fight against inflation, the effects will be anticipated and expectations about future (spot) exchange rates will lead to immediate asset substitution over frontiers. The speed of adjustment of portfolios (stocks of internationally diversified financial assets) is much higher than adjustment of the flows in the product markets. Moreover, the latter may react on the current exchange rate and the former on expected exchange rates. The result could well be that the portfolio holders' expectations are fulfilled nearly instantaneously because a *relatively* marginal volume substitution of currencies will tend to bring about a sufficiently large alteration of the spot exchange rate so as to adjust the share (in value) of the less attractive currency in the portfolio. At that moment, current account adjustment, reacting with a lag of, say, 6–12 months to a given exchange rate will now be upset. It is not excluded that so-called 'overshooting' takes place – that is, the medium-term equilibrium level of the exchange rate (after the current account has had time to adjust to the exchange rate change induced by a previous policy) may be higher/lower than the one imposed by financial capital inflow/outflow due to perceptions about a future political capacity or willingness to fight inflation. This explains in part the persistent problems of the French franc and the Italian lira as well as the sharp decline of the dollar in 1977/78.

As if this were not yet complicated enough, there is also the problem that the trade balance, besides adjusting more slowly, also begins adjusting by moving in the 'wrong' direction in the short run (say, half a year).[20] The reason is that export and import prices may not react simultaneously to, say, a depreciation: the former may be denominated in the depreciating currency while the latter increase immediately. Since volumes of trade will have been contracted some time before, a fall in the terms of trade (being a relative price) with a volume that adjusts only slowly will first cause a deterioration of the trade balance. This is called the J-curve effect. Now, if there is already little confidence in the currency among portfolio holders they may react to this deterioration and further adjust their stock of assets, hence causing further depreciation and imposing a larger real adjustment on the country at stake.

There is the possibility that, due to expectations, differential speeds of adjustment between the current and the capital account, possible overshooting and the J-curve, a country can be entangled in a vicious circle of inflation causing depreciation, which pushes up prices of imports and competing importables, in turn implying a higher price level, in turn leading to 'automatic' price compensations in the wage bill, in turn leading to further depreciation.

A first and essential objective in such a world economy is therefore to reduce inflation in every country. When indulging in the illusionary politics of money creation behind an 'insulating' exchange rate, what one will experience is financial capital mobility and real wage rate rigidity constraining the adjustment possibilities so much that the exchange rate will sharply react.[21]

If different countries, with changing political coalitions, conduct different policies at different times, wild gyrations of exchange rates will become a permanent feature of the 'system'. The adjustment costs and uncertainty in the tradeable goods sector (a large one in open economies) will be high and dis-investment will set in. The aim of reducing inflation is so overriding that the larger part of the responsibility should properly fall on every single country.

Nevertheless there is a need for coordination for the following reasons. The intended speed of reducing inflation and the timing of such domestic programmes, among Western countries, may be such that they can lead to short-term capital movements influencing exchange rates, hence inflicting difficulties on certain countries. Particularly worrisome is the scenario where certain countries switch to a commitment to reflate while others attempt to fight inflation seriously. The case of France in 1981/82 with a rapidly increasing inflation, in part accelerated by two depreciations, and a large deficit on the trade account (in part caused by the J-curve?), was in sharp contrast with many other countries reducing inflation. The recent reversal of policy has yielded some improvement, reducing the tendency of macroeconomic problems to spill over to trade policy and protectionism, even vis-à-vis EC member countries.

Perhaps more important is the need to coordinate the methods of reducing inflation. This problems is most pressing in the case of the US since we still live largely on a dollar standard. Until early 1983 the US chose to follow a strict 'money stock policy' while leaving interest rates for assets of various duration free. The reduction of the growth targets for the money stock over several years' time was independently set by the US authorities. The costs inflicted (especially) on the EC economy have been enormous. First, the level of interest rates was pulled up to a much higher minimum 'plateau'. For countries like those of the Benelux and Germany, with low inflation rates, business investment and construction (and the housing market) collapsed, since the real interest rate rose to some 6–8 percent in a time of weak overall demand and stagnant world trade. Also, (renewal of) government debt became much more expensive exactly at a time when unemployment payments skyrocketed. The painful aspect was that countries with a good inflation record – that is, where inflationary expectations had largely disappeared – had to pay a very high price for a policy established elsewhere, in an attempt to eradicate inflationary expectations in that other country.

Moreover, the EMS countries could not but marginally benefit from the falling real and nominal oil prices, as the dollar climbed up commensurate with the high interest rates in the US. Second, short-term interest rates gyrated enormously dependent on whether consumer credit was squeezed quantitatively or certain other policy intentions were announced. In turn, this caused large fluctuations of the dollar, only to be reversed a few months later when short-term interest rates moved up again.

It would seem therefore that there is a case for multilateral surveillance of, or at least a multilateral veto against, the monetary-cum-exchange rate policies of the major Western economies. Such surveillance would have to encompass the entire set of monetary policies, budgetary deficit policies and the method of financing them, exchange rate intervention and policies with respect to financial capital movements.

How Summitry Has Dealt with Macroeconomic Issues

In contrast to the issues of protectionism, macroeconomic policy cooperation has been dealt with by the summiteers in some detail, occasionally with fairly precise country policy assignments and more than once with attempts to exercise leadership in strengthening specific functions of international economic institutions (i.e. the IMF and the OECD). However, one should not jump to the conclusion that *therefore* macroeconomic cooperation through summits has been (more) effective. I shall discuss the following themes: exchange rate stability, the verbal crusade against inflation, and coordination of contractionary economic policies. In a separate, following section coordinated expansionary policies will be dealt with.

A recurrent theme in economic summitry, indeed a major reason why it all began at Rambouillet, is exchange rate stability. Then, the compromise formula was: 'With regard to monetary problems, we affirm our intention to work for greater stability. This involves efforts to restore greater stability in underlying economic and financial conditions in the world economy. At the same time, our monetary authorities will act to counter disorderly market conditions, or erratic fluctuations in exchange rates.' The summit cleared the way for the Jamaica rewrite of art. IV of the IMF agreement (January 1976; ratified in 1977), to which the declaration explicitly referred. As noted before, the Jamaica rewrite has created what could be characterised as a non-system since it permits any form of exchange rate pegging or floating while the 'firm surveillance' the IMF is supposed to exercise has never been seriously implemented. Quite the contrary, in 1977 and 1978 the dollar nosedived, with nominal exchange rate changes vis-à-vis the Deutsche Mark, the yen and the Swiss franc above 50 percent.[22] In Puerto Rico (1976) the Seven still observed that 'since November (1975), the relationship between the dollar and most of the main currencies has been remarkably stable.' In London, stability in exchange rates as such was not referred to, but in Bonn it received much attention (also due to the preceding Bremen agreement on the EMS, the aim of which was to create a 'zone of monetary stability'). The EMS perhaps more than the summits induced President Carter to announce his 1 November 1978 programme to achieve exchange rate stability (mostly) by fighting inflation, while working on coordinated currency market intervention through the issuing of Carter bonds and large swaps with the Bundesbank and the Swiss central bank. Carter received explicit credit in the Tokyo declaration which, with respect to exchange rate stability, was otherwise repetitive. After another two years of practising benign neglect (some say: aggressive neglect), the US seemed to be prepared to coordinate intervention in currency markets once again whenever 'it is agreed that such intervention is helpful', following the Jurgensen report (April 1983), assigned at Versailles and accepted in Williamsburg. A first coordinated attempt in early August 1983, to stop the dollar from rising, failed hopelessly.

In Versailles a separate declaration on stability in the international monetary system was attached. This declaration repeats certain phrases of earlier summits on the relationship between appropriate overall stabilisation policies and the stability of exchange rates, which is entirely unhelpful in its excessive, indeed concealing, generality. As before, the triple set of objectives of lower inflation, higher employment and growth ought to 'converge' and this would be instrumental to exchange rate stability. From the analysis in the previous section it is evident that such a presentation is misleadingly superficial. One might object and argue that this generality enabled Mitterrand to formally uphold his economic strategy, but that does not render the statement more useful.[23] A much more interesting element is the offer to build a 'quintal key currency system'. As stated before, this idea is still vague, and its demanding requirements are certainly not yet fulfilled.

Having said all this it is nonetheless possible to entertain some hope for the better. One can discern, from Ottawa via Versailles to Williamsburg a prudent but ongoing 'rapprochement' (especially) between the Europeans and the US. One encouraging indication is that the level and volatility of exchange rates has come to be seen more and more as a partial problem, requiring extensive consultations on a whole set of key macroeconomic variables and the policies they are influenced by (as, indeed, the conclusions on pages 128 to 132 suggest). An example will readily clarify this point: given the reiterated intention of all summiteers to curb inflation, a common concern about exchange volatility is inevitable as well, since (say) a rapid and substantial appreciation of the dollar will exert upward pressure on the inflation rates of open economies (in the EC, for instance) through the importables, including oil; but if, in turn, the appreciation is mainly due to the attraction of real interest rates — given a low level of inflation in the US — for financial capital, a common concern for the internal mix of monetary and fiscal policy is a logical consequence as well; the latter can lead to disputes about sterilised versus non-sterilised currency intervention (the latter implying at least some relaxation of monetary policy) and about the size and ways of financing the budget; meanwhile, given the desire to avoid higher inflation, exchange rates in Europe ought to be defended in the short run by jacking up interest rates, in turn affecting investment and employment.

Thus, the Annex to the Williamsburg communiqué recognises the simultaneity of monetary, fiscal, exchange rate, and productivity and employment policies. In this respect, it is less vague than the Versailles statement. In addition, there is a pledge to 'take fully into account the international implications of our own policy decisions'. These attitudes and intentions, and the informal gatherings of finance ministers that, supposedly, should monitor them, are certainly an improvement over the icy atmosphere in Ottawa.

It is perhaps useful to spend a few words on Ottawa, and the proclamations to fight inflation that preceded it. The verbal crusade against inflation is an aspect of macroeconomic consultation, appearing in all nine summit declarations, that is typically written for domestic consumption. Given the ideological cleavages between certain leaders, in certain summits, nothing more than a personal exchange of views and a better understanding of one another's positions could be expected. There is some analogy with incremental protectionism but the analogy should not be pushed too far since the fight against inflation is bound to reach political leaders earlier than the issue of incremental protection. Also, inflation is a macroeconomic issue and can be handled better from the top, if genuinely desired. The proper summit issue is, however, how to coordinate disinflationary policies.

The international repercussions of domestic disinflationary policies began to be considered only rather late in the history of economic summits. At no moment, however, were the permissible limits of national contractionary policies – in so far as they inflicted costs upon other countries – defined.

Whereas the London summit still enounces that 'our most urgent task is to create more jobs while continuing to reduce inflation', the Venice (1980) declaration – for the first time – sees the latter as an 'immediate top priority'. The recognition of the need to 'retain effective international coordination to carry out this policy of restraint' was not followed by any indication about the danger of tough, synchronised anti-inflation policies. A Delphian awareness of the problem can be read from Ottawa's 'highest priority . . . to bring down inflation *and* reduce unemployment' (my emphasis). Profound differences of opinion on the appropriate macroeconomic strategies – most sharply, between expansionist policy in France and tight monetary policy in the US, but also among the four EC countries and, in different ways, between them and the US – made it difficult in Ottawa to agree on a meaningful common text. The excessive reliance on money stock policies in the US, with very high interest rates 'sweating out' inflationary expectations, receives some attention: 'we arc fully aware that levels and movements of interest rates in one country can make stabilisation policies more difficult in other countries by influencing their exchange rates and their economies.' But no coordinated attempt at damage limitation follows; merely, 'that most of us need also to rely on containment of budgetary deficits.' There is no commitment about, or special mention of, the very worrisome US budget deficit forecasts, notwithstanding the explicit desire 'to minimise volatility of interest rates'. The best one can say of the Ottawa gathering is that the leaders assumed the right to persuade one another. Versailles utilised essentially the same language as Ottawa, on this topic, except that it explicitly calls for an 'essential reduction of real interest rates'. Meanwhile simultaneous disinflation had clearly led to a policy record worse than any single country had intended in terms of unemployment, with inflation lower but budget deficits at record levels everywhere.

The Coordination of Expansionary Policies

The coordination of economic expansion has played a role right from the start at Rambouillet, where a reference can be found to 'a responsibility on all countries, especially those with strong balance-of-payments positions and on those with current deficits, to pursue policies which will permit the expansion of world trade to their mutual advantage'. At Puerto Rico, expansion was much discussed but the coordination aspect was merely acknowledged, not tackled.[24]

The contrast with the London commitments of 'our governments to stated economic growth targets or to stabilisation policies' is striking. It is known that the Downing Street summit engaged in a genuine attempt to coordinate growth rates, and the policy assignments thought necessary for them; however, these commitments were never formally published. A conspicuous, and embarrassing, example was the 5 percent growth target for West Germany that turned out to be barely above 2.5 percent.[25] It would be mistaken to attribute this failure to the mismatch of the (secret) growth objectives set at the summit. Rather, it is not in the nature of economic growth objectives that they be 'coordinated' through the setting of country *targets* per year. A more appropriate method is to coordinate the *instrumental* policies so as to ensure both the proper direction and the compatibility of the means.

The instrumental approach was employed in Bonn with explicit country assignments for such policy mixes as would achieve an expected *increase* in the growth rate of GNP, fitting their respective roles in the 'convoy'. The 'locomotive' theory, as somewhat clumsily applied in London, and the comprehensive 'convoy' compromise agreed to in Bonn, are at the same time the most far-reaching instances of discrete macroeconomic coordination ever practised in the post-war Western world and the most controversial ones in terms of accomplishments or effectiveness. This warrants a brief digression, not least because the idea was much discussed in 1983 after having been out of vogue since the Bonn summit.[26]

First, macroeconomic coordination is politically and institutionally very difficult. Political obstacles lie foremost in the crucial importance of domestic electoral programmes that are the basis for (re-) election of politicians in today's mixed economies. Although always comprising a few sweeteners for narrow constituencies or pressure groups, it is particularly employment, price stability and growth policies that tend to dominate national elections. The politicians' attachment to announced macroeconomic policy intentions is often too great to be seen influenced and altered by foreign leaders.[27] Institutionally, it is not easy in different countries to realise the policies decided outside the domestic social networks, still apart from the different positions of independence the central banks in the various summit countries have.

Second, the history of macroeconomic coordination in the European Community is not encouraging. Beginning with the third medium-term programme, EC macroeconomic coordination has been attempted in a consultative framework to little avail. As from 1974, under the EC 'convergence' decision, more frequent consultation has taken place, but it has not gone beyond mere informative discussion. It seems that the Economic Policy Committee has gradually been able to come to more 'convergent' policy convictions within the framework of the EMS but it is exceptionally hard to evaluate these exercises from outside without published literature. The more influential Monetary Committee has successfully pushed for a convergence of inflation at lower rates. Gradually, a more convergent view on the desirability of disinflationary policies has developed, but coordination of expansionary policies has never been accomplished.

Third, the nature of macroeconomic coordination has been vigorously attacked in several ways. In Germany, and elsewhere, the *specific Bonn package* was criticised as 'inflationary' and as a violation of the domestic commitment to reduce the outstanding stock of public debt. This dispute is difficult to resolve as far as inflation is concerned because the 1979 performance of the Germany economy was heavily influenced by the second oil shock. The sensitivity in Germany, however, was apparent from extensive discussion about the proper limits of further expansionary policy.

The practical implementation of attempts, respectively in London and Bonn, to devise a coordinated economic expansion, suffers from three defects that can only be briefly touched upon in this essay.

One is that the locomotive and convoy strategies were not nearly as operational as one would have wished as a summiteer. The central idea is that 'strong' countries should undertake expansionary demand management, preferably via raising public deficits that should be 'accommodated' (financed) by the Central Banks so as to avoid a hike in interest rates. The simultaneous assignment to 'weak' countries is to further suppress inflation by incomes policy and tight money policies. The overall result would then be an international transmission of demand expansion without unduly risking a vicious circle of additional inflation, and new depreciation in the 'weak' countries. Hence, it might also be expected to have a stabilising effect on exchange rates, which, by itself, would restore confidence in the tradeables sectors.

The obvious problem is that of defining 'weak' and 'strong' countries. The OECD takes as criteria for a strong country: having low inflation rates, (high) surpluses on current account and appreciation tendencies for its currency. Of course, what is 'high' and 'low' may be subject to (political) discussion, and different electorates (and central bankers) may have different views. Furthermore, can one assume countries to be permanently 'weak' or 'strong'? Clearly not, as demonstrated by the US which could perhaps be denoted as 'strong' in 1976/77 (although that is debatable for all three criteria) but definitely not in 1978. The aim of the strategy ought not to be to turn 'strong' countries into 'weak' ones, of course; nor is there a firm base for the strategy when the assigned 'locomotive' can become a wagon asking to be pulled ahead by others, in the twelve months up to the next summit.

A second defect of the strategy is its textbook Keynesian approach of demand management. Some of its crucial elements require suppositions that might not have been valid in the 1970s. Especially the presence of inflationary expectations, fed by 'learning' in wage negotiations and in price-setting by business, destroys the old idea that under-utilised capacity prevents an increase in inflation from taking place in the short run. Money and exchange rate illusion will disappear — through indexation procedures, renegotiation clauses, or otherwise — so that budget deficit policy will quickly be read as a signal to anticipate higher inflation. If such inflationary expectations are deeply engrained in the behaviour of economic agents, the relation between inflation and unemployment (the so-called Phillips curve) switches from a negative one into none at all, or (some say) even into a positive one.

A recognition of this view might explain the strong emphasis on disinflation beginning with the Venice summit, with traces already in earlier communiqués. In 1978, however, sensitivity to possibly rising inflation — traditionally great in Germany — made the issue of expansionary policy controversial, whether at the OECD level[28] or in Germany.[29]

The third defect is the likelihood of a rather weak transmission mechanism for employment increases in other countries.[30] Of course, such estimates, based on simulation of transmission via trade in goods and services, can be criticised on various accounts, but even if they represented underestimates of, say, 50 percent, the transmission would still be small. This point of criticism is a serious one, since, even if one believes that inflationary expectations hardly play a role at a certain moment and hence expansionary fiscal policy could be effective, it does not but marginally serve the objective sought. Such a weak transmission gives ammunition to (German) policy-makers in holding that real wage restraint in the 'weak' countries will be much more effective in enhancing employment there than German (or Japanese) fiscal expansion. In a 'convoy' approach, however, this argument loses much of its force. However, it is still true that, under flexible exchange rates, the short-run impact could be relatively weak. With conspicuous plans for fiscal stimuli, much of the hoped-for augmentation of the convoy-leader's demand for foreign exports will be anticipated in the foreign exchange markets. This leads to a fall in the spot rate, giving rise to a J-curve effect in the short run. It implies that, during the implementation lag of the budgetary expansion, strong-country exports become *more* attractive (as their price in foreign currency tends to fall). The import volume effect, caused by internal expansion a little later, will now have a smaller *net* effect abroad. On the other hand, the recessionary circumstances of the late 1970s also warranted policy acts that would increase the confidence of business investors. But this argument, going beyond a simulation exercise, is credible only if investors also believe that inflationary expectations have been 'sweated out', so that fiscal policy might have real effects.

A final point of criticism is that of Vaubel, who holds that international competition in macroeconomic policies is an empirical 'method of discovery' (i.e. Hayek's view on competition as a process), superior to compromising the best policy performance to second-best coordination.[31]

This digression hopefully explains why the taste for new attempts to coordinate expansionary policies had been spoilt for several years. Nonetheless, advocacy of macroeconomic coordination has persisted,[32] particularly in circles where the 1979/80 inflation was explained as cost-push and temporary. After two years of exceptionally tight monetary policies, the issue has returned but in a different shape. Inflationary expectations have indeed been largely, though not completely, 'sweated out' but this time budget deficits have skyrocketed and the only possibility is monetary expansion or a more accommodative financing of the deficit. An important proposal to this effect was made by 26 leading economists.[33] As noted before, since Ottawa the summiteers have moved closer to this position although the key words 'expansion' and 'coordination' still appear to represent heresy for some participants.[34]

Energy

Economic summitry began only after the West had started to realise that there was much more to the energy problem than the Club of Rome's scenario for a very distant future or the military imperatives of supply lines in case of warfare. In Japan – and to a lesser extent, in France – this had always been realised: much of its industrial produce was less intensive in terms of energy, compared to competing products from elsewhere, and the country's export strategy had always been explicitly linked to its extreme energy dependence. The EC had been aware of the danger of insufficient volume availability ever since the Suez crisis of 1956 and the foundation of Euratom, but was lulled into disinterest and neglect during the 1960s when crude oil carried a fixed price payable from rapidly rising incomes. A wasteful disregard, low population density and a harsh climate in large areas of the country, combined with a US dominance in the seven-firm oil oligopoly, effectively blocked any recognition of the 'energy problem' for the US public. As late as early 1979, the first oil crisis was still viewed by the large majority of Americans as a hoax;[35] even in September 1979, this figure had gone down only to 52 percent.[36]

The first oil crisis caused disarray and a primitive selfishness among the OECD countries. Japan swung to a pro-Arab position in the Middle East conflict and sought to obtain long-term barter contracts, exchanging oil supply security for substantial technological aid, turnkey factories and infrastructural construction in Arab countries (and Iran). The US sought to organise a (buyer) monopsony which, for political and economic reasons, was difficult to accept for the more oil-import dependent allies. The Europeans were divided: France refused to cooperate in the newly founded IEA although it eventually agreed to 'collaborate' with the IEA's emergency oil-sharing programme via an aligned EC mechanism; several EC countries scrambled for special supply contracts and off-setting export orders, mostly to little avail; the Netherlands, embargoed for some 2–3 months, was not solemnly supported at the 1973 Copenhagen European Council summit (it *was* effectively helped by the intra-firm sharing-out of oil by the Seven Sisters).

The initial role of the summits in energy, therefore, could not possibly be more than verbal and symbolic. In 1975, a few diplomatic sentences were inserted in the communiqué. The only interesting phrase is a polite reference to international cooperation between consumer and producer countries in the long-term interest of both, a sign of diplomatic accommodation between France and the US. The Puerto Rico and London summits showed no interest in the energy problem, apart from a single, obligatory phrase in the final statement, and the London announcement to couple the commitment to nuclear energy with a study on the minimisation of the risks of nuclear proliferation. This study on the internal aspects of nuclear fuel cycles was available only in Venice – three summits later! – and played a role neither in the core discussion about energy nor in the political debate between the US and Canada on the one side, and the EC, on the other, about the insufficient stringency of controls by importers of uraniumoxid. The verdict on the summiteers' reaction to the first oil crisis is straightforward: they played no leadership role, nor did they really show an awareness of the energy problem beyond the IEA's emergency oil-sharing plans.

This had already changed before the second oil crisis. It had taken the EC four years to align its initially very diverse, national responses to the first oil-price hike. Although the *real* oil price started to decline over 1974–1978, the Community (and Japan) observed with increasing uneasiness the disparity of energy imports over the Atlantic. Between 1973 and 1978, US oil imports increased by 28.5 percent although the OECD imports (excluding the oil-producing UK and Norway) actually fell by 2 percent. Moreover, Canada's oil exports to the US declined sharply and US domestic oil production – discouraged by price controls, which kept the US oil price below the world level – decreased as well. The upshot was that the US alone could be held responsible for a gradual strengthening of OPEC's position in the world oil market despite increasing European production and energy conservation. Since the internal US debate on energy policy was stalemated, the EC found a common ground at the European Council meeting of heads of state and government in Bremen (early July 1978) in combining own EC commitments on energy conservation and imports with a call on the US to initiate likewise an active energy policy with due regard to international interdependence in those matters. In the communiqué of the Bonn summit of the Seven-Plus, two weeks later, the connection is substantially recognised.[37] The US had to pay this political price in exchange for the German and Japanese promises to lead the Western 'convoy' by adopting expansionist macroeconomic policies, a lead that the US was in no position to join given the dramatic fall of the dollar and the large deficit in the balance of payments. For President Carter the EC pressure was probably a welcome support for realising a breakthrough of the domestic energy stalemate. Nonetheless, he exposed himself to a considerable risk of failure, in view of the clear assignments in the Bonn communiqué.

The US promised to take measures before January 1979 so as to save 2.5 million barrels per day on 1985 imports of oil. More precisely, it pledged to build an oil reserve stock of one billion barrels, to increase its coal production by two-thirds, to reduce the marginal energy/output coefficient to 0.8 (with oil consumption growing slower than other energy sources), to keep 1978 and 1979 oil-import levels below the 1977 oil-import level and, finally, to raise the domestic oil price to world levels by 1980. It is clear that these detailed commitments were not merely a matching of the Europeans' Bremen commitments to reduce their 60 percent dependence on imported energy to 50 percent and to realise a marginal energy/output coefficient of 0.8 (both by 1985). The US commitments were part of the comprehensive Bonn package that went beyond the demands of the macroeconomic convoy strategy in committing the US to a more responsible energy policy and the Japanese (besides their macroeconomic promises) to a doubling of their development aid in three years.

The importance of the Bonn summit for energy policy is substantial especially because these commitments were accepted when the world oil market was anything but tight, the OPEC surpluses had largely disappeared and the *real* oil price had started to fall. It would be inappropriate to assert that the summiteers were galvanised into action only by the second oil crisis, which unfolded in 1979. Furthermore, the degree of commitment in as loose a gathering as an economic summit is truly remarkable if one realises that it was accomplished without the pressure of crisis, doom or danger.

By the time of the Tokyo summit outside pressure had suddenly changed into an emerging second oil crisis. The Iranian revolution, late 1978, had led to a temporary interruption of the more than four million barrels per day Iran contributed to world oil exports. As of April 1979 Iranian exports were back at around three million barrels per day. Yet the effects of this relatively minor event were magnified by rash stockpiling by summit countries such as Japan and Germany (and probably others) and by chain reactions on the Rotterdam spot market. As the IEA calculated later, the 'shortfall between OPEC supply and demand during the first quarter of 1979 was approximately 4 percent, and virtually all of this was accounted for by stock-building.'[38] Hence, the second oil crisis was largely self-made through uncoordinated panic measures taken by Western governments and oil companies. The shortfall was so small that the IEA emergency oil-sharing mechanism was not triggered: in other words, an oil crisis appeared to be possible even within the 7 percent supply-shortfall range necessary for an IEA 'emergency'. The Tokyo summit was dramatised by a simultaneous OPEC meeting in Geneva where oil prices were raised from $14.50 to $18.00 a barrel (Arabian light crude), only to be further increased towards the end of 1979. The atmosphere had been further strained by a conspicuous *Newsweek* interview, given by Giscard d'Estaing (then president of the European Council), in which he accused the US of not having taken its last year's commitments seriously. The US, on its part, wanted the EC to establish oil consumption targets *per country*, despite the Community's failure to achieve this at the European Council summit in Strasbourg two weeks earlier.

The Tokyo package in which all summit countries assumed precise oil import commitments for 1979 and for 1985 was no longer an

EC–US affair (as in Bonn). Moreover, the four EC countries and the president of the EC Commission promised to try to convince their EC partners to commit themselves to country targets as well. This imposition of the Western summit on, in fact, the smaller EC countries was a painful process but led to a success towards the end of 1979.

The Venice summit was the last one truly concerned with energy.[39] By the time the summiteers reached the San Giorgio island across the Canal Grande, the oil-price had gone up to $28 per barrel. However, the underlying tensions of the summit had more to do with the disparate reactions to Afghanistan and to the US-hostages in Teheran than with divergent views on long-run energy policy. The long-run strategy chosen focused on the reduction of the marginal energy/output coefficient to 0.6 for 1990, and on the reduction of the share of oil in total energy consumption (1980: 53 percent) to 40 percent in 1990. There was also a vaguer reference to the absolute level of oil consumption in 1990 that ought to be 'considerably' less than the 1980 level.

One major reason for a more conciliatory view of summiteers towards one another surely had to do with the increasing success of conservation measures. Especially the US had piled up an impressive cumulation of energy saving measures such as mandatory fuel efficiency standards for cars (with increasing stringency through 1985), fuel switching in power plants, alternative energy programmes and the phasing out of controls on oil and gas prices.[40]

What summitry has never been able to accomplish is to devise a coordinated stockbuilding programme so as to deal with brief and relatively small supply interruptions, causing huge price increases and great uncertainty. Now that energy conservation, induced supply of oil from new sources and prolonged recessionary circumstances have engendered an unexpectedly large fall in world demand for oil, resulting in decreasing prices, the IEA emergency oil-sharing mechanism is not really what one needs (although it ought to be retained, of course). The gunpowder barrel the Middle East really is can always lead to sudden new interruptions that − small as they might be − should be managed by coordinated supply from previously built-up stocks. And equally important is that oil markets ought to know beforehand that such will be the policy and that stocks will suffice to implement it.

Suggestions and Conclusions

As soon as economic summitry gets beyond the informal exchange of views and the personal accounts of the domestic political constraints of foreign (economic) policy-making, it faces a difficult dilemma: the summit countries can either attempt to exercise leadership in stabilising the Western economy or they can engage in declaratory politics. Both strategies carry considerable costs. The former will entail important domestic political and diplomatic costs before hammering out a package agreeable to the Seven-Plus; subsequently, painful actions will have to be undertaken to 'impose' the agreed policy cooperation on the other Western partners. A case in point is the Tokyo summit with which the smaller EC countries found a previous European Council decision *not* to opt for country targets with respect to energy imports reversed in an exclusive Big-Seven gathering in which they were only symbolically represented (namely, by the president of the EC Commission). It is not surprising that this caused irritation.

Declaratory politics seem to come cheap but are widely perceived as futile in a period when leadership is regarded as being crucial to stabilise the Western, if not the world, economy. The costs of repetitive, pompous gatherings being perceived as ineffective debating clubs issuing statements full of generalities should not be underestimated. One may reasonably argue that the highest resort of international politics – summitry – ought to be sparingly used. If heads of state and government really wish to fall back solely on informal contacts, expectations should be scaled down by proclaiming just that. Yet, it is especially here that politicians cannot forgo the splendid opportunities for domestic political publicity in separate press conferences and the like (see also Becker, chapter five in this volume). Furthermore, 'sprovincializzare' may be so dominant a motive for new summiteers that any willingness to hammer out detailed package deals might be lacking. According to Hellmann[41] US sherpa Myer Rashish had signalled long before the Ottawa summit that Reagan would engage neither in quantitative or otherwise binding target setting nor in concrete policy recommendations; the president wanted to go no further than a 'getting to know each other'.

Nonetheless, there are considerable potential advantages in a more assertive role of the economic summiteers in the three large domains discussed above.

In international trade, summits can be exploited much more as an informal institution reaching diplomatic and political compromise solutions or preparing efforts of international rule-making. As pointed out earlier, in a setting of permanent negotiation on the permissible extent of protection, enforcement by judicial review (so-called 'dispute settlement procedures') will be overtaken by political review. As domestic pressures accumulate, inevitably some of the issues will rise to the highest level of political decision-making and it is there that they should be solved.

It is a second-best solution to opt for specific problem-solving in protectionism at summits. But it seems superior to the available alternatives of talking generalities without actually fighting entropy by common leadership, or without ordering trade ministers and trade diplomats to agree to firm, multilateral dispute settlement procedures and respect the outcome. It is precisely because the domestic political origin of the pressures makes it attractive to avoid the automaticity of the international rule of law that trade policy conflicts can be solved only by high-level political review: firmness in resolving the remaining problems at the summit level will provide the badly needed confidence for international trading firms.

If major policy disputes could be solved at summits, it would also become more difficult for smaller countries to engage in free riding. It is true that the more operational and formal economic summits become, the more they will be perceived as directorates, attempting to 'impose' a given bundle of compromises on the smaller countries. Such impositions will be easier, however, the more the Seven-Plus show that they are prepared to commit themselves to clear and long-term solutions that have a 'public good' character for other participants of the trading system.

This is particularly so because the three members of the 'triopoly' (the EC, the USA and Japan) all have great obstacles built into their decision-making with respect to trade policy. In Japan, there are long-term problems of distribution and marketing as well as important cultural and oligopolistic business inhibitions that militate against the notion of 'free market access' without tariffs and other border interventions. Also, a complex, perfectly discriminatory public procurement and R&D policy, set up in consultation with business circles, carves out entire sectors from an open contact with the world economy. In the USA, there are constitutional problems regarding the prerogative of trade policy decisions. Over the last decades an incredibly complex institutional machinery has grown up – with intermittent changes like the Council of International Economic Policy, that lived for five years only; with trade representatives having different authority; with President Reagan attempting to alter the set-up once again in 1983. In the EC, perceptions on protectionism differ among countries and the Committee 113 (preparing trade policy decisions) only too often swings into the protectionist direction in order to pre-empt or minimise the (blackmail of the) damage to the internal market of the EC. Furthermore, a very serious weakness is that the EC itself has no federal customs, neither a common customs code, nor a hierarchical position in directing the implementation of customs procedures. Since modern protection is highly discretionary, the relatively effective, but slow judicial review in the EC is inappropriate to cope with the increasingly numerous tiny infringements of the 'free circulation of goods' within the Community. What is a headache for the Community is of course beyond the potential scope of summitry.

Yet, it is manifest political leadership that can transcend the institutional obstacles and interest-group lobbying. The summits ought to get beyond the generalities on trade and give clear assignments (and not just deadlines, without well-defined goals) to trade ministers and diplomats. Failing this, progress at lower-level commercial diplomacy will be most unlikely, and trade diplomats will have to act as a firebrigade, extinguishing one conflict after the other. No system can be sustained in this fashion.

There is also a role to play in macroeconomic coordination. Approaching the mid-1980s the role of economic summitry should be to increase economic security within the Western economy by firmly preventing a spiralling plunge into a deep depression. In five out of seven summit countries inflation has come down to roughly 3−5 percent; two are struggling to suppress inflation from their present levels of 9 and 14 percent, respectively. Meanwhile, world trade stubbornly refuses to grow. With many NICs having to restrain their exports, and the few Southern 'locomotives' (Mexico, Brazil) having to squeeze imports to pay their debts, the growth of world trade will have to come from the industrialised West. After nearly two years of strangling interest rates, business investment has given way to disinvestment or is limited to necessary replacement. Consumer demand is suppressed by falling wages and falling social security payments. Attempts to decrease budget deficits lead to further contractions of demand. Protectionism is on the rise virtually everywhere and the first recognisable 'competitive depreciation' (Sweden's devaluation of 16 percent in September 1982) ought to alarm the summiteers into exercising positive leadership, soon. This is possible now that US interest rates have fallen and the extraterritorial application of US sanctions against the USSR has been lifted.

The US could attempt to organise a well-considered monetary expansion in concert with other summit countries. In his February 1983 statement to the US Senate, Federal Reserve Board Chairman Paul Volcker clearly signalled that a stringent attachment to money stock policies (especially M1, the so-called base money stock) is no longer possible, due to financial innovation (caused by deregulation) and the lessening of inflationary expectations, and no longer necessary, because of the very large under-utilisation of capacity. The weak recovery, under way in mid-1983, ought not to be strangled.

The EC ought to respond positively. It should also urge the UK to join the EMS, hence creating a firmer link between the more stable SDR, the ECU and policy consultations within the Community, while persuading the French to depreciate slowly in order to undermine their protectionist zeal. The Japanese contribution could consist in further integrating their money and capital markets in the world monetary system, and relaxing the obligation of domestic, institutional portfolio holders to buy *Japanese* government bonds far below world interest rates. This would lead to higher interest rates and a higher yen, hence to less pressure on Atlantic trade accounts. With the much lower interest rates of 1983 this is possible without unduly burdening Japanese firms (that tend to have very high debt ratios) with interest payments. Such a summit deal would be a logical and fruitful follow-up to the agreement to boost the IMF resources, made halfway between the Versailles and Williamsburg summits.

In the energy domain, finally, a period of falling or at best stagnant prices has arrived. It is not likely to last more than a few years. The importance of the downward pressure on oil prices lay especially in the cash flow of firms that needed a further boost after the mild restoration of profits (or the curtailment of losses) in 1982 in the more robust sectors of the Western economy. It also dispelled the near-paralysing uncertainty in energy-intensive sectors (such as chemicals, heavy transport, metals) about the future energy bill and, hence, about the viability of investments. Combined with a cautious strategy of concerted demand expansion, this could eventually lead to badly needed investment both for restructuring and growth. The summiteers could further increase the certainty of investors by devising a mandatory oil-stock management mechanism, triggered by a sudden shortfall of supply due to war. Such a mechanism requires the building of oil-stocks when markets are not tight (in other words, now), the commitment not to employ it as a buffer stock to 'regulate' the 'normal' price changes (this would require OPEC cooperation anyway, but is also besides the purpose) and the automatic but gradual release of supply from stocks in case of *sudden* interruptions of supply.

The record of the Seven-Plus is neither impressive nor is it entirely hopeless, especially in energy and, to a lesser extent, in macroeconomic cooperation. In matters of protectionism – an ideal field for top political leaders to cut through the nitty-gritty of specific products and the parochialism of sectoral desk officers in trade ministries – the summits have at best brought an awareness, a sense of remembering, that protectionism is a zero-sum game. The art of commercial diplomacy is not to announce protection and discuss with foreign governments whether they would opt for 'voluntary' restraint. On the contrary, that art consists of defining a meaningful offer to other trading nations in an understanding of their industrial capacity (and consumer and industrial absorption) in order to achieve appropriate adjustment at home, both as to restructuring and as to increasing (mutual) exports.

The most serious question of today's world economy, however, is still the threat of true depression. In Europe and important NICs (such as Brazil and Mexico) the recovery is hardly noticeable or plainly absent. There remains the danger of faltering business investment and consumer demand, given the measure of insecurity provided. In the macroeconomic sphere, increasing international certainty is a public good that can be realised effectively and more rapidly if the summiteers take the lead and commit themselves to bolder and more concrete initiatives on the demand side. In an era of more 'positive adjustment' and deregulation of the supply side there is every reason to create a climate in which the new environment for business can be exploited by entrepreneurs. Permanent shrinkage of every component of effective demand – whether consumption, public and private investment or exports – fails to provide the necessary business confidence in medium-term investment. Business investment requires a restoration of that confidence. This is a major reason why a cautious summit strategy could be a useful underpinning of economic revival.

Notes

Acknowledgements: The final version of this essay has benefited from discussion in the Working Group and with the participants of the Colloquium on Economic Summits, organised by the European Institute of Public Administration, as well as from comments by George de Menil and Victor Schoofs. The usual disclaimer applies, of course.

1. See the contribution of Robert Putnam, chapter 2 in this volume, for the significance and origins of the Library Group.
2. As is suggested by G. de Menil, 'Si le sommet de Versailles n'avait pas eu lieu', *Commentaire*, no. 20 (Winter 1982/83).
3. See J. Pelkmans, 'How effective is Western economic cooperation?', *Aussenwirtschaft*, vol. 35, no. 2 (June 1980).
4. The best known expounder of this view is Charles Kindleberger. For a good summary see Ch. Kindleberger, 'Dominance and leadership in the international economy', *International Studies Quarterly*, vol. 25, no. 2 (June 1981). See also, inter alia, M. von Neumann-Whitman, 'Leadership without hegemony: our role in the world economy', *Foreign Policy*, no. 20 (Fall 1975).
5. The US, Canada, Japan, Italy, the UK, the Federal Republic of Germany, France, plus the European Community as such (the latter, formally, in matters for which it is competent).
6. One might even argue that US predominance, combined with the unique position of the big five US oil companies, made an IEA superfluous at the time.
7. Certain participants, or their aides, feel that this judgement is incorrect. Ex-President Giscard d'Estaing expresses a belief in the effectiveness of the rejection of protectionism in the communiqué of the London (1977) summit (*The Economist*, 21 May 1983, p. 26). Anthon Solomon, secretary of the US Treasury in the Carter administration, holds an even stronger view; see G. de Menil and A. Solomon, *Economic Summitry* (Council on Foreign Relations, New York, 1983), p. 44.
8. Although the EC immediately interpreted the communiqué in a protectionist way.
9. SITC = Standard International Trade Classification.
10. This point is developed in J. Pelkmans, 'Economic cooperation among Western countries', in R. Gordon and J. Pelkmans, *Challenges to Interdependent Economies* (McGraw-Hill, New York, for the Council on Foreign Relations/The 1980's Project, 1979).
11. In 1967, when the Kennedy Round was concluded, the US still considered shipping and shipbuilding as unnegotiable (despite prohibitive protection) and refused to actually implement the removal of the American Selling Price just agreed. Another example is the US insistence in 1955 on exempting agriculture from GATT Rounds, later exploited by the EC in a most deleterious way.
12. In the appendix to the London summit declaration, the following diplomatic *trouvaille* appears: 'Such progress (in trade liberalisation) should not remove the right of individual countries under existing international agreements to avoid significant market disruption.' What agreements are meant here: art. 19 of the GATT or various 'orderly market agreements' or voluntary, but mutually agreed, export restraints?
13. It should be observed that the dramatic decline of the dollar during 1977/78 had an impact on the US–Japan trade deficit only between the Bonn and Tokyo sum-

mits, cutting it by roughly one-half. Japanese imports also increased due to the fiscal stimulus agreed in Bonn. However, a plunge of the yen made this adjustment very short-lived.

14. Note that the London summit (appendix) utilised the wording 'agreements on the basis of reciprocity among all "industrialised countries"', which is in accordance with GATT, art. 28, and diplomatic negotiation tradition. This is very different from the notion that the US should review its trade policy with an eye to 'reciprocal' application of rules and Codes.

15. For a discussion of the 'reciprocity bills' in the US Senate, see W. Cline, *Reciprocity: A New Approach to World Trade Policy*, Policy Analyses in International Economics, no. 2 (Institute for International Economics, Washington D.C., 1982). However, the danger, though weakened, has not disappeared, in view of Senator Danforth's bill (International Trade and Investment Act), early 1983. See J. Danforth, 'The need for reciprocity legislation', *Economic Impact*, no. 43 (1983/3).

16. *The Economist*, 26 February 1983, p. 24.

17. In the event of a 'fundamental disequilibrium' one could devalue after IMF agreement. Among Western countries the memory of the 1930s was so strong (and, occasionally, the 'pride' of having a 'hard' currency so predominant) that currency pegs were maintained too long.

18. The exceptions to this philosophy (like art. 12, GATT) were clearly tailored to an emergency and, moreover, were temporary.

19. See, inter alia, M. Mussa, 'Macroeconomic interdependence and the exchange-regime', in R. Dornbusch and J. Frenkel (eds.), *International Economic Policy* (Johns Hopkins University Press, Baltimore, 1979); M. Goldstein, 'Have flexible exchange rates handicapped macroeconomic policy?', *Special Papers in International Economics*, no. 14 (June 1980), Princeton (International Finance section); P.R. Allen and P. Kenen, *Asset Markets, Exchange Rates and Economic Integration: A Synthesis* (Cambridge University Press, Cambridge, 1980); R. Bryant, *Money and Monetary Policy in Interdependent Nations* (Brookings Institution, Washington D.C., 1980); and V. Argy, *The Postwar International Money Crisis: An Analysis* (Allen & Unwin, London, 1981).

20. The so-called J-curve.

21. Underlying this perhaps somewhat cryptic statement are two assumptions. One is that fiscal expansion, financed by money creation, cannot but marginally and temporarily 'buy' more employment, even in a closed economy, after so many years of high inflation. In an open economy, it is also unrealistic to assume exchange rate illusion (i.e. to assume that price rises due to depreciation will not or will insufficiently be anticipated). Second, it is bureaucratically difficult and economically unattractive to implement capital export controls, especially for EMS currencies (cf. Italy).

22. Between late Sept. 1977 and 31 Oct. 1978, the yen/dollar rate altered by 51.2%, the Swiss franc/dollar rate by 58.7% and the Deutsche mark/dollar rate by 34.2% (source: OECD, *Economic Outlook*, Dec. 1978, p. 59).

23. Close to hypocritical is the closing sentence where greater exchange rate stability and freer movement of goods and capital are said to mutually strengthen one another. The recent French wave of protection and the severe Italian capital export controls belie this statement.

24. 'The formulation of such expansionary, non-inflationary policies, in the context of growing interdependence, is not possible without taking into account the course of economic activity in other countries' is the clearest statement.

25. The German government surely did not live up to the commitment 'to adopt

further policies if needed to achieve their stated target rates' until the Bonn summit.

26. See for instance, Helmut Schmidt, *The Economist*, 26 February 1983, p. 24; and Henry Owen, in the *International Herald Tribune*, 7 January 1983.

27. This statement needs some qualification. As Putnam suggests in chapter 2 of this book, the domestic-foreign dichotomy is rarely the proper distinction. If a minority view on − in this case − macroeconomic policy is congruent to that of majority views in other summit countries and carries many votes, a government leader may still be compelled to go along with a summit-induced adaptation of policy.

28. See the sharply opposed views of the monetarist P. Korteweg, 'Overhauling the OECD strategy for stabilizing the international economy', Erasmus University (Rotterdam), Discussion paper 7801/M, presented to the Shadow European Economic Policy Committee (29−31 May 1978 in Brussels), holding that no lasting expansion and no lasting employment could be bought by 'locomotives' or 'convoys', and S. Borner, 'Who has the right policy perspective, the OECD or its monetarist critics?' in *Kyklos*, vol. 32, fasc. 1/2 (1979).

29. See, for example, H. Kaufmann, 'Germany's option to be a mini-locomotive: a reassessment of 1977', *Economia Internazionale*, vol. 31, no. 3−4 (Aug.−Nov. 1978) and, by the same author, 'From the "locomotive hypothesis" to "concerted action", the metamorphosis of an idea', *Economia Internazionale*, vol. 32, no. 2−3 (May−Aug. 1979).

30. See D. Gebert and J. Scheide, *Die Lokomotiven-Strategie als wirtschaftspolitisches Konzept* (Sonderpublikationen, Kiel, for the Institut für Weltwirtschaft, 1980), ch. 4, especially pp. 143 ff.

31. R. Vaubel, 'International coordination or competition of national stabilization policies? A welfare-economic approach', revised version of paper presented at the European University Institute's Colloquium on New Approaches to the Study of International Integration, Florence, 1980.

32. See, for instance, A. Shonfield, 'The world economy in 1980', *Foreign Affairs*, vol. 58, no. 3 (1980), and *The Use of Public Power* (Oxford University Press, London, 1983), pp. 47−55; and Bergsten and Klein, in *The Economist*, 23 April 1983.

33. Bergsten and Klein, *The Economist*, 23 April 1983.

34. In the Versailles and Williamsburg declarations, the following words − on macroeconomic policy − can be encountered: cooperation, convergence of policies, close collaboration, consultation process, convergence of economic performance (also, of economic conditions), corrective action. The word 'coordination' only appears with respect to exchange rate intervention.

35. R. Lieber, 'National economic security: the problem of energy', in F. Alting von Geusau and J. Pelkmans (eds.), *National Economic Security* (John F. Kennedy Institute, Tilburg, 1982), p. 213.

36. D. Brown, 'U.S. energy policy in global perspective', in Alting von Geusau and Pelkmans (eds.), *National Economic Security*, p. 71.

37. After stating that they 'are committed to reduce (their) dependence on imported oil' and noting that the EC had 'already agreed at Bremen' on certain specified targets, the section on the US begins as follows: 'Recognising its *particular responsibility* in the energy field, the US will reduce its dependence on imported oil.' (Author's emphasis.)

38. Lieber, 'National economic security: the problem of energy', in Alting von Geusau and Pelkmans (eds.), *National Economic Security*, p. 215.

39. Both the Versailles and the Williamsburg communiqués contain vague declarations of intent on energy conservation and even on improving contact between oil-

producing and oil-consuming countries. However, there is no sense of urgency, which is particularly worrisome for the EC now that the interest in energy policies is waning.

40. Brown, 'U.S. energy policy in global perspective', in Alting von Geusau and Pelkmans (eds.), *National Economic Security*.

41. R. Hellmann, *Weltwirtschaftsgipfel Wozu?* (Nomos, Baden-Baden, 1982), p. 77.

4 POLITICAL ISSUES AT THE SUMMITS: A NEW CONCERT OF POWERS?

William Wallace

> '. . . les princes qui gouvernent la planète . . .'
> André Fontaine, *Le Monde*, 8 September 1982.

There is nothing new about efforts by groups of major powers to organise the international system, in the interests of maintaining international order, as they define it. Where there is one hegemonic power, formal 'groupings' are hardly necessary. Consultations among governments or among heads of government serve to associate secondary powers with the position of their leader and on occasion to modify that position. Where two dominant powers manage to moderate their rivalry, summits serve to register the limits of their sphere of influence and to spell out the rules of superpower rivalry − as at Tilsit in 1807, or at the Soviet−US summits which edged the international system from cold war towards détente. Where power is spread among several countries, international crises or periods of instability give rise to conference diplomacy; sometimes dignified and formalised by such titles as 'The Holy Alliance' or the 'Concert of Powers'.

Some French commentators trace a direct line of descent from the 'Big Three' of Britain, France and the USA, the three Western powers of the wartime alliance, through to the Giscardian concept of political summitry à la Guadeloupe. Given the slower pace of international travel in the 1940s and the 1950s, the Group of Three operated more often at foreign minister and senior official level than among heads of government; in September 1950 the Dutch foreign minister (then Dirk Stikker) was reportedly 'incensed' about 'the Big Three technique of fixing the outcome of larger meetings', as demonstrated by a two-day meeting of the British and French foreign ministers with the US secretary of state in New York in advance of a NATO council meeting. The informal triumvirate died at Suez in 1956, but it had been weakening before then as the disparity between the United States and its two European partners became more apparent; General de Gaulle's attempt to revive it in 1958 was dismissed out of hand. The decline in American dominance over international economic relations since then has been marked by the emergence of economic summitry, to attempt to manage collectively what can no longer be organised by a single leading country.

One underlying question in considering how appropriate it is to extend economic summitry to political and security issues must be whether the shift in military capabilities and political influence – so far as that can be assessed – has been sufficient to support a similar pattern of collective management. Successive US governments have resisted the notion that their reduced economic weight within the international system carried with it a reduction in their political responsibilities or their security role, though calling on their European partners to shoulder a larger share of America's 'global burden', more commensurate with their economic capacities. But European governments have shown little enthusiasm for taking on additional responsibilities outside their own region, certainly not as part of a restricted group of powers; Japan has shown no enthusiasm whatsoever. Consultation, yes; joint action, forcible if necessary, as in earlier Concerts of Power, no. Is there a firm enough basis yet for political summitry, either in America's willingness to listen to its partners, or in its partners' willingness to assist the USA in what it conceives as its global role?

Why Revive Political Summits?

Experience so far of political summitry among the major Western industrialised countries has been so limited that this paper must necessarily focus more on issues of principle and future development than on the assessment of the record so far. Guadeloupe provides one model: a deliberately informal and unstructured meeting, not intended to lead to any ringing public pronouncements or major new commitments. Venice offers an alternative model: a larger group, treating (or registering) decisions on policy towards the Middle East, and discussing urgent and immediate problems for common action in East–West relations.

Guadeloupe offers one justification for political summitry: the utility of informal and off-the-record conversations, bilateral and multilateral, among responsible government leaders to enable each of them to add a sense of personal contact, understanding – perhaps even of mutual trust – to the formal and impersonal reports which they gain from their own administrations and from each others' embassies. The 'Gymnich' style of meeting of responsible politicians chatting round the fireside with officials rigorously excluded, has a powerful and widening appeal. It has spread among the Ten European Community governments to finance ministers, ministers of agriculture, employment and justice. On the initiative of the German Government, it has now been instituted among the foreign ministers of the NATO states.

In a sense, this type of activity serves the same function in the contemporary international system as royal weddings and funerals did in the nineteenth-century European system. Once heads of state and government are all together in one place, a great deal of useful informal business can be transacted, contacts made or developed, impressions changed or confirmed. The political conversations which took place around such state occasions as President Sadat's funeral or that of President de Gaulle were of the same order. It is, arguably, of particular importance in fostering informal conversations among top leaders on political issues, because questions of ideology, assumptions about the nature of international order or about the characteristics of other governments' behaviour, directly affect foreign policy decisions. Meetings such as this enable the major heads of government at least to understand each other's stereotypes a little better, perhaps even to modify them a little. The relative infrequency in the modern international system of 'occasions' which serve to bring them all together makes it useful to create the occasion instead. Their superiority over a succession of bilateral meetings rests as much in the convenience of being able to conduct a series of conversations at the same time and in the same place as in the multilateral discussions themselves. If there were regular heads of government meetings within the NATO framework, or if it were the custom for heads of government (like their foreign ministers) to gather in New York in the early weeks of the United Nations General Assembly, much of this informal exchange could take place more discreetly – though the atmosphere of the country house weekend (or, as at Guadeloupe, the Beach Hotel) is considered by proponents of such meetings to be the most conducive to relaxed conversations.

There are a number of evident disadvantages to this style of diplomacy. Its success depends partly upon continuity in office, allowing leaders to build up personal relations over time and over a series of such meetings. French presidents, with seven-year terms, seem assured of continuity. Japanese prime ministers, within a system which operates on a principle of rotation, lack any such assurance.

Canadian, Italian, even British prime ministers have less certainty of long periods in office. Democracy – particularly parliamentary democracy in multi-party systems – does not fit well with summitry of this sort. The stability of political elites, the *cursus honorum* of those who hoped to rise to prime ministerial and presidential positions, provided in the 1950s and 1960s a succession of heads of government with an accumulation of international experience from previous ministerial posts. The more disturbed political and economic conditions of the 1970s brought more frequently to high office men and women who lacked much international contact or experience.

Secondly, informality can lead to misunderstanding as well as to understanding. The Macmillan–de Gaulle conversations at Rambouillet in 1962 were a classic example of informality, with irritating and constricting officials excluded; and they gave rise to an equally classic misunderstanding between the two governments. There was an informal and private meeting between Mussolini and Hitler which both considered to have gone 'very well' but after which the Italian and German foreign ministries were reduced to asking each other what they thought had been discussed or decided. Officials constrain ministers and prime ministers; the larger each national team, the more formal the meeting becomes. But prime ministerial memories are not always perfect, nor their grasp of the issues which they choose to discuss always as firm as they believe. Besides, they may discover around the fireside that they positively dislike each other; an infusion of personal relations into intergovernmental relations which (as some recent examples indicate) does not help Western coordination.

Venice offers an alternative set of justifications for political summitry; the impossibility of separating political issues from economic ones in concerting approaches to a turbulent international system, and the need therefore to deal with problems in the round. Export credits, energy supplies, technology transfer, even agricultural trade, are all political issues when seen in East–West terms at a time of deteriorating relations with the Soviet Union. They have increasingly become politically charged in relations with the Middle East countries. It makes as little sense to preserve an artificial distinction between the two at the level of Western summitry as it does within Western Europe – though within Western Europe they are still brought together fully only at the 'summit' level of the European Council, with the division between political cooperation and the Community to some extent paralleling the division between NATO political consultations and the OECD.

The disadvantages accompanying this are largely matters of time and intellectual overload. It was, arguably, possible in the nineteenth century for the leaders of Europe to meet and dispose of the problems of the globe. But the world is now a great deal more complicated than before the First World War, and even the most intelligent and widely travelled national leader must face great difficulty in mastering his brief. The subject matter of economic summitry is complex enough without adding a further tangle of political issues; and there is a limit to how long heads of government can stay away from their capitals, or how often they can be brought together. The world is not a chessboard; but political summitry can encourage the sense that smaller powers are pieces to be moved around, not specific sets of actors whose interests and demands are not easily ignored.

The nineteenth-century partition of Africa could grandly ignore the wishes or reactions of the natives to European decisions. Twentieth-century summiteers, competing to sell arms, power stations and educational packages to regimes of the left, centre and right throughout the world, cannot afford to be quite so sweeping. Failure to understand the local dynamics of conflicts, in South-East Asia and Central America for example, has led Western policy-makers astray on a number of occasions since the Second World War.

Yet there exists no other forum for global political consultations which can meet the demand − if governments now recognise such a demand − to concert the Western response to interconnected crises outside the North Atlantic area. This is not an entirely novel idea: de Gaulle's 1958 proposals included the suggestion that the Alliance should be extended to cover the Middle East and Africa, with 'agreement among the principal participants' on the Western response. Britain's withdrawal from east of Suez at the end of the 1960s, and France's limitation of its extra-European security commitments to Africa, left the United States for the first time in the 1970s as the only Western power with the capability and the willingness to play a security role in the Middle East and Asia. In their turn, the Europeans lack a convenient forum − if they wish to have one − through which collectively to exert pressure on US policy towards Latin America. It is more difficult to set up new international organisations − or to alter the terms of reference, and perhaps the membership, of NATO − than to establish new meetings of this kind; the very success of European Political Cooperation in evolving an effective infrastructure and a real convergence of views out of an initial series of ministerial conferences shows what an informal approach can achieve.

There are, of course, also disadvantages in this approach. Concerted Western responses are easiest to achieve in the face of clear and evident threats; belief in, or rather over-estimation of, the 'global Soviet threat' provides a simpler basis for common action than a careful examination of the distinctive problems of Namibia, Yemen or Nicaragua. The public image of a concerted Western response presents also a ready target to frustrated nationalists within a turbulent world, all too ready to see imperialism as the source of their difficulties. Iranian leaders were quick to claim that the Guadeloupe summit was a pretext for Western 'plots' against their revolution.

In particular, there exists no other forum for associating Japan with the management of the international political system. The interconnection between economic and political instability, the use of economic assistance (to Turkey, Egypt and Pakistan, for instance) and of economic sanctions as instruments of foreign policy, and the importance of Japan's economic links with the Third World, all make it essential to draw Japan more actively into global *political* as well as economic management; the ambiguities and uncertainties of Japan's response make it more useful to proceed informally, by associating the Japanese prime minister with a series of relatively unstructured conferences.

A further, European, justification for seven-nation summitry is the desirability – or necessity – of bringing pressure to bear upon the United States government at the highest level to influence the way in which it exercises its global responsibilities. Bilateral conversations may help to 'educate' American leaders to European interests and approaches to international problems; but multilateral gatherings, with the three (or four) major European powers able to operate together, offers the prospect of bringing greater influence to bear. There are echoes of the old British attitudes to the 'special relationship' here, with the underlying assumption that the approaches of European leaders to international problems are more sophisticated than those of American leaders. Certainly the French concept of Guadeloupe-type summitry reflected a similar approach – adding the realistic assumption that the weight of German support was necessary to enable the President of France to talk to the President of the United States on an equal footing. With the three (or four) most important European states participating we have, within an informal framework, the Atlantic partnership (or the Atlantic 'director-ate') which governments on both sides of the Atlantic have been calling for for over twenty years. The question arises however of whether influence is best brought to bear so publicly. The major European governments concerted their determined efforts to get their point of view across to the new Reagan administration, in the winter of 1980 −81, through the less formal and less visible process of successive visits by the foreign ministers of Britain, Italy and Federal Germany to Washington, all bearing the same message. Informal conversations do not involve either side in being seen to be influenced by the other; do formal summits risk arousing domestic resistance to leaders who 'give way' to foreign pressure?

How Should Political Summitry Be Organised?

So far, seven-nation political summitry has been organised on only the most rudimentary basis. The addition of 'political representatives' to the preparatory meetings has provided the bare bones of an infrastructure; but Ottawa and Versailles have built very little on the foundations of Venice, and sceptical officials have referred to their political dimension as 'cocktail party discussion'. What level of future organisation is thought to be desirable depends primarily upon the main objective of this new form of political summitry. Informal consultations, on the Guadeloupe model, can only be obstructed by too much official preparation and note-taking. Global political management, on the other hand, would lead towards the emergence of an infrastructure potentially as complex and as time-consuming as that which now underpins European Political Cooperation − and one which, unavoidably, would displace EPC as the main framework for coordinating multilaterally the foreign policies of the larger European states.

How should this form of political summitry be linked to other channels of political consultation? Though there exists no formal organisation for intergovernmental consultation among Western countries on global political and security issues comparable to the OECD in the economic field, there are a number of formal and informal bodies which to some extent fill this need. On East–West relations, NATO links European governments to the US administration on a basis of continuing information exchange and consultation. On this and most other international issues, European Political

Cooperation brings the Ten together. A formal link between the EPC framework and the US administration was established under the Ottawa agreement of 1974, though it has operated only patchily since the end of the Nixon-Ford administration. There have been tentative suggestions from the Japanese Foreign Ministry since the beginning of 1980 that they would like some comparable arrangement — most explicit in the uninvited arrival of the Japanese foreign minister at an EPC ministerial meeting later that year. Other less formal groups also bring together the 'principal nations'. The Berlin Group, with the same members as those whose heads of government attended the Guadeloupe summit, discusses East—West relations in Central Europe; it also provides convenient, and discreet, opportunities for discussing other issues among a restricted group. The Namibia Contact Group brings these four and Canada to bear on a specific problem of international political cooperation.

There is no necessary trade-off between these other forms of consultations and seven-nation summitry; indeed, they are essentially complementary, with Western summitry adding an extra dimension — perhaps even an overall political direction — to such lower level contacts. The same foreign ministers, the same senior officials, circulate from meeting to meeting and group to group, providing a thread of continuity which arguably renders any more formal links unnecessary. The trade-off comes when factors of time, attention-span, patience and overload come in. The emergence of European Political Cooperation as a preferred forum for consultation on, for instance, the CSCE had the unavoidable consequence of downgrading the importance (and the frequency) of NATO consultations on such issues. There is a limit to the amount of redundancy in repeated consultations which busy politicians and officials will stand.

How formal a structure does such political consultation need to underpin it? Various observers — the 1981 Four-Institutes' report on *Western Security*, Professor Brzezinski in a conference at IFRI in Paris in 1981 — have called for 'some type of a permanent, though small, secretariat' as part of a more systematic pattern of preparation and implementation of Western political summitry. In the previous paragraphs it was noted that consultations among the principal Atlantic nations already exist on a wide range of issues, though they do not include Japan to any significant extent. A new structure should therefore be small, avoid duplicating existing consultations, and concerned above all with bringing Japan into global political consultation — if the other 'principal nations' are agreed that Japanese involvement is an essential part of political summitry.

The experiences of European Political Cooperation, and of the NATO secretariat, raise some large question marks as to the utility and desirability of permanent or 'international' secretariats. The weakness of NATO, for some critics, has been that its international secretariat is cut off from direct political responsibilities; the strength of EPC, for them, is that all those involved are directly in touch with member governments and directly responsible for national policy. There are some obvious limitations in transferring the EPC model to a global level – the most immediate of which is the far greater difficulty of arranging and maintaining regular meetings among responsible officials across the far greater distances which are involved in collaboration with the USA and Japan. There would most probably have to be some permanent US and Japanese 'missions' in Europe, if Europe were to be the location for consultations, perhaps consisting of senior officials of ambassadorial rank, regularly travelling back to their national capitals, and assisted by a small staff. From this to an international secretariat is a large jump – which, the experience of the last thirty years suggests, the governments involved should be extremely reluctant to make.

How frequent should political summits be – and should they be regular or *ad hoc*? The European Council meets three times a year to handle its agenda of political and economic issues; the foreign ministers of the Ten who prepare its work meet, in one forum or another, at least a dozen times a year, and their political directors even more frequently. Political summitry on an annual basis risks failing to fulfill even the aim of fostering informal contacts and understanding; the continuity of membership, once one moves beyond the Guadeloupe Four, would threaten to be extremely low. If political and economic summitry is to be continued, the length of the agenda dictates at least two meetings a year. If the major governments involved are aiming for a concert of powers, then these meetings must be on a regular and continuing basis, with an extensive infrastructure of information exchange and preparation of common positions which would – in effect – come to resemble the EPC framework at the Atlantic level (and thus, probably, partly displace that framework itself, at the European level). If they are aiming, more modestly, at informal consultation and occasional crisis management, then there are stronger arguments for flexibility: for an annual meeting, with the possibility of convening additional meetings at shorter notice should circumstances (and a number of the governments concerned) demand it.

How visible should political consultations be? That depends, fundamentally, on what the main purposes of political summitry are seen to be. Informal exchanges of view, as argued above, are much easier within a framework of confidentiality; though the experience of Guadeloupe demonstrated how difficult it is for elected national leaders to resist the demands of their press corps and the attractions of domestic publicity and achieve the degree of confidentiality and privacy which marks the Gymnich meetings. If summits, on the other hand, are intended in part to signal to other countries and other groups of countries a concerted Western position on major international issues, then visibility is an advantage – apart from its evident advantages in educating and informing domestic opinion about the international responsibilities which their own governments have to shoulder.

Other problems follow from the visible image of a coordinated group of powers working to promote their own interests within the international political system. The experience of EPC is, again, of relevance: a succession of demands by third countries and groups of countries for consultative arrangements, starting with Dr. Kissinger's demand for privileged access for the US administration in April 1973 and the request by Arab foreign ministers for a group-to-group dialogue (which they intended to be fundamentally political), presented at Copenhagen in November 1973. In later years the Canadians, the Norwegians, the Turks and the Japanese have all asked for some form of consultation; and the ASEAN countries have, like the Arab League, pursued a political dialogue through economic channels. Western summitry, if it developed far, would thus take the world further towards bloc-to-bloc diplomacy, and would impose additional burdens of consultation and negotiation on the governments of the Atlantic grouping, as they responded to demands for reassurance, concessions, or negotiations from other groups.

In practice, of course, a degree of visibility is unavoidable in meetings between heads of government; and a degree of confidentiality is easy to arrange once they meet. It is impossible for heads of government to meet each other in secret, as restricted groups of finance and foreign ministers from the same countries have managed to do over the past few years. Press attention is constant, calendars are avidly followed, and unexplained absences an incentive to investigate. Once they have arrived, however, it is easy to talk in private about subjects not on the public agenda. Shared concerns about domestic developments in friendly countries, political contingencies which it is thought better not to admit to before a threatened crisis erupts, can readily be discussed over dinner or round the table without being included in the public briefings or communiqués.

The Problem of Numbers

The awkward question of size and participants raises separate, but linked, questions of European participation and non-European participation. Both raise questions of the optimum size of the group and the necessary qualifications for entry. Here again one is faced with a difficult trade-off between the informality of small groups and the costs of excluding other significant international actors, between the utility of summits as confidential forums for private discussion and their value as visible symbols of Western solidarity. Some of those associated with the Guadeloupe summit have claimed that it would have been impossible to discuss so openly such intensely sensitive issues as the modernisation of NATO's intermediate nuclear weapons forces, or Western approaches to arms control negotiations with the Soviet Union, in as large a meeting as the Venice summit – let alone in the formal and crowded atmosphere of a NATO heads-of-government meeting. But the costs of appearing to settle issues vital to the whole of the NATO alliance in a restricted *directoire* were reflected in the shaky commitment of several small alliance governments to nuclear weapons modernisation, and the contribution which this image of decisions imposed from above in accordance with the attitudes of a few dominant powers made to popular pressures in these countries to opt out of their alliance 'responsibilities'.

Restricted membership meetings, with varying degrees of secrecy, have become a feature of European – as well as of Atlantic – cooperation in foreign and security policy in recent years. Within the last five years there has been a tendency for the governments (and in particular the foreign ministries) of France, Germany and Britain to prefer smaller groupings of European Political Cooperation as a framework for international consultation and crisis management. The reasons for this are evident: irritation at the 'moralism' of some smaller countries on policy towards South Africa, boredom at the slow pace of the *tour de table à dix*, a feeling that serious business is more easily conducted among serious powers. Further development of Western political summitry would increase that tendency. The danger for European Political Cooperation – and for European cooperation as a whole — is that such a divergence between the larger and the smaller member governments would only increase the 'irresponsibility' of the smaller states over foreign policy issues on which they were barely consulted, and reinforce the impression of the larger governments that 'Europe' is a matter of the larger states providing economic benefits for the smaller *without* the latter accepting political obligations in return.

The existence of the 'Berlin Group', which brings together Britain, France, Federal Germany and the United States to discuss the security of Berlin and the wider context of East–West relations, has provided a convenient and private framework for the three 'big' European states to talk with each other and to exchange views with the United States. Italy, naturally absent from a group which owes its formal existence to a preoccupation with the central front, has strongly objected to its exclusion when it has suspected that these consultations had spread to wider issues of Soviet foreign policy. If such a restricted group were to act as a focus for discussion and concerting of actions on Mediterranean problems, Africa or the Middle East, it would become far less natural to exclude Italy — with its active diplomacy in those regions, its willingness to commit troops (as in the Lebanon) where necessary, its strong commercial ties and its increasing importance as an arms supplier. Once in the Community as well as in NATO, a Spanish government might also press its claims for what would unavoidably be seen as 'a seat at the top table'.

If European collaboration on foreign policy is not to be undermined by such developments, it becomes vital to ensure that Western summitry and European Political Cooperation are carefully linked together. *Visible* consultations with the smaller, non-participating states, both through EPC ministerial meetings and through ministerial visits to individual capitals, are thus an essential mechanism for maintaining a shared sense of responsibility and European solidarity. This, in turn, carries its costs in the additional burden which an expansion of Western summitry would thus place on the leaders of the larger European states.

The question of extra-European participation is of a different order. It is, arguably, strongly in the European interest to involve Japan in political consultations with the United States, as a means of increasing the weight of allied influence on American policy — provided that the Europeans are prepared to invest some effort in the pursuit of a political dialogue with Japan, and the Japanese willing to respond. Beyond that, it seems to be in the Europeans' interest to limit the size of the group. If Canada, why not Australia? If Australia, why not . . . and so on. Once one has countries of the size of Australia and Canada participating in the summits, the case for excluding the Netherlands becomes weak, the case for excluding Spain is difficult to sustain. There is some utility in holding occasional summit meetings of all the NATO member governments, with the major non-NATO OECD members added; it would have a certain symbolic value for the smaller states, and would provide the opportunity for extensive informal exchanges. But it would be a very different form of exercise from those envisaged by the participants in Guadeloupe or Venice.

The Experience So Far

Heads of state and government sit on the top of a lively and active transnational debate within the foreign policy elites of Western Europe and North America on Soviet intentions, on the balance of military forces, on the appropriate Western responses. Occasional meetings of these leaders may usefully serve to focus this debate, to compare different approaches and to pull together the different strands. How effectively each summit can serve such a purpose will depend – as always, in political as well as in economic summitry – on the personal preferences and preconceptions of those involved, their willingness to think in the longer as well as the shorter terms, their openness to the nuances of each other's arguments. As in economic summitry, as well, effectiveness requires careful preparation: more careful preparation than the single preliminary discussion among officials, perhaps a month beforehand, which has apparently been the pattern so far for the political dimension of the summits of the Seven. European Political Cooperation, with its established – if underutilised – consultative links with the US administration, provides an available framework for such preparation. There is as yet no similar link with Japan – though hints have been repeatedly dropped from Tokyo in the past two years that such a link would be warmly welcomed. Rather than weaken the existing structure of European collaboration on foreign policy issues, the European participants in the Western summits should work to adapt the machinery they have to fulfill this additional role.

The experience of the Williamsburg summit of May 1983 reinforces these conclusions. Preparations for the political discussions which were anticipated were minimal. American officials had argued over whether to press the political dimension of East–West trade again, but in the light of the previous year's experience wiser counsel prevailed. There were hints in American pre-summit briefings that the US administration would like to discuss the Middle East situation, but that they anticipated resistance from their partners to too large a political dimension at a primarily economic summit. At the one preliminary meeting of Political Directors, in early May, the Canadians – with US support – proposed a declaration on nuclear missile deployment and arms control, one of the central concerns of the Guadeloupe four-power summit of four and a half years earlier. But this met with resistance from the French and Germans, and the participants arrived in Williamsburg without an agreed political theme or text.

Two days later the seven heads of government issued, alongside their economic communiqué, a 'Statement on Arms Control', which reasserted the 'Western' commitment to pursue lower levels of armaments in relations with the USSR, but meanwhile to prepare to deploy the intermediate-range missiles which NATO had agreed to position within Western Europe from the end of 1983. This declaration, hailed as the 'success' of the summit, served as a visible symbol of Western solidarity, both to the Soviet leadership and to the electorates of West European countries. It signalled to the Japanese the increasing association between Japan and its Western partners on security issues – welcome to some, highly unwelcome to others. But it was a last-minute declaration. The issue was raised by Mrs. Thatcher and President Reagan on the first evening of the conference. Overcoming the reluctance of President Mitterrand, the agreement in principle was passed on to the foreign ministers for drafting; but their initial draft did not meet with the approval of all the heads of government. The agreed text emerged seven hours later than intended, with a stronger emphasis on the commitment to arms reduction than its Anglo-Saxon initiators had envisaged, and – in deference to French and Japanese reservations – without any reference to the North Atlantic Alliance.

When heads of government meet together, they naturally talk about the issues uppermost in their minds. At Williamsburg the subject of Lebanon was raised both in bilateral and multilateral conversations, as an immediate problem with implications for regional and global security, in which American, French, Italian and British troops were already contributing to peacekeeping forces. The forthcoming deployment of intermediate-range missiles in Europe was a direct and central concern to five of the seven participants at Williamsburg, and an indirect concern to Japan in the event of negotiations on arms reductions in Europe leading to a displacement of Soviet missiles towards the Far East. The discussion, with all its differences of perspective, appeared to have brought home once again to the Americans the importance of pursuing negotiations on arms reductions in parallel with deployment, and to have underlined for the French and the Japanese the need to accept that 'the security of our countries is indivisible and must be approached on a global basis'. The utility of producing a published statement lay partly in the discipline of forcing the participants to define their agreed line, partly in the signal which it gave to the Soviet Union, and − at least as important − partly in the signal which it gave to public opinion in Western Europe, the United States and Japan.

Would it have been 'better' if such an outcome had been planned more fully in advance? The immediate circumstances of the Williamsburg summit were, after all, the occasion for the declaration: a Soviet statement on the East−West nuclear balance, issued the day before the summit began, to which this could be presented as a response; the particular circumstances of the British election campaign, in which nuclear weapons had become a significant issue. Long months of planning would have drawn in other issues, would have produced a longer and more intricate declaration, and might well have inhibited such a free and open discussion at Williamsburg. Discussions on the issue had been continuing, at different levels, within the NATO framework, as well as within bilateral conversations among the Europeans and between European governments, the United States, and Japan. At Williamsburg it was therefore easy to raise the issue, to identify the main points at stake, and to argue the case for a public statement − without the necessity, or the burden, of substantial preparatory meetings within a framework specially created for the purpose.

Yet the Williamsburg statement on arms control established another precedent for seven-nation summitry. It registered acceptance that such summits had political purposes, even if their main function remained economic. It repeated the precedent of the Venice summit in making a public statement on a major international political issue, though on the basis of informal discussions more reminiscent of Guadeloupe. The participants will have drawn different conclusions from this experience; but one hopes that they would agree not only to continuing an exchange of views on political issues, but also to regarding the exchange of views as more important than the necessary preparation and publication of statements on the maintenance and future of the international political order.

5 BETWEEN IMAGE AND SUBSTANCE: THE ROLE OF THE MEDIA

Kurt Becker

When the heads of state and government of the major Western industrial powers met for their first conference at Rambouillet in 1975, they were advocates of a non-spectacular summit. They did not tend to pompous publicity. Originally, they did not even want press conferences. They regarded the remoteness of a château as a suitable site to discuss confidentially and openheartedly, at the highest level, without cabinet members or advisers. Foreign ministers and finance ministers were in fact supposed to hold their talks separately.

The objective agreed upon was the exchange of views and assessments of the long-term consequences of the oil shock in an atmosphere of familiarity. Priority was also given to monetary problems. Valéry Giscard d'Estaing, host in Rambouillet and inventor of this configuration of a summit, had been inspired to take this initiative by the encouraging experience of the 'Library Group. He wanted to revive that style of conversation and to put it on a higher level and, perhaps, to sustain as president his personal responsibility in the field of world economic and monetary affairs. Chancellor Helmut Schmidt, a former member of the Library Group as well, endorsed Giscard's idea. Schmidt had in fact often contemplated the indisputable benefits to be gained from a dialogue among heads of state and government and the highly effective political interplay it could produce. In his view, the summiteers would as a result feel more secure on the general drift of the others' policies.

In their final session, the summiteers of Rambouillet began to waver in their original aversion to a press conference. They were impressed by the throngs of journalists waiting outside the conference building, and did not want to arouse the media's indignation. So they made up their minds to meet the media in separate national briefings. But they very soon realised the risks of separate approaches, different statements, diverging emphasis and varying conclusions, which could lead to counter-productive effects. Ultimately the summiteers were prudent enough to agree on an improvised joint press conference in the nearby Mairie of Rambouillet.

From then on the summiteers abandoned their discretion, as was confirmed the next year in Puerto Rico. The 1976 summit turned out, however, to be rather ineffectual as far as worldwide publicity was concerned. The United States was the only country in which the meeting was given a fair amount of coverage. The United States was facing presidential elections, and the American organisers produced a summit designed to satisfy primarily, if not solely, the needs of US television in terms of spectacle and timing. The lobby of the hotel in Puerto Rico resembled, in fact, a huge television studio.

The summit of the Seven completely changed its procedures and its image in 1977 in London. It is since then that we have the type of international conference we are now accustomed to. Two circumstances gave added impulse to public interest in the London summit.

Jimmy Carter had become president of the United States five months prior to the summit. It was his first trip to Europe and everybody was curious about his appearance, his style and his approach to world economics. Among the proposals he had brought with him was an urgent appeal to Germany and Japan to adopt a reflationary policy. He suggested that both economies should function like locomotives, leading the recovery of the Western economy which at the time was still plagued by deep recession. It was thought that Carter's strategy might lead to a spectacular confrontation between him and Schmidt. However, the statesmen avoided any collision and agreed the next year (1978) in Bonn on one of the most remarkable package deals ever to be hatched at a summit.

Secondly, there was the close sequence of two summits in London – the third economic summit conference of the Seven and the spring ministerial meeting of the North Atlantic Council attended by the heads of government of the NATO countries – which naturally escalated public interest and concern.

Since 1977 the summits have been attended by voluminous delegations. The traditional participation of two cabinet members alongside the heads of state and government was extended by affiliation of economic ministers and an increasing number of bureaucrats. By far more than a thousand journalists hurried to the summit. This explosion did not occur by accident. It was the result of both the governments' desire for publicity and the media's intention to treat the conference as one of the most outstanding events of the year.

On Ronald Reagan's trip to Europe in 1982, during which he attended the summits in Versailles (summit of the Seven) and in Bonn (summit of NATO heads of state and government) and paid visits to London and Rome, the president was escorted by eight hundred journalists, including photographers and television crews. In 1983 an estimated four thousand media observers attended the summit in Williamsburg. The summiteers have been making use of the media to a growing extent. Self-representation and self-assertion have become significant features of the conference. The governments take care of transport and accommodation for the journalists. They hire briefing rooms and television studios in advance. The host nation arranges for all the facilities required to secure efficient press coverage.

Neither press nor television nor radio broadcasting stations dare to neglect individual presence on the spot with their own staff members or special correspondents. Competition and rivalry among the media is tough. The professional reputation of journalists and media is at stake with regard to getting scoops and exclusive interviews. The same applies to comprehensive reports according to schedule.

The Gospel of Summitry: The Communiqué

One noteworthy by-product of the enormous publicity has been the fast-growing importance of the communiqué. It has become the key document of the summit in the eyes of both the governments and the media. Members of the participating governments and diplomats refer to, and commentators and analysts from the press comment on and publish, primarily the contents of the communiqué, comparing them to the results and substance of past summits, if they recall them, leaving aside or treating as secondary the debates in the plenary sessions, background briefings and press cuttings of interviews in the archives. One reason for this − a very regrettable one − might be that, apart from some summiteers, sherpas, high-ranking advisers and top journalists, only a few participants and observers of the summit have acquired comprehensive knowledge of the process. Or is it just that experience shows that, after all, results count only if they are mentioned in the communiqué? In any case, it is clear that the summiteers' intentions and propositions, considerations and resistances tend to lose all relevance if they are not mirrored in the communiqué.

Because the communiqué has become the gospel of summitry, the summiteers concentrate on its language. The communiqué thus inevitably ends up resembling a carefully prepared catalogue of all the problems that have been discussed or at least mentioned in the debate as deserving public attention. The communiqué summarises views, assessments and objectives, disregarding the different doctrines of the summiteers. It is patchwork. Decisions on a package deal, like the one worked out in Bonn (1978), remain an exception. The summiteers are very cautious, they prefer to make non-committal statements of intention rather than forge clearly defined decisions.

The media have accepted the outstanding importance of the communiqué. As the final stage of the conference approaches, they switch over and from then on collect news and background exclusively from the perspective of the wording of the communiqué. Many serious newspapers publish the full text of the communiqué while others print at least the most illuminating passages.

The Spokesmen

A spokesman's importance as a mediator of information on and off the record depends on his status in the government he speaks for. In general, it is he who controls the mainstream of news from the moment the summiteers raise the curtain on the opening ceremony. In the weeks prior to the summit he devotes himself to building up a public consensus around the position of his government. Interviews given by the heads of state and government and news and comments inspired by spokesmen or cabinet members are part of the routine of the preparatory work. To a certain extent, governments struggle for their success at the summit through press campaigns, addressed not only to the nation but to summit partners as well. This indirect dialogue between statesmen through the media is part of the preliminary tactics of summitry.

But from the evening before the summit begins until the concluding press conference is held, the spokesman is the only link between the summit and the media. At the final joint press conferences additional information is rarely disclosed, and the large concert halls or similar buildings in which they take place do anything but create an atmosphere of intimacy. As a rule the summiteers confine themselves to formal statements along the lines of the communiqué. An exceptional case was the press conference in Bonn, at which Helmut Schmidt submitted an excellent summary of the summit's decisions. The same is true of Ottawa where Pierre Trudeau wound up the debate on the international state of affairs under difficult circumstances.

After the session, the heads of state and government meet with their national press corps, emphasising the achievements of the conference in general and their personal commitments in particular. This dialogue with the media and the contents of the communiqué dominate the news published and broadcast immediately after the conference.

The summiteers take a tremendous interest in getting positive headlines in the news. An objective of preference, however, is a personal appearance on the television screen. A television interview seems to be crucial for an emotional domestic response. A summiteer cannot alter the facts, but in presenting his individual version of the conference he may be successful in emphasising the essentials. Commentators of the press like to follow these live interviews in the conference studios, either to compare the individual leader's view with the official tendency and their own comments or to control facts and figures. The summiteers never neglect their contacts with the printed media, but they are primarily attracted by television, as if it were a superior court. It is odd that while television rarely cites news or comments published by the press, the newspapers give high priority to what statesmen say in a television interview, even if they do not go beyond the statements made in their press conferences. The summiteers know from experience that their performance on television will also produce news in the press. Even if they are in a hurry after the conference they will be aware of this benefit and will never pass up the opportunity to appear on the television screen.

During the conference the summiteers usually contact journalists, if at all, solely on a confidential basis, and only if the newsman belongs to the restricted circle of conference veterans and distinguished professionals. Apart from this exception, a spokesman is the only official source. He operates a shuttle service between his delegation and the media. His success depends partly on his thorough knowledge of the complete spectrum of problems under discussion. Prior to the conference he gets the various files that are prepared for the top members of the delegation. He has no access to the session room, but he meets with his head of state or government several times a day. He is also in close contact with the other cabinet members, the sherpa and the note-taker. A spokesman is a participant in the preparatory talks of the delegation. He is briefed on the fireside chats at night, where the heads of state and government are among themselves before the foreign secretaries join the party, and he learns the substance of bilateral conversations. So, the problem is not so much what he is able to deliver as information, but how far he will go in revealing what he knows. He has to keep in mind the media's tendency to overestimate and to exaggerate details reported out of context.

Before the summit, each government holds a number of deep briefings in an effort to explain its position and the nature of the problems on the agenda. If they did not do so, there would probably be an extreme lack of balance between the governments' and the media's knowledge and awareness of the complexity of the issues under discussion which could lead to misjudgement and misinterpretation. The main objective of a spokesman is to obtain a maximum of support from the media for the benefit of his government by delivering a maximum of information. He has to contribute as much as possible to the raw material from which the media create their news. The press expect him to defend this main purpose of his activities even against the wishes of members of the delegation, who are generally in favour of greater restraint. While the summit is under way, top members of the delegation tend to view any information given to the media as potentially damaging to the negotiations. They therefore tend to carefully select information and also to over-rate the effectiveness of denials.

A comparison between the merits of 'too much' and those of 'too little' information leads to the conclusion that an insufficient flow of news and background serves little purpose for it will induce the media to fill the gaps with − often misleading − speculation. The less the media are informed by their 'own' national delegation, the more they are prepared to listen to rumours and unqualified news, if not gossip. The prevailing judgement among experienced journalists of different nationality is that the Americans and Germans are in the lead with respect to frankness and detailed information. The Americans, of course, derive profit from their status as a world power, which insures careful attention in any case.

In Venice and in Ottawa the summiteers assembled in strict isolation. Pierre Trudeau, the Canadian host, was eager to create an atmosphere very similar to the one Giscard had in mind when he first proposed the summits. He chose Montebello with its gigantic bloque house, fifty miles from Ottawa, as the location for the summit. He wanted the leaders to work undisturbed by the media and the bulk of the bureaucrats, who had to stay in Ottawa. Journalists were allowed to circulate only at some distance from the fences surrounding the conference building. The spokesmen went to Ottawa by helicopter twice a day or even more often.

In Ottawa the media depended completely on the spokesmen for information. But US Secretary of State Alexander Haig went to Ottawa several times to inform the American media on the state of affairs while the summiteers continued their discussions in the wilderness of the province of Quebec. Haig was one of the busiest spokesmen in Versailles as well, conveying messages and highlights of the conference to the journalists on a number of occasions. The media appreciated the news straight from the horse's mouth, and Haig gained favourable publicity. Like Haig, many other cabinet ministers contacted the media in Versailles, as was their habit at many summits.

In Williamsburg President Reagan urged the heads of state and government not to contact the press. Cabinet members were not bound to this rule, however. And so it was US Secretary of State George Shultz who gave an official briefing to inform the media about the summit declaration on security policy.

If controversy, conflict or dissent among the summiteers becomes obvious, and if these sensational aspects of the summit are scaled down by the spokesmen – rightly or wrongly – the hothouses of the press ghetto produce an atmosphere in which speculative news spreads like wildfire. It is often built on the basis of leaks and indiscretions. The discussion in Versailles on East–West trade and the completely divergent positions of Reagan and Mitterrand in this field provoked sensational reports of a split within the West. No spokesman is able to reconcile conflicting ideas, and if statesmen themselves rush into print, it stands to reason that the media should deal primarily with the spectacular news that is available. The Versailles incident may be regarded as a significant example of the evident limits of keeping the flow of information under control.

What Catches the Headlines

As it has become the habit of the summits to give priority to short-term issues, the media no longer expect any profound discussions on long-term problems. Consequently, they hardly take notice of those issues on the agenda which really deserve public attention but which do not produce controversy or decisions for the near future. The press does publish comments and analyses on long-term problems, like energy and the shortcomings of the West's industrial structure, the need for a reallocation of resources and the North–South conflict. However, articles on such topics are rarely published in the context of the summit or referring to them. Some vague phrases in the Versailles communiqué on energy and the North–South issue were mentioned in the media, but the journalists learned through leaks or suspected by instinct that the summiteers did not really seriously discuss these matters. The heads of state and government just completed the communiqué with a truism.

François Mitterrand, an excellent orator, gave a lecture in Versailles on modern technology and its impact on policy-making. He wanted to extend the agenda beyond the usual topics, but he got little response, apart from some ironic remarks by President Reagan. Only very few international newspapers quoted some condensed passages of the technology part of Mitterrand's speech. The summits should not, of course, be mistaken for a seminars. But it is disappointing that the summiteers are apparently unable to plunge into long-term issues. The media have become accustomed to this, though from time to time they do regret and criticise this inability. The media are not, however, exerting the sort of pressure that might induce the summiteers to revise the conference's agenda.

The fundamental change since Rambouillet is evident. It is in particular the striking unwillingness of the summiteers to agree on concerted actions and joint policies. The success of the summits in Bonn and Tokyo, which produced strategies aimed at economic recovery and energy saving, respectively, remains unparalleled. However, since the second oil price explosion, the dilemma of domestic politics and Western interdependence has increasingly affected the summits. The media have reported and criticised this state of disarray and the lack of cohesion which are impairing the decision-making process and have called for an energetic effort to solve the problems of industrial growth and unemployment, of unbalanced trade and erratic exchange rate fluctuations – without knowing the remedy, however. Because of the absence of coordinated policies and a common approach to the solution of urgent issues, the tendency of the summiteers to a phoney consensus in the communiqué has become a significant feature.

On the other hand, there have been some positive changes, too. The media welcomed the inclusion in the agenda of discussions on international crises and on the partners' assessments of the threat from the Soviet bloc in the context of East–West relations in general. The summit in Venice might be regarded as a decisive turning point. Half a year after the Soviet invasion of Afghanistan, the summiteers took the opportunity to analyse the international state of affairs. As they continue to discuss foreign affairs by exchanging views and considerations, a sensible balance between the political and economic aspects of security policy has been established at the summits. In this respect, the Williamsburg summit produced an outstanding event: the passing of a declaration on the West's security policy and its arms control policy that was endorsed even by the Japanese prime minister. The media support this process. In their perception, the model of the 1979 four-power summit in Guadeloupe (United States, France, Germany, Britain) with its political *tour d'horizon* ought to be adopted by the summit of the Seven as a promising procedure for high-level consultation, both in the plenary session and in bilateral conversations.

This evolution contributed to a considerable extent to the image of the summit in Williamsburg and its publicity which focused at least as much on security policy as on economics. The Seven do not want their annual meeting to become a formal institution, a sort of directorate of the West, but public expectation and speculation is in favour of a Western institution for international crisis management.

Confidentiality

A specific problem of the summit is whether it is possible to keep the discussions confidential. The answer is ambiguous.

The discussions in the plenary session can probably not be considered confidential. The delegations are too voluminous, and the statesmen speak from papers prepared for them by their aides. There is no genuine dialogue; the summiteers speak neither spontaneously nor to the point. The summiteers themselves want the essence of their interventions to be publicised because of the domestic resonance. The spokesmen brief the media immediately, at least on the remarks of their principal. By tacit agreement among the delegations, detailed hints on the other summiteers' speeches are not given during these briefings. But a spokesman has to explain the context, and so some fragments of the whole debate are disclosed. There are very few secrets left.

The disadvantages of this procedure are obvious. The summiteers behave very carefully, aware of the risks of a misleading publication of their interventions. Another disadvantage: the journalists very seldom know exactly what the summiteers of other delegations said. So, very often, the reproduction of a debate in the media resembles a sort of bizarre mosaic.

Well-reputed journalists are sometimes informed about the course of the fireside conversations, where the heads of state and government are among themselves. But the summiteers usually surrender information at their own discretion only in cases of bilateral conversations behind the scene or in the corridors. Approximately fifty bilateral meetings between summiteers contribute to the real importance of the summit. If anything about these strictly confidential chats becomes known, it occurs by tacit agreement of the participants, by accident or by subtle leaking.

The summit of the Seven is an outstanding social event too. Well-known statesmen arouse the curiosity of people – how do they behave among themselves or what are they doing privately, if they have some time to spare? The media like to cover these aspects of a summit and to publish human-touch stories. Many journalists go to the airport to catch a glimpse of the summiteers on their arrival. They wait for motorcades at hotels and conference buildings. In this respect, Versailles was unique. The beauty of the gardens and the feudal pomp of the Palace fascinated the media, television in particular. Descriptions of the grandest surroundings the annual meeting of the major industrial countries have ever enjoyed, the menu of Versailles and the gracious toasts at the glittering dinners were published everywhere. The summiteers appreciate this valuable contribution to their publicity. Their daily appearance on the television screen, among leading statesmen, ensures domestic popularity.

Domestic Concerns

Summits serve increasingly as a political instrument to meet domestic requirements, either to force national consensus or to give evidence of an effective performance on the international stage, struggling to protect national interests. The media convey the messages, while at the same time harshly criticising the decay of the summits.

This development, too, affects the drafting of the communiqué. The sherpas, who are in charge of this work, more and more frequently accept the 'generous cooperation' of the summit participants, completing the communiqué with a specific passage one of them desires for domestic purposes and omitting certain wordings which might not go down well with another's electorate. The result is annoying. Diverging views and strategies, different priorities and even contradictions make up the communiqué. The media attack this practice year after year, but have become accustomed to the give-and-take of the summiteers on which the final statement is based.

The temptation to use the summit for domestic purposes is only one aspect. We can also observe, vice versa, the determination of statesmen to use national consensus, reflected by the media, as a leverage at the summit, to influence the contents of the communiqué or the readiness of other delegations to compromise.

At any rate, the media are the means of delivery. They participate in the struggle for national bargaining power at the summit and in the feedback, sometimes without being aware of doing so. But the role of the media in the context of the summits should not be overrated. It is true, governments feel very vulnerable to press campaigns abroad, if they are involved, and also to a lack of support from their national press. The summiteers carefully consider the media's comments. Sometimes they come to the conclusion, under the pressure of a media campaign, that it would be better to drop a project or to put more emphasis on a claim.

A successful summit presupposes results which fulfill public expectations. This raises a severe problem. Before the summit, national governments tend to tell the people and the media what their own desires and objectives are, thus creating an atmosphere of expectation and trust that ignores the positions of the other governments and the necessity of a compromise. Consequently, public opinion is misled in the first stage and hence disappointed in the results at the end of the conference. Many summiteers may therefore be tempted not only to discuss their positions and problems among themselves but also to address the media on these points. President Reagan agreed in Versailles on a compromise with regard to constraints in East–West trade. But because of the domestic debate in the national media stimulated by the White House and the Pentagon, this compromise did not come up to public expectations in the United States. So the president felt himself obliged to surrender to the public criticism and to proclaim an embargo – extraterritorial and retroactive – in the context of the Soviet gas pipeline deal, though he had not mentioned the possibility of such tough action with a single word at

the Versailles summit. This is a significant example of the consequences of a domestic approach to the media prior to a summit,
which roused unjustified expectations to such an extent that the
president had to resort to subsequent measures.

A summary analysis of the role of the media leads to the following
conclusions.

– The media contribute to the image of the summit as the most
important annual conference by publishing news and reports in
great detail and at great length.

– The descriptions of the events and the assessments of the results
are sometimes misleading in detail, but, all considered, tend to be
true in general terms.

– The media express criticism within reasonable limits. Many
comments are written on a high level by experienced and well-in-
formed journalists. The media push the governments to make every
effort to achieve a favourable outcome of the summit, but do not
hesitate to emphasise failures and shortcomings. Without any doubt
the media are a mighty power at the conference table.

– Reporting on the summit, the media create a greater public
awareness of worldwide problems. Even if no strategy for dealing
with the recession and unemployment emerges at the summit, the
public gets a wider view of political and economic interdependence.
Security is no longer regarded solely in terms of military policy and
defence. The people learn through the media that security is a much
more complex matter, which also embraces aspects of economic and
social stability.

– The media stimulate domestic debates about the main topics on
the summit's agenda by discussing the international state of affairs
in the economic field.

– Analysis of the international press by the governments leads to
valuable recognition of political tendencies within the West which
governments do not learn through bilateral talks at the summit or
through ambassadors.

The criticisms in the media usually reflect the same dissatisfac-
tions expressed by many insiders: inability and unwillingness of the
summiteers to come up with decisions, lack of commitment, vague
guidelines in the communiqué. This is true with respect to all the
problems currently afflicting the Western states and governments,
ranging from unemployment to budget deficits, from high interest
rates to slow or stagnant industrial growth.

But in the final analysis the media's reports include a lot of positive assessments, too, like the value of personal contacts, leading to familiarity among the summiteers, pressure to discuss common problems and to reaffirm the principles and values of Western societies. None of the Seven can act against the others' vital interests in the long run. Sweeping neglect may be practised temporarily, but no government can run with its head against a wall.

Apart from the well-known deficiencies of the media, there is one important point that arouses justified discontent. In general, the majority of correspondents covering the summits relies on their national delegation. Even well-reputed international newspapers rarely supply their readers with a complete picture of the many components of the summit proceedings, describing the different approaches of the delegations to the single issues. As a matter of fact, the flow of information rests on a system of seven separately operating delegations and spokesmen, without a minimum of interplay. To get an appropriate insight on the summit, one has to read newspapers from different countries. Only some international news agencies do attempt right from the start of the conference to give a comprehensive survey. But they tend to present only current news without sufficient background information.

The small community of experts and individuals who take a particular interest in the summits deplore these circumstances. On the other hand, media experts know from experience in summitry that the alternative of a joint spokesman would be very unsatisfactory. He would not be entitled to disclose any information of value that was not agreed upon by the Seven. The result would be a presentation of trivialities, a statesman-like reaffirmation of Western unity or bone-dry information on the topics under discussion.

Even the joint press conference of the heads of state and government delivers little genuine information. But they, at least, give their audience a first-hand impression of their mood and pronounce some phrases that can be quoted.

There is a broad consensus among the media people that the summiteers favour playing up the spectacular side of their annual meeting. They seem to be concentrating more and more on its impact on the public, if that has not become the main purpose. Even Ronald Reagan's sincere attempt in Williamsburg to scale down the Versailles effect could not alter the nature of the summit.

Everybody, including government insiders, is convinced that the summit process needs to be reformed. The media's criticism is therefore well-founded, and rigorous. But, at the same time, most media people find it hard to imagine that the West could resolve, or even manage, its problems if the summits of the Seven were no longer held. The media count on the heads of state and government working together, and, conversely, the governments count on the media. The media have become an integrated part of summitry, and summitry has become an integral part of the Western system.

6 THE EUROPEAN COMMUNITY AND THE SEVEN

Gianni Bonvicini and Wolfgang Wessels

New structures and organisations — especially those which are created in an *ad hoc*, voluntaristic fashion by an elite club — automatically become a cause for concern, in particular for those who are excluded and for older organisations which see them as a threat to their *domaine reservé*. The annual economic summits of the seven major industrial democracies were (and to a certain extent still are) perceived by non-participating Western countries and the European Community as a possible threat to their role as decision-makers in world and European economic affairs. The circumstances surrounding the first summit gathering reinforced suspicions that the heads of government of the largest EC member states would take decisions without sufficiently consulting with their partners. The summits of the Seven were supposed to be highly confidential with a flexible agenda that could include any relevant international issue (and the original conception of just an exchange of views raised additional doubts). Without a defined relationship with existing bodies like the Organisation for Economic Cooperation and Development, the International Monetary Fund and the European Community, in particular, the Western summits were viewed by many as necessary in principle but a threat and disturbance in practice. Would this new body not dominate all other set-ups and lead *de facto* to a sort of 'directorate' of the most powerful? Was it not the Gaullist vision reformulated in new terms; a practice that would undermine the principle of equal participation of all countries of the Western world?

The issue was raised within the European Community, especially by the smaller countries and the Community institutions — the European Parliament and the Commission, in particular. Western summitry was seen not as just another decision-making forum but as a rival of, or even a substitute for, the Community as the major body through which decisions on European economic policy are made.

For more than two years these major doubts were expressed in the question of whether and how the Community would be represented at the summits.

Procedural solutions to the issue were found in 1977 and have worked without major problems since then. Indeed, the Community's participation in the preparatory phase and in the summits themselves has run more smoothly than expected, indicating that both sides may have overestimated a number of problems. Community involvement has developed and continues to evolve along a pattern which is typical of West European foreign policy-making in the second half of the seventies and early eighties. Western summitry and the Community both have a role to play in the complex and chaotic realm of international economic policy-making, which is more than ever before conditioned by the growing interdependence of the Western economies and the continuing, or even increasing, reassertion of national governments as stabilisers of their respective welfare societies. The increase in the number of independent units in the international system, combined with the breakdown of binding rules and the waning of natural leadership, has made it more imperative than in the fifties and sixties to develop effective consensus-building procedures. The Western summits and the EC are both playing their parts in a multilevel and continuous process – each with different roles and characteristics, both necessary for Western Europe. Thus, after overcoming some diplomatic rigidities, the two structures have become complementary for the Community countries. As long as there is no basic change in the patterns of conflict and cooperation in the Western world leading to a new role for the summits, and as long as there is no *saut qualitative* of the Community, the relationship between the two structures seems to need no major improvements.

European Foreign Policy:
Towards a New 'Actor' in the International System?

The role of the Community and its member states in the summits of the Seven is part of an overall evolution of West European foreign policy-making. The balance sheet of common or coordinated foreign policy activities of the Community and its member states in the seventies and early eighties looks at first sight ambiguous. On one side, the geographical and functional scope of the external relations of the Community based on the legal provisions of the Rome Treaties have been expanded considerably,[1] as have the coordinated activities of the member states in the framework of European Political

Cooperation (EPC)[2] dealing with nearly all international issues at the diplomatic level. Is this an evolution towards a foreign policy 'unit', a 'world power – albeit a civilian power'[3] or towards a new 'coherent and purposeful actor'[4] which would also lead 'naturally' to the participation of the Community as such in the Western summits?

Firstly, the international role of the Community can be seen as the result of a certain – nearly automatic – logic, a spill-over from Community treaties and subsequent common and coordinated activities into new areas or into new organisational set-ups like Western summitry.[5]

Secondly, other observers see the national foreign policy activities of the member states not as obsolete,[6] not as being replaced by the Community, but as continuing and even thriving. Seen from this perspective, the EC and EPC are but limited instruments of national actors, who use them if and to the extent that they are useful for national interests. The restricted participation and the limited role of the Community in Western summits is thus ultimately the result of a sort of cost-benefit analysis on the part of the national actors.

Thirdly, the foreign policy networks of the Community and the Western summits are part of an interdependent system ruled by a certain 'regime'.[7] The interdependence of economic, diplomatic and security problems, which reduces the capacity of nation states to act autonomously in internal and external affairs, demands subtle management with certain norms, principles and decision-making procedures. The EC and EPC – like the Western summits – are partly competitive, partly complementary, components of this system. The role and the participation of the EC is therefore more the result of a struggle between member states of the EC and within the bureaucratic substructures of the member states.

For our purposes, these views and perspectives raise the following questions:

1. Which forces and arguments pressed for and which resisted participation of the Community in the Western summits? Which of the above theories is valid and might thus also be of importance for the present and future role of the Community within the Western summits?

2. Is there one persistent role of the Community within the summit process or are there different patterns according to the subjects dealt with?

3. What effect does this participation have on the decision-

making process of the Community and its relevance in solving certain problems? Is there conflict or complementarity? Is the role of the participating member states greatly enhanced vis-à-vis that of the non-participating member states?

4. What impact does the EC's participation have on summitry? Is there an international regime with mutually consistent norms and decision-making patterns?

5. In which direction should and will the Community participation evolve – taking the different scenarios for summitry structures and functions into consideration?

The Historical Debate: Three Schools of Thought

The tensions between the evolution of common and coordinated West European foreign policy-making, on the one hand, and the persistent and even increasing role of national governments – especially of the larger member states – on the other hand, were felt once more as soon as it became clear that the Western economic summits would become a regular event. Beyond the immediate problem of the participation of the Community, this debate was taken by some as a case central to the issue of the direction in which foreign policy-making in Western Europe should and would evolve.

Only because of the importance of this in principle for West European foreign policy, it should be explained that this problem was exclusively an intra-Community conflict. The extra-European participants were not opposed to Community participation.

The question of the participation of the European Community as such was articulated concretely on the eve of the second gathering, in Puerto Rico (27–28 June 1976).

At the first summit, the previous year at Rambouillet, the problem had been barely touched on. In the final communiqué, point 15, the six participants (Canada had not been invited) made a generic reference to the fact that 'we intend to intensify our cooperation on all these problems in the framework of existing institutions as well as in all the relevant international organisations'. Apart from everything else, the sensation was that the gathering would remain an isolated event, with no regular sequel. Only after the convening of the Puerto Rico summit by US President Ford did the Europeans begin to seriously pose the dual question of: a) how to allow for participation of the excluded countries, currently referred to as the non-participating states, and b) what kind of representation to attribute to the Community.

The debate which started to turn around these questions was controversial, reflecting not only the existence of different doctrines on European foreign policy-making but also the uncertainties about the role the Western summits should and could play. There were and are three different schools of thinking:

1. Community 'orthodoxy' demanded that in economic questions only the Community (and not the member states) should 'speak with one voice',[8] i.c. that a 'bicephalous' delegation headed by the presidents of the Commission and of the European Council should represent the Community on the basis of a mandate passed by the Council of Ministers and the European Council, respectively. This solution would be in line with the normal procedures for Community negotiations leading to treaties with third countries.[9]

This school of thought argued that the existing *acquis communautaire* and the *finalité politique* of Community activities, confirmed in the conceptions of a 'European Union' (Paris 1972) and of a 'European identity' in world affairs (Copenhagen 1973), made a single and coherent position in these Western summits imperative. The balance of power would and should shift away from national governments to Community bodies. The participation of national leaders except for the president of the European Council would be made nearly superfluous as national powers were replaced or substituted by Community competences.

Alongside these advocates of a more united Community were some smaller Community countries which regarded this procedure as the only way to ensure that they were in the game and would not become just pawns or 'non-participating decision-takers'.[10] It was also argued that if these countries continued to be excluded they would eventually become 'irresponsible' free riders of the international system who would not feel obliged to follow common Western lines. The two opening questions − representation of the smaller countries and representation of the Community − would be solved *uno acto*, by adopting an integrated approach, levelling off the differences in power between larger and smaller countries.

This school of thought was not only progressive in terms of integration policy but at the same time moved on the defensive against a 'principal nation approach',[11] as Western summitry was perceived as not the only attempt of the major countries to organise international affairs in a restricted club. The meeting of the five finance ministers (US, German, French, British and Japanese), the four-power Berlin group, the four-power Guadeloupe summit, the regular bilateral summit meetings of the four major West European countries, the suggestion of Giscard d'Estaing that a *directoire* be created within the Community, and trilateral secret meetings of the foreign ministers of France, the Federal Republic of Germany and the United Kingdom were some of the developments or attempts to keep the smaller countries and the Community out of the decision-making circle.

In the Western summits, this kind of Community representation would have led to a rather inflexible position as the Community delegation would have to stick to its mandate. Experience in other international forums has demonstrated that the Community and the Ten are slow in reaching decisions and that, once established, their stances are rigid, which is best explained by the consensus principle of internal Community decision-making. This school of thought implicitly assumes that summitry will take at least *de facto* binding decisions in the economic field.

2. Opposite to this school of thought was the argument of the French president. His Library Group concept of Western summitry[12] stressed the informal character of the meeting which was not supposed to lead to any decisions within the competences of the Community. The informal exchange of views among the highest responsibles should not be disturbed by additional participants who could not speak for anyone. Those who are able and prepared to take decisions should cooperate; excluded should be those who complicate affairs without being able to contribute to problem-solving. Behind this position lies the French – or better – the Gaullist view that only the representatives or the 'incarnations' of national sovereignties have the right and are able to shape international events. The Commission just does not have direct and basic legitimation as this can only be based on national sovereignty. Giscard, perhaps less doctrinaire than his predecessors, stuck less to the normative argument of national sovereignty than to the efficiency criteria in his reasoning.

Even in the case that only the 'club' (Library Group) concept of Western summitry had been implemented, repercussions for the Community and the smaller member states were to be expected. Even without any formal decisions, convergences or divergences of views in this club would have had positive or negative effects on the whole OECD group and on Community policies. Because the Western summits so often lay the ground for decision-making on economic questions, the Community is in one way or another directly concerned. Non-participation of the Community would reduce the relevance of the West European framework in solving major economic problems. This exclusion of the Community might induce a dynamic process by which the Community would be regarded internally and externally as being of secondary and declining importance. Within the Community, the balance of power would shift even more away from the Community bodies to the larger member states. The two opening questions regarding the Community — representation of the EC and representation of the smaller countries — are considered as irrelevant by this school of thought; they are useless questions which need no answers.

3. Another line of thinking recommended a middle-of-the-road position which would allow participation of the presidents of the European Council and of the Commission not based on a binding and complete mandate, but reflecting Community positions and opinions where necessary and useful. This position was also in line with certain pragmatic developments in the Community's foreign policy-making: the Commission had progressively been accepted as an 'invited guest' at meetings of (intergovernmental) European Political Cooperation; the president of the Commission was also taking part in the restricted meetings of the European Council, even in the highly confidential 'fireside chats'.[13] This school of thought reflects the pragmatic and evolutionary development of the West European foreign policy-making structure and of Community institutions in general. The legally limited scope of the Community's competences, economic interdependencies and the need to find joint solutions to common problems have led to a 'pooling of national and Community sovereignties',[14] a combining of national and Community powers (not a replacement of one by the other). This school of thought responds to the opening question with a 'parallel' approach — the participation of Community representatives is added without eliminating that of the larger member states. In terms of equal weight, the problem of representation of the smaller countries is not sufficiently solved, as the Commission or the presidency of the European Council can only present the Community's position, not explicitly the position of the smaller countries, whereas the larger countries can bring forward their national positions and thus at least have the possibility of circumventing the common position. An element of equalisation was introduced with the decision to al-

low the participation of the president of the European Council even if he was the representative of a smaller country. The proponents of this school could argue that, in a dynamic perspective, the Community countries would develop some sort of *communauté de vue* sharing the same basic conceptions though without a formally fixed and binding mandate or unified institutions.[15]

These schools of thought were clearly present in the political discussions on the participation of the Community in the Western summits. Of the Community institutions, the European Parliament was the most active in the debate. During its 16 June 1976 session, two central questions were put to the president-in-office of the Council of Ministers, who just happened to be Gaston Thorn of Luxembourg, the representative of the Community's smallest member state. One concerned the role of the smaller countries, while the other dealt with the Community's representation. Thorn's reply, quite *communautaire*, was that the real problem was not representation of the smaller countries but representation of the Community as such: to add some kind of representation for the smaller countries would in fact mean recognising the existence of the two kinds of member state, first-class and second-class. The questioner, Berkhouwer of the Netherlands, was even more emphatic, calling the drawing of a distinction between major and minor countries a violation of the Treaty of Rome. However, just ten days before the Puerto Rico summit, Thorn had to declare that he had not yet managed to put the question formally on the agenda of the Council of Foreign Ministers.

A second point raised by Thorn was that there could not be a sort of delegation of powers to the four major partners, who had no right to represent the others and probably had no intention of doing so either. The path to follow, therefore, was towards a presence of the Community 'in areas of its competence and with respect for the procedures that characterise it'. The smaller countries had problems in trusting their larger partners, as was indicated by the specific question raised by Patijn of the Netherlands whether, on receipt of the invitation to take part in the summit, the four had made representation of the European Community a precondition. Thorn was forced to reply in the negative. This exclusion added to a general feeling of disappointment and frustration on the part of the EC's smaller countries, which is felt not only in the framework of the EC but also in the NATO sphere (deployment of European theatre strategic missiles, for instance).

Through diplomatic channels, some non-participating EC member states had made known − prior to the Puerto Rico summit − that they would not accept a proposal to have the presidents of the Council and the Commission represent the Community. They demanded representation on the basis of a Community mandate. They also demanded that the procedures of Community representation be obligatorily fixed for the following meetings.[16] These demands were not accepted by most of the larger countries, especially France, with the result that the Community was not represented at Puerto Rico. Some of the blame for this was put on the formalistic attitude of the Dutch government.[17] The final communiqué of Puerto Rico made only a slightly more explicit reference to the EC: 'Those among us whose countries are members of the European Economic Community intend to make their efforts within its framework.' This sentence was to be repeated in virtually all subsequent communiqués. At the meeting of the body most appropriate to deal with the question − the European Council − which took place in the immediate aftermath of the Puerto Rico summit, the problem was not really taken up as other questions − in this case, the national distribution of seats in the European Parliament − were regarded as more important. Thus, the rather intense dispute over representation of the Community at the summits of the Seven did not find its way into the deliberations of the European Council. The president of the Council, the Dutch Prime Minister Den Uyl, explained at the end of the meeting that the heads of government had agreed without explicit discussion that consultations should take place prior to such summits and that, in the future, Community procedure should be respected if powers and competences of the Community are involved.[18] This position was repeated by the acting president of the Council of Ministers, Brinkhorst, in the European Parliament. When specifically asked if this procedure had been accepted as such, Brinkhorst replied that the formulation (issued by the Dutch presidency) was not being questioned by the other participants.[19]

At the next European Council meeting in London, the heads of government agreed to intensify economic coordination among the industrial democracies via the Western summit, which was also to serve as the forum for an intensive debate with the new US President.[20] Once again, however, the intra-Community procedures for participation were not fixed, though it was agreed to call another meeting of the European Council before the next summit of the Seven.

The European Parliament, in the course of the 14–15 December debate on the two new questions, heard from the president of the Commission and the president of the Council of Ministers that the EC would be represented at the next summit (which at that time was expected to be held in Tokyo, not London, as was later decided). To ward off the risk of further disappointment, the European Parliament decided to present a resolution, which was approved unanimously and with the full backing of the European Commission itself, on the eve of the European Council meeting in Rome in March 1977. The resolution insisted that the Community, Council and Commission be represented at the London economic summit, given that: a) matters of interest to the Community were to be dealt with; b) the Community is committed to speaking with a single voice on the international scene.

However, at the Rome European Council meeting held prior to the Western summit in London (May 1977) the same tensions came up again. The Benelux countries now demanded participation of the presidents of the Commission and the Council, who were to speak for the Community in cases in which Community competences were involved. Giscard d'Estaing remained hostile, stressing in a letter to the president of the Commission, Jenkins, that the London summit was a meeting of heads of state and government which would take no decisions on affairs of Community competence.[21]

The Dutch Parliament demanded the boycott of the meeting of the European Council in Rome if the participation of the Community was not accepted. The Dutch finance minister even threatened financial sanctions.

At the European Council meeting, a preliminary agreement, which was not to serve as 'precedence', was found within a short period of time. According to this agreement, the presidents of the Council and the Commission were to be invited to the 'technical' (Giscard d'Estaing) parts of the conference in which the questions within the 'competences of the Community' were to be discussed; as examples, deliberations on international trade and the North–South dialogue were mentioned.

But what are the Community's areas of competence? The president of the Commission did not participate in the meetings of the first day, 7 May, during which the international economic and monetary situation was discussed. But he was present on 8 May for the discussions on balance-of-payments deficits, international trade negotiations and energy problems. The most generous concession

was that the president of the Commission was allowed to dine together with the Seven on the eve of the summit.

It was clear that this sub-division of topics was simply a political
act of caution in the face of Giscard d'Estaing's opposition to the
Community's participation. As a sign of protest, Giscard did not attend the opening dinner.

In Autumn 1977, the foreign ministers came up with a satisfactory
procedure. With this procedure, the participation of the presidents
of the European Council and of the Commission was guaranteed,
except where political deliberations were involved. This solution was
found without any major dispute. The opposing forces had apparently realised that this *modus vivendi* would serve their interests
without making a major case for or against a certain model of West
European decision-making. Experience at summitry, and in other
forums and organisations, has proved this parallel approach to be
efficient. Moreover, this solution leaves the question of the final
form of the participation of the Community institutions open.

The Community's Participation: The Parallel Approach in Practice

With the procedure agreed upon by the Community, the Commission was fully accepted and has become a regular participant in the
summits. The president of the Commission, his sherpa (who has up
to now been his chef de cabinet), alternating vice-presidents and
Commission officials have been present at all the meetings at their
respective levels. Minor attempts to downgrade the role of the president of the Commission (offering him no microphone, excluding
him from the official photograph, preventing him from speaking,
etc.) have been handled in various ways by the changing presidencies
of the Western summits. At least the German and Italian governments as hosts of the summits in Bonn and Venice played an effective role in having the president of the Commission fully accepted.
In the process of constant involvement, the Commission seems to
have emancipated itself, taking on a role in its own right and with
a certain degree of autonomy, i.e. the informality of the deliberations has made it possible for the Commission to develop conceptions of its own which might not yet represent the position of the
Community as such. The Commission has played a major role especially in the areas of trade policy, North–South relations and
macroeconomic policies. There seems to be a tendency for the Commission to constantly enlarge its area of involvement.

The presidency of the European Council, also foreseen as a participant at the summits, did not raise any problems until the Versailles meeting in June 1982 (see table 6.1). Until that time the presidency of the Council had always been present in its own right as a 'major' country. The suspicion that the Western summit meetings were scheduled in such a way that the Council presidency, which rotates every six months, would always be in the hands of a major Community country is officially denied but seems to have some truth to it. In 1982 the situation changed as two smaller Community countries were holding the presidency. France as the host of the Western summit that year raised certain objections to adding another participant to the club, pointing to logistical problems. The rules were clear, however, and with Belgium holding the Council presidency it was difficult to prevent 'old friends' from joining the preparations and the deliberations of the summit.

Table 6.1: European Council Presidencies at the Time of the Summits

City of Host Country	Summit Date	Council Presidency
Rambouillet	November 1975	Italy
Puerto Rico	June 1976	Luxembourg
London	May 1977	UK
Bonn	July 1978	W. Germany
Tokyo	June 1979	France
Venice	June 1980	Italy
Ottawa	July 1981	UK
Versailles	June 1982	Belgium
Williamsburg	May 1983	W. Germany

Over time this procedural problem has also been eased – for example, Denmark, which held the presidency of the Council in the second half of 1982, participated in the preparations for the Williamsburg summit which took place during that period. This could be considered an example of the good functioning of the so-called 'troika system' (whereby the previous, the present and the future presidencies work together) proposed in the London Report of October 1981, to improve cooperation in the context of European Political Cooperation.

In the preparation period (for example, in meetings with the US president) and in the deliberations themselves, the president of the European Council normally illustrates Community positions, without however restricting his interventions only to the common European denominator. Some European Council presidents apparently have taken their Community responsibility more seriously than others.

Just as the participation of the two representatives of the Community has been resolved satisfactorily, so apparently has the involvement of the smaller non-participating EC member states in the decision-making process. The Commission reports to all Community bodies (especially the COREPER and the Council of Ministers) on the preparations and the results of the summits. Questions can be raised and suggestions can be given by all member states of the Community. The European Council, the regular meeting of the Community heads of government, normally spends some time discussing the forthcoming summit.

The intensity of discussion on the Western summits as such seems not to be very high in most Community bodies. A major protest by the non-participating member states was raised only after the Tokyo summit, at which a preceding energy-saving decision of the European Council in Strasbourg was overruled. The non-participating countries are apparently not really forcing debates about the agendas of the Western summits. This low level of engagement is attributable, however, less to a lack of interest in the proceedings of the Western summits than to the fact that the issues concerning the international economic system that are on the agendas of the various Community bodies are already included on the summit agendas. The topics of the Western summits are part of an ongoing process of debate which is taking place regularly within the Community with the full participation of all the member states. Therefore, the positions of the Community for the Western summits do not normally need to be worked out specifically for that occasion as they can be derived from the constant exchange of views which goes on in the Community framework. The EC thus does not develop a clear mandate in the strictly legal sense, but instead presents the member states' converging (or sometimes diverging) views.

The procedural problems of the Community's participation in the summits is no longer a major point of conflict for the Community or for the Seven; far more crucial will be the quetion of whether there is an evolution towards a *communauté de vue* among the Community summiteers on the major issues related to the international economic system.

As far as *the Community and the topics of the Western summits* are concerned, the maintenance of free trade, respect for the rules of anti-protectionism and multilateral trade talks form the core of Community competences; the Community has exclusive powers in this field, and it is normally the Commission that negotiates for the Community. It is therefore natural that the Commission should be highly involved. The Commission has in fact presented preparatory papers in this area (something no member state has done) and has played a major role in the sherpas' discussions on the multilateral trade negotiations. The Community position has not always been firm and unambiguous, however, and differences between Bonn and Paris have also emerged at the Western summits. Where the West Europeans have taken a strong common stand is in exerting pressure on Japan to open its market. The Community members have also been united in their reluctance to use East–West trade as a political instrument. They reacted in common against US pressure, especially in the case of export credits for the USSR and in the natural gas pipeline affair. The same happened on the eve of the Williamsburg summit when the Community participants rejected the American proposal to include trade issues on the agenda, which the Europeans considered a matter for the GATT negotiations.

Regarding *energy policy*, the Community does not have any exclusive competences and the attempts to develop a common EC energy strategy have produced only limited results. Other forums like the International Energy Agency are certainly more important in developing concrete instruments and binding rules. In the summitry process, the Commission was active to a certain degree when energy issues were involved, but the secretariat of the IEA clearly played a larger role. On energy questions the Community has served more as a framework for building a sort of 'coalition' of the European countries, through which some preparatory work could be done. The Tokyo summit indicated the possibilities and the limits of this 'coalition' approach by the Community. Though there were common European interests, especially vis-à-vis the United States (energy saving via deregulation) the European coalition was not firm; some countries used the interests of non-Community participants in the summits to strengthen their position vis-à-vis their Community partners. In the field of nuclear export policy, France and the Federal Republic of Germany took a common stand opposed to that of the United States.

In the deliberations on *macroeconomic and monetary policies*, the

Community has limited powers of consultation and coordination. The European Monetary System (EMS) has forced the member states (except for the United Kingdom and Greece which are not fully participating in the system) to agree on exchange rate adaptations and has led to intensified consultations on macroeconomic policies, but major decisions in this area are still made in the national capitals. At the summits, the Community member states have on several occasions shared the same interests when it comes to monetary questions; the EC member states have, for example, pressed the United States to give up its policy of benign neglect in letting the US dollar float downwards (in the Carter days) or upwards (in the Reagan days). Though the Europeans' position on the reform of the international monetary system has been far from consistent, they have been united in urging the United States to assume its responsibility and work towards greater stability of the currency system.

Concerning guidelines for macroeconomic behaviour and concrete government actions, changing coalitions within the Community camp can be found. In the debate over whether inflation or unemployment should be fought first and the trade-offs involved, a general consensus developed in the second half of the seventies that the fight against inflation was also the most effective instrument against unemployment (London 1977). In Versailles (1982) Mitterrand set different priorities, but they did not prevail in the face of the general acceptance of 'Reaganomics'.

Apart from this broad consensus on certain macroeconomic issues, at the London summit a major debate on the locomotive theory took place, which would ultimately lead to the 'convoy decision' taken in Bonn (1978). The pressure put on West Germany and Japan at the 1977 summit of the Seven to stimulate their economies was applied in the Community framework, too – especially at the Bremen meeting of the European Council (Spring 1978). Bonn was unable to convince its Community partners to form a united defensive front against the US pressure. Indeed, the member states' acceptance of Schmidt's proposal to create the European Monetary System was linked to Bonn's willingness to stimulate the Community economy. In this case, the Community served as an important framework through which to mobilise pressure on one member state, which was seconded in the preparations for the Western summit.

In the field of macroeconomic policy the Community members have also been united in putting pressure on the Reagan administration to introduce measures to reduce the high US interest rate.

In the area of the North–South dialogue the Community position was rather unified, at least in terms of procedure. The member states argued for an open attitude and for the convening of the Cancun summit of developed and developing countries against the negative attitudes of the United States. On substantive issues, however, their positions have not always been united.

With regard to political-diplomatic declarations, the Community, in the strictest sense, cannot get involved as this is outside its field of competence. However, most topics taken up at the Western summits have been on the agenda of European Political Cooperation, through which the foreign offices of the Ten work together. EPC declarations have not, however, played a major role. The president of the European Council, who would be the only one entitled to present the common views of the Ten, has usually been reluctant to do so, normally preferring to stress the position of his own government.

In the foreign policy area, summitry has produced some declarations of general consensus, like those on refugees, air piracy, the seizure of US diplomatic personnel as hostages, terrorism. More controversial points which showed up US–European cleavages were East–West relations, especially with regard to the assessment of détente policy after the Soviet invasion of Afghanistan and the common Western reactions to this invasion and to the developments in Poland; similar difficulties came up in Williamsburg when the Americans pressed the Europeans to accept a declaration in the field of security, namely, the question of deployment of the Euromissiles. Differences have also surfaced in the context of Middle East policy.

Though the representation of Community policies as such by the presidents of the European Council and of the Commission has been limited due to the fact that there has not been and should not be a mandate, on most topics a high degree of 'likemindedness' among the Community members has been demonstrated, i.e. the positions of the Community governments have followed – even without a formal mandate – common lines which are both a reflection of some basic 'European interests' and the result of a long and complex process of deliberations within the Community. Strong and 'extreme' US positions have apparently served in many cases to bring the European partners to more converging positions than could be expected from internal deliberations within the Community context. At the same time, the Community countries have not developed into a unified coalition with the same position on each and every question. Not only on the procedural side but also in terms of substance, no direct Community mandate has been developed, though the coherence of European positions is greater than could be expected considering the preparation procedures and the concrete positions taken within the Community.

A building of Community coalitions would meet with strong opposition from the other participants in the summits, who would be concerned over the loss of flexibility and informality. Community positions presented as not 'negotiable' at the summits would block the summitry process. The only example of this kind – the energy decision of the Strasbourg meeting of the European Council – was rapidly put aside in the subsequent deliberations of the summit of the Seven. Such coalitions would also be refused by the participating Community heads of government, who do not like to stick to a common fixed line, as they want to keep their freedom of manoeuvre.

Looking at the substance of the policies which the Community countries have put forward in the context of Western summitry, the Community as such and the non-participating member states have normally had no reason for complaint; the participating Community countries have in several cases reflected the common perceptions of the EC member states or have even accepted Community policies as such; in cases of divergences among member states, the smaller members' positions have normally been somewhere 'in-between' the divergences of the larger participating countries. Except with regard to the energy decisions taken at the Tokyo summit, the non-participating EC member states have not raised objections.

A cleavage between the larger and smaller member states which could be accentuated by Western summitry is seldom found in the Community – at least not in the area of economic policy. Problems have occurred and could occur in the field of what is misleadingly called 'high politics', i.e. in the security area, in which the larger EC member states might feel obliged, because of internal conviction or external pressure, to take active positions which the smaller countries might like to avoid.

If the Western summits were to deal more intensively with such topics, the differences in weight and in status among the EC member states might be aggravated as a consequence of the deficits in the political cooperation apparatus of the Ten, in which it has been difficult to discuss security questions in a broader sense, as the debate on the Genscher-Colombo initiative clearly indicates. These deficiencies in EPC are also due to the unwillingness of the smaller countries to deal with security questions – thus reinforcing the tendency towards a 'principal nation approach'.

The Impact of Western Summitry on the Community

To analyse and assess the impact of Western summitry on the Community is, first of all, a question of the yardstick used, as indicated in the schools of thought mentioned earlier.

The 'federalists', who evaluate all European steps in the perspective of progress towards a federation with strong European institutions and a minor role for the nation states, would argue that the role of the European nation state, especially of the larger member states, is reinforced by the Western summitry process. A European 'concert of power' instead of an integrated unit is perceived as being a possible consequence of such European participation in the Western summits. The participation of the Commission – according to the federalists – can only be seen as an alibi. The Western summits in this form are clearly detrimental to the cause of European integration.

From the perspective of the champions of 'national sovereignty', European participation in Western summitry is adequate; the Community has been given the role it has always played – that of a useful coalition under the control of the member governments. The participation of the Commission is a deviation from the path of rigid intergovernmentalism, but the real effects are seen as differentiated and in a dynamic perspective, i.e. less in static constitutional terms.

With the breakdown of the post-war 'regimes' which regulated international trade and the energy sector, the monetary system and economic policies, as well as the bipolar political systems, the need for constant and more interventionist management of the Western system has been growing. No binding rules nor 'natural' leadership has emerged in place of the eroded international system, while the number of actors and interdependence among the Western countries have increased. National governments depend for their political survival on the (positive) effects of actions taken by other actors outside their direct influence. All these factors urge a policy of permanent consensus building. The Western summits are but the most explicit indicator of the changes taking place in the method of handling the international system. Taking this development as given, the Community member states had to increase their common or coordinated activities if they wanted to give their grouping a prominent role in dealing with the new or more acute problems they faced. With the Community summits of the Hague in 1969, Paris in 1972, Copenhagen in 1973 and Paris in 1974, as well as with the creation of the European Council, the governments of the member states clearly gave the Community an important yet not exclusive role in tackling the member states' common problems. As many problems — like the security of the Western states' energy supplies — cannot be approached adequately at the Community level only, additional and sometimes more important forums had to be created or used more extensively. Seen from the national capitals, the problem-solving strategies are thus multifaceted and diversified; the usefulness of the Community level for devising and implementing a certain policy is assessed on each occasion. In this perspective, the Western summits have had different effects.

1. The regular meetings of the Western summits 'forced' all Community countries to elaborate some common guidelines for international economic policies; though the discussion on economic policies within the Community is certainly not induced only by Western summitry, the summits have nevertheless been an added pressure for the debates which take place in the European Council at the highest level. The scope and relevance of Community discussions has thus, at least in some respects, increased. So far, the Western summits have not reduced the importance of the Community as a problem-solving arena nor have they replaced Community decisions. There is a common understanding among all Community countries that the international economic problems need to be dealt with at a high level among the OECD countries. Summitry, up to now, has not taken decisions which would make the Community useless, obsolete or irrelevant.

2. The high-level deliberations of the summits on international economic policies have strangely enough strengthened the *de facto* role of the Commission by actively involving it internally in the Community preparations and externally in the discussions and bargaining processes of summitry itself. The president of the Commission now has access to a high-ranking network of relations from which he had previously been excluded. The role of the president of the Commission in the Western summitry process, like his role in the European Council, has not been fixed in a way which would fit in with a federal concept; the repeated demonstration in the second half of the seventies and early eighties that such a role was an illusion has however been balanced by an increase in his *de facto* influence as an *additional* member of the highest club.

3. The relations between participating and non-participating Community countries seem not to have deteriorated after the *modus vivendi* was found. The non-participating countries apparently have

felt sufficiently involved in the preparation and implementation of summit decisions. This attitude has certainly been due at least in part to the non-committal character of the summit deliberations.

Both the Community and the Western summits are vital elements in the management of international economic policies − as up to now the relationship has clearly been more one of a complementary division of labour and less one of competition in different avenues.

The Future Role of the Community in Western Summitry: Scenarios and Options

Speculating about the future is as stimulating and necessary as it is dangerous and limited. We know that we have to deal with too many unknown variables to be able to make an unequivocal prognosis of future events; at the same time, we should not refrain from 'educated guesses', as they might lead to more thorough reflections about the possibilities and options ahead − knowing that decisions affecting the future course of Community foreign policies and Western management will lead in one direction or another. More concretely, if the role of Western summitry remains in its present framework, then we do not need to look for major changes within the Community. If, however, the nature of summitry changes due to political and economic developments in the international system, then the Community's involvement will have to change, too. Speculating about the future can imply both some thoughts about what *might* happen and preferences about what *ought* to be. Both perspectives have to be combined to develop some realistic options.

Scenario A: Evolution of the Present Pattern

In this scenario the present complex network for exchanging information, consultation, coordination and decision-making becomes more refined. This tendency implies that Western summitry and the Community (including EPC) are strengthened and made more efficient without altering the institutional *status quo*, i.e. control by nation states. If Western summitry becomes an increasingly important decision-making body, summitry and the Community may be able to steer clear of conflict, as long as the Community preparations for the summits do not evolve towards some form of mandate. The more important Western summitry becomes as a decision-making body, the more the Community will need to intensify its internal consensus-building procedures, if and in so far as the Community remains an important forum for coordinating national policies (which is assumed in this scenario).

If instead a mandate were given, this would reduce the flexibility of the participating member states and would change the character of summitry from a 'club' to a negotiation procedure. In such a case, the organisational and political infrastructure of Western summitry might be strengthened to prepare meetings within 'square brackets' so that the heads of government would have to solve 'only' the most crucial items. In this process, the Community could become more directly involved as a negotiating unit.

If the Western summits should also increase their consultations and perhaps consensus formation in the field of diplomacy and security, the Community members would have to adapt their mechanism of political cooperation to this function.

In this scenario the whole process of Western policy-making would become more burdensome and complex, which would certainly be against the avowed preferences of the heads of government. But as the development of the European Council (which is, of course, in a different situation) demonstrates, there might be an increasing need for the heads of government to take decisions rather than make only general statements. If the heads of government were not willing to take up a decision-making function, the risk of a collapse of the Western network for managing the international system and of a consequent emergence of new 'regimes' might increase.

Scenario B: Creation of New Systems of Fixed and Binding Rules

In this scenario, Western summitry outlives its usefulness, at least for economic questions, as fixed, automatic and binding rules for international economic life, a 'new Bretton Woods system', are established or developed in some way or other which makes a regular involvement of the highest political leaders superfluous. This would also reduce the Community's engagement in these issues, making the whole problem become less and less relevant.

In this scenario, the need or the wish to reinforce political consultations, especially regarding relations with the East bloc, might increase, however. In this case, the Ten would have to reinforce their political cooperation mechanism.

This scenario looks rather unrealistic, though, as the preconditions for creating such a system of fixed and binding rules do not seem to exist.

Scenario C: A New Atlanticism

In this scenario, Western summitry becomes a vital and central part of the capitalistic world in managing its interdependencies and external challenges. The ambiguities of using several forums and differentiated strategies are supplanted by a strong drive towards a common OECD approach to economic and political problems. Summitry is used not only for consultation and limited actions but also for taking decisions on problems affecting the whole of the Western world.

In such a scenario, the Community might evolve in one of two directions. One is the trilateral option by which the Community, in some form a coherent and purposeful actor, becomes as a unit the partner of the US and Japan. In this option the Community would need to reinforce its internal procedures and external coherence. In the second option the Community is reduced to secondary importance, as the participating EC member states rank Western summitry as *the* major forum for decision-making in which they do not want to be limited by their Community obligations. In such a case, Western summitry might be the major factor setting off a strong process of erosion of the Community.

Scenario D: A Divided Summitry

This scenario describes a situation in which the Western countries are increasingly divided into two or more groups (e.g. US vs. Community). Cleavages across different sectors of policies would not necessarily be overlapping, making the constellations of interests flexible, but would probably be mutually reinforcing, thus leading to persistent coalitions. Summitry would become less an attempt to solve common problems and more an arena of confrontation. In such a scenario a Community favouring détente, mild protectionism and a social-democratic approach to solving economic and social problems could be one of the coalitions confronting the US and/or Japan; however, the Community itself might be split with some member states joining the coalition of the anti-protectionist, monetarist, 'hard-line' forces.

Scenario E: A Strengthened Community

In this scenario, summitry would have to live with a more unified European position, achieved either through a strengthened *communauté de vue* which leaves the member states as the principal actors or through a more unitary institutional set-up establishing some sort of European federation. In the context of Western summitry this might lead to either better 'bilateral' coordination, as the number of opinions is reduced, or to more intense conflicts, as the European position becomes more doctrinaire and less flexible because of a slow and cumbersome internal consensus-building procedure.

In this scenario, changes would not be taking place within the Western management process which would be forcing the Community to adapt to a new situation; developments endogenous to the Community itself would instead be inducing evolutions in Western summitry.

A crucial factor, in any event, will be the national actors' perceptions of, and the strategies used or discarded by them in, certain forums. The strategies will depend on the coalitions of interests they perceive useful and capable of being built up.

Thus, unless major changes occur in the economic and political environment, both the Community with its European Council and Western summitry will perpetuate their existence, as they offer the national actors possibilities and options to look for coalitions in the international system and for national struggles. The *status quo* in institutional terms therefore looks rather stable.

Notes

1. The literature on this subject has also grown considerably; see for example Edmund Wellenstein, *25 Years of External Relations of the Community* (Community Press Office, Luxembourg, 1982); Werner J. Feld (ed.), *Western Europe's Global Reach: Regional Cooperation and Worldwide Aspirations* (Pergamon Press, New York, 1982); and one of the latest surveys: Reinhardt Rummel, *Zusammengesetzte Aussenpolitik: West-Europa als internationaler Akteur* (N.P. Engel Verlag, Kehl am Rhein, 1982).

2. See especially David Allen, Reinhardt Rummel and Wolfgang Wessels (eds.), *European Political Cooperation: Towards a Foreign Policy for Western Europe* (Butterworths, European Studies, London, 1982).

3. Werner Feld, 'Introduction', in Feld (ed.), *Western Europe's Global Reach*, p. 10.

4. See Michael S. Dolan and James A. Caporaso, 'The External Relations of the European Community', in *The Annals of the American Academy of Political and Social Science*, November 1978, p. 136; for a critical position see Paul Taylor, *Limits to European Integration* (Croom Helm, Beckenham, 1983), pp. 118–163.

5. For the spill-over theorem see Philippe C. Schmitter, 'Three Neofunctionalist Hypotheses about International Integration', in *International Organization*, vol. 23, no. 1 (Winter 1969), pp. 161–166; and concerning the 'Sachlogik', Walter Hallstein, *Die Europäische Gemeinschaft*, 5th Edn. (Econ, Düsseldorf, 1979), p. 22. For a critique of these theories see Wolfgang Wessels, 'The European Political Cooperation: Model or Nuisance for a New Institutional Equilibrium', in R. Kovar (ed.), *The Community Institutions on the Threshold of the 1980's: In Search of a New Balance* (Be Temple, Bruges, 1981).

6. For this option see especially Stanley Hoffmann, 'Reflections on the Nation-State in Western Europe Today', in *Journal of Common Market Studies*, vol. 21, no. 1–2 (Sept.-Dec. 1982), pp. 21–39.

7. As basic literature on these notions and theories see Robert O. Keohane and Joseph S. Nye, *Power and Interdependence: World Politics in Transition* (Little, Brown & Co., Boston, Toronto, 1977), and the special volume on the 'International Regime', *International Organization*, no. 2, 1982.

8. On this notion see the declaration of the 1972 Paris summit of the nine heads of government of the EC countries.

9. 'Bicephal' representation is often necessary, because there are 'mixed' national and Community competences.

10. On this notion see Robert Putnam, chapter 2 in this volume.

11. This notion is used extensively in the report of four European research institutes coauthored by Kaiser, Lord, de Montbrial and West, *Western Security: What has changed? What should be done?* (The Royal Institute of International Affairs, London, 1981).

12. On this notion see Putnam, chapter 2 of this book.

13. See Wolfgang Wessels, *Der Europäische Rat: Stabilisierung statt Integration. Geschichte, Entwicklung und Zukunft der EG-Gipfelkonferenzen* (Europa Union Verlag, Bonn, 1980), p. 258.

14. Besides the already mentioned mix of Community and national competences established in the Treaties and the participation of the Commission in EPC, we find formulas like 'the Council and the representatives of Member States meeting within the Council' in areas like education and environment.

15. On this notion of a *communauté de vue* see Wolfgang Wessels, 'European Political Cooperation: A New Approach to European Foreign Policy', in Allen, Rummel and Wessels (eds.), *European Political Cooperation*, p. 6.

16. According to *Agence Europe*, 14/15 June 1976, these demands were presented at the informal meetings of the foreign ministers of the Nine in Semmingen.

17. See *Frankfurter Allgemeine Zeitung*, 29 June 1976.

18. See Wessels, *Der Europäische Rat*, p. 179. Apparently this point was not generally accepted; Chancellor Schmidt explained at his press conference after the European Council meeting that this question was not mentioned at all, whereas Prime Minister Callaghan demonstrated his diplomatic 'skills' by saying that although he knew the subject had been mentioned, he had no clear recollection of the agreement since he did not have his earphones on. In any case, there was no published conclusion of the presidency on this question.

19. See the proceedings of the European Parliament, 15 September 1976, p. 122.

20. *Agence Europe*, 26 March 1977, p. 6.
21. *Agence Europe*, 10 March 1977.

7 A FALL AFTER THE RISE?
THE POLITICAL OPTIONS FOR EUROPE

Cesare Merlini

Analyses converge in saying that the annual summit meeting of the seven major industrialised countries of the world, however oscillating the effectiveness of the single meeting, has become an important new body in international relations.

Decisions are held up for months awaiting negotiation or sanction at the summit. A growing multitude of media men — in the thousands range — assemble around the heads of government, ready to look at the communiqué through a microscope and hoping for a scoop out of some personal conflict between them. Unpopular policies are pushed down the throats of public opinion when they have been decided at the summit and the authority of leaders is judged by their performance there. The worldwide attention the summit of the Seven attracts is a confirmation of the dominant role played by the Western industrialised democracies. Their role has, in fact, been challenged less than expected, culturally as well as politically and economically, either by the communist East, a strategic contender, or by the developing or poor South, a demographic power.

The novelty of the summits does not lie in the fact that they are held at the highest level; kings, plenipotentiaries, dictators and heads of government have met throughout history. The real innovation is that the leaders of the seven major industrialised democracies now meet on a regular basis and with a consolidated membership, in a forum which has a more or less direct and effective relationship with the existing institutions and alliances that link the participating countries among themselves and with others. But while there is a convergence in considering the summits of the Seven a new and important forum, opinion is divided when it comes to explaining the origins of Western summitry, its relevance and novel aspects.

Some emphasise the importance of establishing personal contact among the Western leaders as a means of reviving relations which have been dulled in the routine work of the above mentioned institutions and of bilateral and multilateral diplomacy. Western solidarity is enhanced by the heads of government getting to know each other better and realising that, whether they like it or not, they are all in the same boat. Public opinion needs to be able to identify power with individuals. It is also contended by this school of thought that it is good for the Americans to see their president in the role of a world leader; it is comforting for the French to see their *chef de l'état* taken into account; and it is consoling for the Italians to see that their *presidente del consiglio* is participating. Finally, it is positive for the Japanese to see their prime minister in the company of Western leaders, even though he represents a country located in the Far East. Leaders, it is said, must be educated, especially if they are brand new in power, and if their previous career has been somewhat parochial. They learn more in a two-day summit meeting than in months of heavy lecturing by diplomatic aides and foreign policy advisers.

The summit was born in fact out of the initiative of two European leaders, namely Giscard and Schmidt, who had established a constructive and sympathetic personal relationship when they were finance ministers. It is the well-known 'Library Group' model, whose validity has been verified *a contrario* by the apparent weakening of the effectiveness of summits when well-acquainted leaders leave the scene to other less experienced and apparently less compatible fellows.

This approach, which emphasises subjective factors linked to the leaders' personal participation, is seen by others as an explanation of *how* the summit process originated but not *why*. The real origin of these meetings, according to this second school of thought, resides in such objective factors as the need to 'manage the increasing interdependence' of the Western economies more adequately than was being done by the existing international institutions, to compensate for the decline of the United States through 'collective leadership', to reverse the widespread economic slowdown by means of 'trilateral solidarity' and to assemble around a supposedly decisive table 'the principal countries', including the newcomer, Japan, which at the time seemed reluctant to become involved in Western cooperation.

The subjectivist approach does not take into account, it is said, that despite the crowds which gather from time to time around the Pope and other remaining traces of personal leadership, there is a depersonalisation of politics, a fragmentation of power pyramids which has deprived the apex of the plenipotentiary authority it once enjoyed. The complexity of the political and institutional structures of our advanced states injects into the summit process the multiple interactions of domestic politics and Western interdependence, as is described by Robert Putnam.[1] Even in the Third World, there are fewer charismatic leaders today than in the past.

Western interdependence is mostly, but not exclusively, economic. In looking at the extension of summits to political matters, William Wallace mentions two models: the Guadeloupe one, where a restricted circle of leaders confidentially discusses a number of current hot issues (subjectivist approach), and the Venice model, where the summit is forced to take into account the inseparable nature of economic and political issues, dealing with them in plenary sessions and treating them as such in a final communiqué (objectivist approach).[2] It is this second model, the 'objectivists' contend, that has gradually prevailed in more recent summit meetings, including Williamsburg.

These two interpretations of the origins of the summits of the Seven need not be considered as alternative and incompatible. History shows that events and invididuals inextricably combine and influence one another. It is inherent in the summit concept to mix – in Putnam's words – 'fostering of personal understanding' and 'resolution of prisoners' dilemmas', i.e. the subjectivist approach on one side, and 'energising of the policy process' and 'justification of internationally desirable policies' at home or 'accommodation of divergent policies' and enhancement of 'policy coordination' among states, i.e. the objectivist approach on the other.

The distinction is relevant, however, in so far as it comes up again when the lines of desirable development of the summit process are discussed. The subjectivists wish a return to the fireside chat among leaders, a drastic shrinkage of delegations, the shortening, or even the abolition, of the communiqué together with a decimation of the media crowd. The objectivists claim that such fireside chats have in fact never existed and that the current complexity of the meetings can be reduced but not avoided. Some go further and suggest a more structured procedure for the work of the sherpas and associated technical groups prior and subsequent to the meetings, the convening of ministerial meetings (as Washington did in anticipation of Williamsburg, with the tepid participation of the Europeans), and even some form of institutionalisation, secretariat or the like.

Such suggestions heighten the sensitivity and the concern of both the existing institutions and those Western countries which are not part of the summit. They are afraid this might lead to the creation of a superstructure that would reduce the effectiveness of, and the interest in, such bodies as the OECD or the IMF or others (even the Atlantic Alliance if political and strategic matters are increasingly dealt with) and which would, by the same token, increase the distance between the 'Big Seven' and the others. Subjectivists thus seem to abound among officials of small countries and international institutions.

The Decline of the United States' Role

I share more of the objectivist than of the subjectivist approach. The origins of the summit of the Seven date back to the decline, or even the crumbling, of the Western system that had developed over a quarter of a century after World War II. During that period the nearly unchallenged US predominance combined with a relatively enlightened American leadership to create or relaunch, with an attendant devolution of power, a number of cooperative institutions of different size and competence. Priority was given to them rather than to the pure and simple reinforcement of hegemony. These institutions or alliances or agreements constituted what I have called elsewhere the 'systemic factors'[3] of the development of the West and the establishment of the 'Pax Americana'. Their working benefited from – and by the same token was criticised because of – the inspiration, political influence, financial support and, sometimes, ultimate guaranty provided by the United States.

I will not discuss here the interesting subject of how this American leadership developed in a substantially bipartisan way out of federalist thought associated with puritan moralism, how it combined enlightened and far-sighted concepts with obscurantist waves at home, or support for anti-colonialist movements with exacerbated anti-communist policies. One feature of particular relevance was the US backing of the European integration movement, envisaging federal targets that went beyond what the Europeans themselves were ready to achieve. It also helped the development of Japan, later to become a formidable economic rival alongside the European Community.

Although signs of it had been visible before, between the two wars, it was quite an innovative approach and as such was resisted by those accustomed to thinking in terms of traditional power politics. An outstanding example was General de Gaulle who, though wholeheartedly a Westerner, stubbornly resisted US predominance and consistently disliked the cooperative institutions that were established under its influence before he came to power. He abhorred them all, however weak their power over governments, whether at the European level (he called Community bureaucrats a bunch of *technocrates apatrides*), at the Atlantic level (he pulled France out of NATO) or at the world level (he called the UN a *machin*, a French way of identifying something you do not even remember the name of). On the contrary, de Gaulle loved summitry, which was far more consistent with his approach. He unsuccessfully tried to revive the Big Three to enhance Western solidarity, and other summit formulas to re-open East–West relations. East–West summitry did eventually take place but mostly in a bilateral form, between the two superpowers, to the General's disappointment.

With or without de Gaulle's opposition, this American-led system was sliding downward by the end of the '60s. The relative power of the United States was declining with respect to that of its Western partners in economic terms and to that of its Eastern rivals in strategic terms. The economic decline culminated in the unilateral measures of August 1971 and the strategic uncertainty in the Vietnam syndrome some years later. This decline of the United States' power could not but affect international institutions and agreements since no other country or group of countries was in a position to take up the leading role. Three schools of thought gradually became more outspoken in the United States: a) the hegemonistic one, which, contrary to common wisdom, thought that the previous period had not served the country's interests and that less 'naive' foreign policies had to be put into action (this school of thought would become particularly vociferous during Reagan's campaign); b) the isolationist one, which lamented that the US was no longer paid back for its 'generosity' (this school of thought was present in the Carter electorate); c) the power politics one, which thought something had to be done to stop the decline and to restore authority, at the expense of Western leadership if necessary (actually it did not believe in leadership without authority). This third line of thought was represented in particular by the other great 'realpolitiker' of the post-war period, Henry Kissinger. The 'pentapolar world' spoken of by Richard Nixon, soon to be followed by the 'Year of Europe', reflected an awareness on the part of the Americans of their decline and, at the same time, was a form of calling the bluff, in so far as there was one, of such 'poles' as the Community and Japan, two strategic dwarves, or of the Soviet Union and China, two economic dwarves, in comparison with the United States, which was still definitely a global power.

Kissinge: oo had little sympathy for cooperative international institutions, void as they are of the 'soul' of national sovereignty. He too rather liked summitry. That such an idea appealed to a man known for his cultural debt to Metternich and to the Restoration period should not come as a surprise to anybody. Referring to September 1971 and to the troubled Western relations following Washington's economic measures of August, Kissinger writes in his memoirs: 'To bring matters to a head, I recommended to Nixon that he intervene personally with the European heads of state. My original idea was a summit of the Western leaders.'[4] The idea did not materialise at the time. So, when the first oil shock came, Western cohesion had already been affected by unilateralism in its 'systemic factors' while no alternative instrument was available for action. What happened had an element of paradox: an administration which was no longer institution-oriented came up with the proposal for the International Energy Agency which was accepted by the others, except post-Gaullist France, which gave a typically Gaullist response in refusing to join.

But summitry was in the air, as perhaps the inevitable answer to the changes that had taken place. Even after de Gaulle France retained its preference for summitry. The waning of the US leadership and the associated decline of international institutions induced Paris to reassess the risks of excessive autonomy and, at the same time, to welcome the fact that American diplomacy was moving closer to its own preferred methods. This was the beginning of an important rapprochement.

Europe at the Summits

The initiative for the summit came from Europe, and namely from France (with German backing right from the start), with typical European, and namely French, ambiguities. On one side it was stimulated by a growing uneasiness about what was perceived as the United States' loss of control. The Western economic system, already shaken at its core by the dismantling of the monetary system, was also severely hit by the energy crisis. There was in Europe − it is true − a certain degree of confidence in Kissinger and his ability to decouple the continuing dialogue with the East from the effort to overcome the Vietnam impasse; but men come and go (and Kissinger did go, shortly thereafter) while problems remain. In fact, the gravity of the problems grew as US ability, and indeed willingness, to manage the crisis declined. The European countries were particularly sensitive to the security side. While they were displaying, separately or cooperatively, a new foreign policy activism (Ostpolitik, development aid coupled with growing interventionism in the Third World) they were also discovering the degree of their dependence on oil and, hence, their vulnerability. Thus action had to be taken in such a way as to involve the United States (and Japan, which was strong enough to contribute and affected enough by the oil shortage to have to cooperate), but without giving it the sole responsibility.

On the other side, by resorting to summitry, Europe was basically helping to re-establish a power hierarchy which reconfirmed the fact that, despite everything, the United States remained the major world power. Though Europe took the initiative, giving itself the numerical majority at the summit meeting, it cut out the smaller members, thus halving that same Community which was one of the main origins of the redistribution of world power that had made multilateral summitry necessary. At first there was some uncertainty about whether Italy would be invited. Opposition to its participation came mainly from France which did not want to see diluted the concept of truly Big Powers (a concept reminiscent of Gaullism and well-rooted in French diplomacy). Italy had to rely on others, especially the United States, in order to have its seat at the table confirmed, with the result that a small but not negligible indebtedness was created. Initially Paris also tenaciously opposed an invitation to the representatives of the Community,[5] but eventually their participation too became assured, with no opposition on the part of Washington. At the summits, however, the role of the president of the EC's Commission, whether meant to represent the Community as such or to give a sense of indirect participation to the smaller member countries, has been clearly marginal and substantially ineffective for both purposes.

In summitry, more than in other articulated and institutionalised forums, the relevance of what is said during the meeting is directly dependent on the political importance of the one who speaks. It makes little sense, therefore, to assume that the higher the number of European leaders sitting at the summit table the stronger the influence Europe has in the summit deliberations. The European leaders, like the others, go there with overwhelmingly national preoccupations and with cooperative or competitive aims that transcend the

Community dimension. The concept of summitry, moreover, is scarcely compatible with the idea of representation of the non-participating countries. This problem, which exists only for the European leaders (the other summit leaders represent nobody but themselves) is irresolvable.

Thus, whether or not Europe eventually gets closer to that famous 'speaking with one voice' depends less on how many are at the summit and more on the degree of preliminary concertation that can be achieved in the Community forums. At a number of summit meetings the Community and the four participating European countries have in effect displayed a certain degree of harmony in their positions both prior to and during the deliberations, which did not prove detrimental to the success of the meetings themselves. This, however, does not happen without irritating the other summit partners, who claim that the Europeans, when closing ranks, lose negotiating flexibility. It was Kissinger who said, not necessarily referring only to the summits, that the United States found it intolerable that the Europeans should come with a pre-set position agreed − possibly painfully − among themselves and defend it, asking that it not be put into question; rather they should consult, he said, with the US first. This is to put the finger on the issue of the priority the Europeans themselves attribute to Community solidarity in the broader framework of Western solidarity, and which the others recognise. As recalled above, in the pre-Kissinger times the Americans did recognise this priority.

What about the Europeans? Since the 1950s the Community institutions have undergone a process of weakening, which has taken place in two stages. In the first one, President de Gaulle, who had supervised the taking-off of the Common Market during the 1958–1968 decade in which he held power, prevented these institutions from acquiring the characteristics of supranationality and irreversibility the Monnet-inspired founding fathers wanted to give them. The General's action against the 'systemic factors', mentioned above, was hence naturally more effective in the European dimension, where France was dominant at that time (Britain having chosen to stay out and Germany being the vanquished party in the war) and where American support could not but be marginal and sometimes even counterproductive, in so far as it heightened French sensitivity about national independence. In fact, supranationality and American dominance were the chief arguments of French opponents, first, of the European Defence Community (which was buried in 1954) and later of the Euratom (which took off half-emptied in 1958 together with the EEC).

In the second phase, still in course, summitry is sucking the blood out of Community institutions. The Community summit, the so-called European Council, was created a few years before the Western one, with the purpose, in principle, of restoring momentum to the process of integration, which was being affected by the consequences of the first phase (and of the enlargement to Britain). It has indeed restored momentum occasionally, but at the same time it has created an intergovernmental forum to which all the difficult issues are sent not only for decision but also, and increasingly, for negotiation, thus subtracting them from the action of the competent Community bodies. It thus *de facto* represents a return to multibilateral diplomacy among the capitals, which the treaties had tried to bypass and overcome. The beginning and development of the summit of the Seven has reinforced this intergovernmental approach in the European Community.

There is a certain parallelism between European and Western summitry, especially in two major respects: first, in the complex relationship with existing institutions, a relationship of complementarity, but increasingly also of substitution and hence competition; second, in the extension from economic matters to political ones.[6] One difference, not a minor one, is that the problem of membership does not exist in the Community where all members participate in the European Council summits.

Thus the four European participants dispose of a machinery to consult among themselves and with the other Community members, in order to build, if they want, common positions to be defended at the summits of the Seven and common instruments for implementing the policies decided at the summits. They have done so on a number of occasions, as has already been recalled, and the summit itself has profited from this cohesive contribution of the European participants. The Tokyo summit can be considered as an example and one might argue that the scarce capacity Washington displayed at that time to lead the group must have helped.

Frequently, in the view of those who support a more structured Western summitry, involving diplomats and/or ministers, European cooperation not only has an influence but should also serve as a model.[7]

Italy at the Summits

Italy's presence at the summit table is not only a remarkable diplomatic success story, but also marks a turning point in the country's foreign policy. The question had frequently been raised in the domestic political debate over whether Italy, a typical medium power, should aim at being the first of the small countries or the last of the big ones. The tragic outcome of World War II and the associated collapse of Mussolini vaccinated the country against excessive national ambitions.

The post-war phase of Western institutional creativity helped the country out of the dilemma. The achievement of some degree of European supranational integration not only made the distinction between small and big countries less relevant, but also gradually determined the outcome of another traditional debate concerning Italy's foreign policy: whether to choose a Mediterranean vocation or a European one. Moreover, the Atlantic Alliance, which Rome was invited to join after some initial uncertainties, provided a security framework with the accepted leadership of one country, the United States, and with the others on a more or less equal footing. Italy faithfully espoused the Community and the Alliance and gradually learned to become an active member of both. These treaties had been signed amidst sharp divisions within the country, but later on the consensus became almost general.

The decline of this institutionalised, multilateral system, the hierarchisation of state powers and the development of summitry posed in new terms the issue of what the Italians call their *collocazione internazionale*, their position in the international arena. At the same time rapid economic growth had generated profound social transformations which in turn had favoured political displacements, especially on the left.

The international set of links that had helped the Italian Socialists become a government party in the '60s was no longer solid enough in the '70s when Eurocommunism showed up. For the West, then, Italy became not only a partner but also a problem. The debate on whether the Italian prime minister should be invited to the summit was influenced by the existence of this problem no less than by the country's status in terms of dimensions, power and economic strength.

The participation in the oligarchy of the Seven, once confirmed, became the third cornerstone of Italian foreign policy, together with membership in the European Community and in the Atlantic Alliance. Over the past decade the country has shown increasing interest in international problems and a new inclination to contribute to their solution (see for instance its participation in the multilateral peacekeeping forces in the Sinai and Lebanon). Whether this increasing interest is a result of its participation in the summits is open to discussion. One could note that some countries which have been excluded from the summits because they are small have not displayed the same inclination in the same period.

The picture, however, is not entirely bright for Italy either. The approach adopted by the Western world in the '70s and early '80s to deal with the international economic problems has made it increasingly difficult for it to be towed by the leading industrialised countries. One outstanding example is the effect of volatile exchange rates on the fate of the *lira* and the consequent, predominantly negative, effects on the domestic economy. Greater indebtedness and higher inflation rates than those of its partners inevitably make Italy's foreign policy less credible and could also raise the suspicion that the country leaders are trying to divert attention from their failure to curb inflation and contain the public deficit by putting greater emphasis on foreign policy. Continuing internal consensus is required in order to keep the Italian House in sufficient order (broad political support has been vital not only for economic policy, but also for the fight against terrorism) and to take the appropriate foreign policy steps. As far as the latter is concerned, convergence with, and support from, the European Community partners has in most cases been essential for gaining the necessary majority and containing opposition within mild terms. The Middle East and deployment of the Euromissiles are examples.

Moreover, the main domestic political knot has remained: the Communists continue to win the votes of more or less one-third of the electorate, thus neither has their weight been reduced so far nor have they yet been fully accepted in the democratic area (i.e. they are not yet considered fully eligible for government at the national level). The decline of integrative factors, which implies a stronger influence of bilateral relations, has reinforced the perception that such a relevant internal transformation is incompatible in the present international framework.

Finally, foreign policy activism, if not associated with a new development of integrative factors, can also have a negative side if it enhances new nationalistic ambitions, which may go either towards preferential bilateral relations with the United States when conservatives prevail or towards more neutralist and Third World orientations when leftists prevail.

What a Stronger Japan Means

The participation of the Japanese prime minister in the summits of the Seven deserves now some specific attention. First of all, it should be realised that the United States' historical relationship with Japan is much less important than the one existing with Europe. Secondly, in the immediate post-war period the 'Pearl Harbour effect' made American attitudes towards Japan less sympathetic than those for Europe, more than half of which had been an ally. Thirdly, the rivalry with the Soviet Union, initially mostly a land power, made Europe a strategic priority.

But over time and with a number of changes taking place in the Far East, from the rise of communist China as a nuclear power to the extraordinary economic development of Japan itself, Tokyo became a fundamenal partner, in political and strategic no less than economic terms, and multiple private and public links developed at an accelerated pace.

Japan, however, had been very much on the sidelines throughout that first post-war period during which, as has been said, the Western system developed around the Atlantic axis with a high degree of institutionalisation. Also culturally Japan felt it had little in common with the Atlantic approach.

When this system declined and the new phase of Western and international relations began to take shape in the early seventies, the Japanese leadership was still very reluctant to become involved in formal cooperation that would require a more active contribution from them. Meeting for the first time in Tokyo in 1973, the promoters of the Trilateral Commission, which in a way anticipated on a private basis the composition of the future summits, met with Japanese business, cultural and political leaders who with few exceptions stubbornly resisted the idea of a common forum. The Japanese stressed over and over again their 'particular situation' in the face of what they perceived to be a Western failure to understand.

There was, however, substantial agreement between Europe and the United States in insisting with the Japanese that they should now 'come on board'. Tokyo had the stakes and the strength to share the political responsibility (and eventually the strategic burden) and not only the advantages of a free market. In addition there was a growing American interest in the Pacific as a consequence of the economic and strategic developments there. For Europe, too, Japan was becoming an important partner with some relevant common interests, like those in the Middle East, and was thus also a potential ally in dealing with the United States. This has been the case, for instance, in a number of energy-related problems, like access to Arab oil and Soviet natural gas. At the same time Europe and the United States share preoccupations about Japanese dynamism in penetrating foreign markets, which has been at the origin of recurrent tensions.

The accumulation and interweaving of these many factors has been such as to induce the Japanese to gradually but fundamentally alter their attitude at successive summits, from Rambouillet to Williamsburg. This evolution, one of the most relevant on the international scene, has taken place in three directions: a) acceptance and formulation of shared rules of conduct; b) participation in more or less institutionalised forms of multilateral consultation and decision-making; c) shared perceptions of the common security problems. Japan has also developed a regional sphere of influence, but to an extent which, especially to the eyes of the Europeans who have multiple and sophisticated regional relations, still appears much too modest. All this amounts to a reduced Japanese specificity.

One current scenario predicts that the United States will become further Pacific-oriented during the remaining years of this century. It assumes that the Americans, either attracted by the country of the rising sun or disenchanted with Europe, or both, would gradually move away from that trans-Atlantic partnership, which had never been completely achieved, to become a 'superpower between two oceans', with either hegemonistic or isolationist overtones, and eventually establish a preferential trans-Pacific system of relations.

Whether one buys the whole scenario or not, there is no doubt Japan poses a complex foreign policy challenge to Western Europe, and that in dealing with it the usual problems of the degree of commonality in attitudes and as to instruments will inevitably arise.

Rising Doubts About Neo-Mercantilism

Summitry has reflected, even symbolised, the changing approach of the West in dealing with the new and complex problems which began to emerge on the world scene in the early '70s. Since then the trend has been towards facing them one by one on an *ad hoc*, piecemeal basis. Pragmatism has been the philosophy and damage limitation the objective. Damage has in fact been limited. Not a few had predicted the collapse of the Western system under the impact of the economic down-trend and the two oil shocks. Certainly, our societies were wounded as massive unemployment and the questioning of the resilience of the welfare system show. But, despite the collapse of the dollar-based monetary system and protectionist pressures, trade and associated interdependence are higher today than they were ten years ago; technological development and the associated transition away from oil (especially Middle East oil) has taken place.

What has happened then? It has happened that those instruments that were conceived in the West, under American leadership, to enhance, but also to master interdependence, have either disappeared or, more frequently, have taken a back-bench position, leaving the forefront to national diplomacy. Beggar-thy-neighbour policies have burgeoned. Leaders have given way to bargainers. Transnational forces have ceased to develop, and, with the decline of international institutions, the means of controlling them have declined too. Power hierarchy has been stressed with the consequence of reducing the sense of participation of the medium and small countries, a hitherto important asset for the Western system. All together, this is less a new approach than a return to a more traditional one.

At the centre of this neo-mercantilistic situation — as it has been called — are the fluctuating exchange rates. In the beginning they were presented as the winning solution. But repeated resort to competitive monetary manoeuvres, frequent forgoing of adjustment of balance-of-payments disequilibria and the growing need to finance deficits, with the associated uncontrolled expansion of international and domestic indebtedness, gradually dispelled such undue complacency.

Summitry has been central in helping the West to live through the tensions inevitably generated by this state of affairs but has also been unable, possibly by nature, to indicate any solution which goes to the roots of the tensions themselves. Two statesmen who consider themselves the founding fathers of the summits of the Seven, Giscard and Schmidt, have pointed out in separate internationally published reports the shortcomings of the fluctuating exchange rates, which they themselves had done much to establish.[8] The former points out that the current economic recovery cannot be but conjunctural while the structural problems remain, and require solutions like a new international monetary system, a popular French refrain. The Western economic recovery, says the latter, must be led by the United States, but not the way it is done now, at the expense of the others.

These and other signs seem to signal the beginning of a dissatisfaction with the results, and a lack of confidence in the future, of continuing pragmatism and *ad hoc-ery*. Nostalgia for the good old days is also expressed whenever the need for massive transfers of funds is required and a 'new Marshall Plan' is invoked or whenever the evils of monetary disorder are more evident and a 'new Bretton Woods' is called for. But both achievements depended on the role the United States was playing at that time. Three fundamental and interrelated questions must therefore be asked: a) Does nostalgia go so far as to wish that the US take on again a dominant role? b) Is that role conceivable without a scaling down of the roles of the other Western countries? c) Would those who run the United States today use their dominance in the same wise and uncharacteristic way as did their predecessors in the early post-war years?

United States: Priority to the Strategic Threat

With the Reagan administration, the purpose of American politics has become to restore American dominance, or, as the ruling circles put it, to restore the authority of, and respect for, America. The administration started with a weak economy and has concentrated obsessively on the area in which the United States is indispensable for the West: strategic confrontation with the East. The Soviet Union, they say, must be matched where it is strong: militarily. They discharged out of hand the European proposals for a broader, the so-called 'comprehensive security', approach, that would challenge the Soviet Union where it is weak: economically. At the same time, the economy at home has been stimulated through fiscal means and thanks to a large influx of capital from abroad, making the dollar strong and overvalued. Thus, part of the widening public deficit resulting from the US defence and fiscal policies is being paid for by its partners.

Confrontation with the Warsaw Pact has become a doctrine, in so far as doctrine means a constant line of interpretation of events with associated rules of conduct. The interpretation is: the Soviet empire is threatening us with destruction but suffers from dramatic weaknesses that can be used to bring it to its knees. The rules are: military build-up and sanctions. It is a sort of 'either them or us'; the contrary of coexistence. There are, of course, nuances, which range from ideology to pragmatism, in the stands of the conservatives around the president. Moreover, the doctrinaire approach to East–West relations actually goes back to the previous administration because of the influence of Carter's national security adviser, Zbigniew Brzezinski.

The point here is that there has been a shift in the approach. During the first post-war period the Western system, which was giving itself a sophisticated and institutional structure, confronted the then ideological, rather than strategic, challenge from the East with cold war instruments. Later, faced with the new global power of the Soviet Union and relatively assured of its own cohesion, it gradually adopted more conciliatory stances and détente developed. The 'troubled partnership' between Europe and the United States was strained by differences but could survive them, also because relations with the East were conducted with flexibility and using a piecemeal approach. Coexistence did not really translate into a common doctrine (except perhaps for West Germany). Now that *ad hoc-ery* has permeated West–West relations, doctrine is being suggested, or rather forcefully induced, in conducting East–West relations.

The Europeans, perceiving a new threat from the Soviet Union now that it is 'modernising' its weaponry and increasingly aware of the threat posed by the proliferation of conflicts in places of vital importance to them, still want, with nuances from one country to another, a strong America. But they are concerned, again with nuances, about *that* strong America, about the costs that are involved for them, about the US caricaturisation of the Soviet threat and about the lack of sophistication the current US administration displays in facing the complexities of the problems surrounding us.

The Europeans' past ambiguities have not disappeared. Being invited to become stronger themselves and to contribute more effectively to Western security, they have given, and still give, partial answers. A new activism in foreign policy has developed, as already mentioned. Defence budgets have been increased, but to the point where the conflict between the associated expenditure and the economic requirements of the welfare state, exasperated by high unemployment, has made them level off.

Public opinion in more or less all the European countries is divided. There is a certain amount of support for more active foreign policies, even with the related and necessary military implications, especially in Britain, France and Italy. But there are strong reservations, too, especially in terms of an increased concern about nuclear armaments and high military expenditure (two concerns which are to a certain extent contradictory in that a substitution of nuclear capabilities with a buildup of conventional forces would involve higher costs). One powerful argument for those opposing more active policies − a wide spectrum of positions going from cautious conditionality to extravagant forms of unilateralism − is the absence, or at least the scarce relevance, of a European approach and set of policies distinct from those of the United States. The fact is that, despite an appreciable degree of cooperation in the framework of a Community which is less economic and more political than the one conceived in the treaties, every state remains the basic actor on the international scene and has not enough strength and resources to work out concepts and carry out policies that would make a European position more clearly identifiable.

The summit meetings of the Seven, that are becoming more political in nature, are bound to reflect this state of affairs. It is true that economic and strategic matters are increasingly linked, as East−West trade and energy transfers demonstrate, but this does not help very much, because of the two above-mentioned 'structural' problems: one in European−American and the other in intra-European relations. In Versailles the resulting contradictions affected the outcome of the meeting. In Williamsburg things improved, but perhaps more in the sense of shelving problems than of solving them.

Which Priorities for Europe?

The regular convening of the summits of the Seven came as a way out of the impasse determined by the decline of the post-war Western approach to international relations. It has considerably helped the West to live through a decade made difficult by repeated energy crises and negative economic conditions which America, Western Europe and Japan were all less equipped to confront cooperatively. But it has not helped to reverse the trend towards fragmentation, which is one of the main causes of Western weakness.

Such fragmentation makes it hard to use economic recovery when it shows up − in the United States, first of all − so that all may profit from it. The instruments to minimise negative impacts on the others and optimise 'locomotive' effects are less efficient than in the past or, in the case of monetary relations, nearly non-existent. Problems, then, grow in dimension and make solutions going to the roots of them appear much too ambitious in the absence of appropriate leadership.

There are now increasingly numerous signs of dissatisfaction with the lack of systemisation in the new approach, that Western summitry somehow symbolises. Reference is made to the need for more structural solutions, using as an example and, indeed, as a model the achievements of the post-war times. The repetition of this model is not, however, easy to conceive if one country, or indeed one political class inside the Western countries, does not play a leading role. The resumption of such a role by the United States raises serious doubts because of the degree of irreversibility of the many factors of redistribution of power throughout the world, in military, political and economic terms.

Moreover, the kind of international dominance the current majority in the United States seemingly wants to pursue does not respond to the requirements of a more structured and cohesive Western system. Seeking hegemony is likely to be better served by bilateral relations. Because of the contingencies, a stronger America, strategically and economically, may be welcome here and there, but it will generate new kinds of strains in the West. It will, in particular, have divisive effects on Europe, because of the emphasis on bilateralism and because the degree of acceptance or refusal will vary from country to country and from time to time.

In the absence of a leading role by the United States, Western summitry has been seen as the embryo of a substitute formula: 'collective leadership'. This remains however an empty formula, because it does not answer the basic political question of where the power lies. Neither power devolution nor power distribution is sufficient to make collective leadership conceivable. Power devolution through common institutions has in fact been reduced. Power redistribution among a number of countries requires a minimum of agreement about the respective roles. It poses above all the problem of the Europeans' role.

The triple process that has taken place in Western Europe after World War II, of a) re-acquisition of international status (especially for Germany and Italy), b) reconstruction and economic development, and c) integration in the Community, has been carried forward with the underlying aspiration to catch up with the United States. The uncertainties as to the reality of Europe as a world 'pole' mostly reside in the partial achievement of European integration.

One possible aspiration of an eventual United Europe (evident especially in France) would be to supplement or even to substitute the American role. This implies a certain degree of opposition to the United States, and consequently a reduced cohesion of the West. This view has not prevailed and in fact European solidarity has so far remained one step ahead of Western solidarity and when the latter has been in trouble the former has had problems too. The original American attitude towards European federalism explains to an extent this situation.

The less divisive line of action pursued by the Europeans has thus been to complement the United States. This applies in particular to their presence at the summits. However, two kinds of problem make the continuation of this line less and less probable: a) the new way of seeing Western relations in the United States: disenchantment with Europe, increasing dislike of the one-step-ahead philosophy, and opposition to devolution or distribution of power; and b) the fact that the process of integration in the Community (see c) above) has been stalled for many years. To give it new momentum would require the completion of economic unity, the development of a specific approach to security[9] and institutional reform.[10] The prospects for such progress are not bright today, but the option is still in Europe's hands. Where they have less influence, and fundamental uncertainties, is on the future course of the United States.

For the foreseeable future, the seven countries who sit at the summit table and a number of other Western countries will continue, as the communiqués relentlessly remind us, to share common values, a high degree of interdependence and the same threats to their security. They are, in short, on the same boat: for the time being, a rocking boat in stormy seas.

Notes

1. See Robert Putnam, chapter 2 in this book.
2. See William Wallace, chapter 4 in this book.
3. See Cesare Merlini, 'Que nous reservent les années 80?' in *Politique Internationale*, no. 8 (summer 1980), p. 197.
4. See Henry Kissinger, *White House Years* (Little, Brown & Co., New York, 1979), p. 958.

5. See Gianni Bonvicini and Wolfgang Wessels, chapter 6 in this book.

6. See Wallace, chapter 4 and Bonvicini and Wessels, chapter 6 in this book.

7. See for instance the Report to the Trilateral Commission by E. Ortona, R. Schatzel and N. Ushiba, *The Problem of International Consultations* (Trilateral Commission, New York, 1976).

8. For the English versions see *The Economist*, 26 February and 21 May 1983.

9. The development of a specific European approach to security is treated in a small book I have written in coauthorship with K. Kaiser, Th. de Montbrial, W. Wallace and E.P. Wellenstein and published in seven languages; in English with the title *The European Community: Progress or Decline?* (Royal Institute of International Affairs, London, 1983).

10. In the European Parliament a resolution was passed in September 1983 envisaging a new institutional treaty among the Community members.